CUBANS
IN
AMERICA

CUBANS
— IN —
AMERICA

A Vibrant History of a People in Exile

Alex Antón

and

Roger E. Hernández

KENSINGTON BOOKS
http://www.kensingtonbooks.com

KENSINGTON BOOKS are published by

Kensington Publishing Corp.
850 Third Avenue
New York, NY 10022

All Kensington titles, imprints and distributed lines are available at special quantity discounts for bulk purchases for sales promotion, premiums, fund-raising, educational or institutional use.

Special book excerpts or customized printings can also be created to fit specific needs. For details, write or phone the office of the Kensington Special Sales Manager: Kensington Publishing Corp., 850 Third Avenue, New York, NY 10022, Attn. Special Sales Department. Phone: 1-800-221-2647.

Kensington and the K logo Reg. U.S. Pat. & TM Off.

ISBN 1-57566-678-2

First Hardcover Printing: May 2002
First Trade Paperback Printing: May 2003
10 9 8 7 6 5 4 3 2 1

Printed in the United States of America

Design by Leonard Telesca

To Papi, who taught me to be a man. To Mami, who taught me to be.
To my wife, Dianne, who puts up with it all. And to my children, Elena and Ben. May they also grow up to love Cuba.

—Roger E. Hernández

To my wife, Betty, and our sons, Alex and Adrian. For my father, Eduardo, and my mother, Mercy, who instilled in me a profound love for Cuba.

—Alex Antón

Contents

Acknowledgments   *ix*

Author's Foreword   *xiii*

Introduction   *xvii*

SECTION I

BEGINNINGS TO REPUBLIC

CHAPTER 1: The First Cubans 1492–1789   3

CHAPTER 2: *Exilios* Begin 1789–1868   26

CHAPTER 3: Wars and Independence 1868–1902   50

SECTION II

REPUBLIC TO REVOLUTION

CHAPTER 4: Immigrant Years 1902–1952   99

CHAPTER 5: Fighting the Sergeant 1952–1958   126

SECTION III

REVOLUTION TO EXILE

CHAPTER 6: Castro's Takeover 1959–1965   146

CHAPTER 7: Freedom Flights 1965–1973   166

CHAPTER 8: Living in America 1973–1980   183

CHAPTER 9: Mariel and the Rise of Cuban-Americans 1980–1989   201

CHAPTER 10: Rafters and Bittersweet Dreams 1990–Present   228

Bibliography   *275*

Index   *281*

Acknowledgments

We would like to express our gratitude to everyone who assisted us in the completion of this book. Although it is impossible to thank individually the many people who helped, encouraged, and cheered us on, we would like to express a heartfelt appreciation to our friends, colleagues, and family:

Ramiro Ortíz, President of SunTrust Bank, and Msgr. Franklyn M. Casale, president of St. Thomas University, were both present at the beginning and encouraged us to the very end, always giving valuable advice and backing throughout the entire process.

Alberto Ibargüen, Publisher of the *Miami Herald,* and Esperanza de Varona, director of the Cuban Heritage Collection at the University of Miami, both provided many of the photos and illustrations that appear throughout the book. In particular, our thanks to Lissette Esquizábal, at the *Herald*'s photo department, whose patience and support made all the difference. Thanks, too, to Eduardo Gil at the Montclair State University Library, Danilo Figueredo at the Bloomfield College Library, and Charles Kingsley at the St. Augustine Historical Society.

Several people read the manuscript at various stages and made important suggestions, including Antonio de la Cova, professor of history at Rose-Hulman Institute of Technology in Indiana; Romel Hernández, journalist and writer extraordinaire; Frank de Varona, professor of education at Florida International University; Dr. Luis Aguilar León, professor emeritus, Georgetown University; Dr. Jaime Suchlicki, Director of the Cuban and Cuban-American Studies Center at the University of Miami; Dr. Luis Botifoll, banker; Dr. Nestor Carbonell, executive and author.

We would like to thank all the folks at St. Thomas University: specifically, Beverly Bacharach, the vice president of St. Thomas University's development office, the president's office, and their respective staffs.

Also, thank you to New Jersey Institute of Technology, particularly Karl Schweizer and Norbert Elliot at the Department of Humanities and Social Sciences and to Bloomfield College, specially President Jack Noonan and Guillermo Jimenez. Their generosity and support made writing this book immeasurably easier.

Many people believed in the project and offered their insights and valuable observations: Juan and Marta Gutiérrez, Jose Sánchez, Carlos Saladrigas, Jose Arriola, Rosa Carbonell, Carlos Manuel de Céspedes, Jerónimo Esteve-Abril, Jerónimo Esteve Jr., Dr. Aida Levitán, Dr. Alberto and Maria Luzarraga, Carlos Planas, Ana Gloria Rivas-Vásquez, Ysrael Seinuk, Jorge Calvo, Augusto Casamayor, Frank Navarro, Isabel de Céspedes, Miguel Angel and Rosa Rodríguez, Fernando Marquet, Gilberto de Cárdenas, Dr. Waldo Laurencio, George Díaz, Juan P. Loumiet, Cesar Alvarez, Carlos Palomares, Eloy Cepero, Willy Bermello, Charlie Martínez, Jose Bared, Manuel Jorge Cutillas, Román and Elena Martínez, Angel Hernández, Sergio Pino, Jorge Mas Santos, Jorge Rodríguez Márquez, Armando Codina, Leslie Pantín, Carlos Arboleya, George Feldenkreis, Alberto Dosal, Jose Cancela, Dr. Horacio Aguirre, Rafael Sánchez-Aballi, Jack Gibson, Oscar and Elena Echevarría, Susan Smith, Enrique and the Alejo family, Georgina and Francisco Angones, Mariano Echevarría, Larry Garmany, Salomon Garazi, Rafael Méndez, Domingo Moreira, Vicente Puig, Diego Suárez, Gonzalo Valdés-Fauli, Mario and Maria Fernández, Iraida Iturralde, Jose Aguirre, Iraida and Jorge Méndez, Tony Argiz, Alfonso Cueto, José Lamas, Gus Machado, Arnaldo Monzón, and Oscar Abello.

A special thanks to our agent Nancy Love for believing in the book and to our editors Tracy Bernstein and Paul Dinas, whose patience, encouragement, and devotion we deeply appreciated.

Roger E. Hernández
Alex Antón

I am very grateful to my family. My wife, Betty, my boys Alex and Adrian, and to the rest of my extended family. I love them all very much and thank them for the support they have given me through the years.

Alex Antón

I want to say a special thank you to Dianne, my wife, who managed to keep the household together without much help from me as I wrote all day and often into the night, at a time when her responsibilities at her own job increased tremendously. And she didn't even complain.

Well, not much. But I would not have even started this book without her by my side.

Roger E. Hernández

Authors' Foreword

Like so many other Cuban-Americans, we were deeply troubled by the national criticism our community took during the final days of the heartrending saga of Elián González. Both of us understood that those who believed the boy belonged with his father had a powerful argument. But it was difficult for us to understand the triumphant glee with which editorials across the nation and even the Clinton White House trumpeted the return of Elián to his father, Juan Miguel.

It was not an occasion for joy. Yes, the boy was back with his dad. But we were infinitely saddened to know that his father intended to take him to live under a tyranny we knew all too well. Cuban-Americans know its oppression deep in our collective soul, having lived it directly or through our parents' stories of freedom extinguished. Elián's mother, Elisabet Brotons, gave her life so her son would not have to endure the suffocation and hopelessness that more than one million Cubans in America had also left behind. We would not go back to those miseries. We did not want Elián to go back, either.

But he went. And what became clear was that this involved more than the tragic fate of one child. Through the entire ordeal, there was little sympathy for Cubans who wanted the boy to live in freedom, and few efforts to explain why the case became such a wrenching emotional issue for an entire people. Instead, Cuban-Americans were branded as right wing fanatics, strident zealots obsessed with the kind of anticommunism that should have gone out of fashion with the

The anguish of Cubans in America reflected in a family's emotional response to news of the raid that took Elián González to his father—and back to Cuba.
(Courtesy *Miami Herald*)

end of the Cold War. It was as if it were somehow wrong to oppose the longest-running dictatorship in the Western Hemisphere.

Something needs to be explained.

Cubans have been exemplary immigrants, fully within the spirit of the American Dream. Cubans have made important contributions in just about every sphere of American life—in business, the arts, entertainment, sports, politics, academia. Although many who came during the early Castro years arrived penniless, Cuban-Americans can boast now of having a standard of living on a par with the broad American norm. Quite an accomplishment in just one generation.

Yet there remains an essential sorrow. Cubans have been coming to the United States to escape oppressive governments on the island since the days of the

Spanish colony in the nineteenth century. The exodus that began with the Castro Revolution of 1959 is of course by far the largest. But sadly, it is only the latest. The path to exile is a Cuban tradition as old as the Cuban nation itself.

Thus, men and women of all ages, of every social class and skin color, born here or arrived just yesterday, were overcome with grief when Elián was taken away. It was a reminder that the fight to see a Cuba where basic human rights are respected still looms large, four decades after the revolution. It is an inherited struggle that also consumed our exiled ancestors in the United States beginning almost 180 years ago.

As a new century dawns, a generation that was young and vigorous when it left for exile, believing in a quick return to the island they love, has grown old. Elderly Cubans are dying in a nation they have also come to love for offering the liberties denied in the land of their birth—but a nation that will always remain foreign to them.

Their children and grandchildren, brought up in the United States, are coming to grips with what it means to be an American of Cuban origin. And yet a third group, those who arrived from the island recently, are trying to understand how life works in the United States, a country so radically different from the Cuba in which they lived.

We want our book to tell their stories. When America asks, "Who are these Cubans, and what do they want?" we hope *Cubans in America* will at least begin to answer their questions.

Roger E. Hernández and Alex Antón

Introduction

Cubans in America is an authoritative, informative, and interesting analysis of the impact that Cubans and Cuban migration has had on the United States. The authors have interwoven the history of Spain, Cuba, and the United States to present a fascinating account of the events and personalities that influenced the Cuban experience in the United States.

The book traces this history from the earlier years when Florida and Cuba were part of Spain. It discusses the British occupation of Havana, the actual beginning of the relationship between the island and its northern neighbor and the growth of that relationship after the U.S. intervention in Cuba and Cuban independence in 1902.

The Cuban Republic's close connection to the United States facilitated the movement of the two countries' populations. Friendly political and economic relations increased tourism both ways. Cubans visited Miami and traveled and studied in the United States. Americans basked in the sun on beautiful beaches of Cuba.

The Castro revolution changed all of this. As the regime became more radical, nationalized private property, increased repression, silenced opposition, and moved into the communist camp, thousands of Cubans fled, primarily to the United States. What started as a trickle of refugees in the early 1960s became a veritable flood by the middle of the decade. Over 1.2 million Cubans found refuge in Miami, New York, New Jersey, Puerto Rico, and many other places or countries willing to take them.

In the United States they grew roots and prospered. Not only did many people realize the American dream of living in freedom with prosperity, but they made major contributions to American life and culture. In the arts, music, medicine, and in American intellectual life in general, Cubans have added much to American society.

Cubans in America is a testimony to the contributions of this enterprising migration. Like others before, it has enriched a country already rich in diversity.

Jaime Suchlicki
Professor and Director
Institute for Cuban and Cuban American Studies
Coral Gables, Florida

BEGINNINGS TO REPUBLIC

CHAPTER 1

The First Cubans

1492–1789

The aroma of fresh tobacco fills a room where cigar makers sit elbow-to-elbow at long tables, expertly rolling the filler in moist brown leaves, then shaping it and cutting it into panetelas and coronas destined to go up in smoke. As they work, they listen to news from Cuba, then they talk, sometimes with pain, sometimes with passion, about the homeland they lost and the political power that rules it.

The scene could have taken place in the Lower Manhattan of the 1890s or the Miami of the new century. One hundred years ago a *lector* would have read aloud from one of the many Cuban exile newspapers; today, the workers might listen to one of the many Cuban exile radio stations. Back then, the discussion would have centered on Spanish colonial rule; today, it is about Fidel Castro's regime. The details change but the longing to see their homeland free remains the same.

To most Americans (probably to most Cubans, too), the Cuban presence in the United States begins with the exodus after Fidel Castro's revolution, *el exilio*. Indeed, more than a million Cubans arrived during this period of exile—desperate asylum-seekers shortly after Castro took power in 1959, families who filled the Freedom Flights in the mid-sixties and early seventies, the teeming masses crowded in boats during the Mariel boatlift of 1980, and the tens of thousands who made it across the Florida Straits floating on inner tubes during the "rafter crisis" of the 1990s. Never before had Cubans made such an impact on the United States. And never before had Americans been so aware of Cubans.

The Cuban exile experience forms a historic cycle at once uniquely Cuban and deeply human: The generations-long saga of a search for freedom, and the tragedy of a people who for nearly two centuries have found that freedom in the United States but not in their beloved island.

The story, however, does not begin with exile. It starts when Cuba and Florida were both Spanish colonies, before Cubans felt the first stirrings of sovereign nationhood, and before the English had begun to colonize North America.

It was geography that dictated early relations between Cuba and Florida. The island of Cuba was discovered by Columbus on his first trip in 1492, and a few years later there were a number of Spanish settlements, one of which would become the capital of Havana. The Conquistadores soon learned that the straits separating Cuba from the continent were not a difficult journey for Spanish galleons. In 1513 Juan Ponce de León, sailing out of Puerto Rico on his quest for the Fountain of Youth, set foot in what is now the United States. He was followed by explorers based in Havana. Pánfilo de Narváez landed in Tampa Bay in 1528 and his lieutenant Alvar Nuñez Cabeza de Vaca spent eight years on an epic overland trek that stretched from Florida to northern Mexico. Hernando de Soto arrived in Florida in 1539 and explored as far as present-day Little Rock, Arkansas and Chicago, Illinois.

Several members of that expedition were natives of Cuba. Garcilaso de la Vega's chronicle of de Soto's adventures mentions two specifically: Pedro Morón and Diego de Oliva. During an attack by a band of Indians, de Soto ordered the two Cuban natives to remove branches blocking a bridge the soldiers needed to cross. Morón and de Oliva dove into the water and swam toward the bridge as arrows landed all around them. They were wounded, but made their way to safety. They are the first natives of Cuba known to have set foot in North America.

However, none of those expeditions resulted in permanent settlements. That would change on September 8, 1565, when Pedro Menéndez de Avilés established the first permanent European settlement in what is now the United States. Spain's San Agustín colony was established on the east coast of Florida forty-two years before the English colony at Jamestown and fifty-five years before the Pilgrims landed at Plymouth Rock.

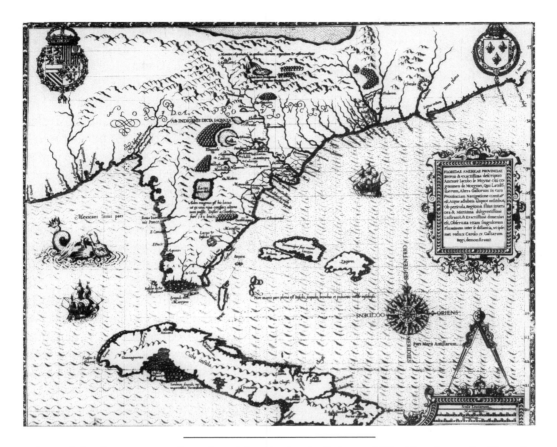

One of the first maps to show Spanish colonies in Cuba and Florida, drawn by French artist Jacques Le Moyne in the 1560s. (St. Augustine Historical Society)

THE COLONY AT ST. AUGUSTINE

Although natives of Cuba surely visited St. Augustine during the first decades of colonization, no records have been found of Cubans actually living in Spanish Florida during those early years. Cuba was still being colonized by Spaniards and populated by their native-born descendants, who kept themselves busy enough settling Cuba itself. Besides, there was no consciousness of being Cuban—those born on the island were considered Spaniards, so bureaucrats who kept records

Pedro Menéndez de Avilés, Spanish explorer who in 1565 founded St. Augustine, the first permanent European settlement in the United States. (Cuban Heritage Collection, University of Miami)

may have given little thought to distinguishing whether a particular colonist was born on the island or in Spain.

But the close relations that developed early on between St. Augustine and Havana suggests natives of Cuba traveled to Florida regularly. Soldiers, priests, and government officials from Havana, whether born in Cuba or Spain, were often sent to Florida on assignment. For them, life was difficult. The newcomers found plenty of fishing all around the narrow peninsula on which they had chosen to build their town, but much of the soil was either sandy, marshy, or forested—unsuited for farming or stock-raising. To make a plot fit for planting, colonists labored under the broiling Florida sun, first chopping down trees and then digging deep to hack away the matted tangle of pine and palmetto roots. Even when the soil was cleared, it was infertile. Only maize and squash produced minimally decent yields, wrote an anonymous visitor in 1570, "up to twenty pounds of maize and no more; although, they say, one (settler) sowed forty or fifty pounds one year."

To St. Augustine, Then Back to Havana

By the mid-1600s the Havana–St. Augustine connection was well established. Historian William B. Griffin notes it was customary for Cuban priests and military officers to be sent to St. Augustine to prove themselves. The idea was to stay just long enough to earn a promotion, then return to Havana. And no wonder people were eager to go back. While St. Augustine was a backwater, Havana was a cosmopolitan center of trade, the third most important city in the New World. Every year since the middle of the sixteenth century, Spanish galleons laden with gold and silver from the mines of Mexico and Peru assembled at

The Maxtas map of St. Augustine, 1593. To the left *of the central fortress is the settlement itself, with colonists' houses and the hard-won fields of maize;* to the upper right *is an Indian village. The North or Tolomato River,* bottom, *actually runs parallel to the Matanzas River,* right. (St. Augustine Historical Society)

Havana Harbor before making the transatlantic crossing. There they waited, the size of the treasure fleet growing as more ships arrived, until Spanish warships escorted the convoy across the pirate-infested ocean. And while the fleet waited, Havana enriched itself by providing sailors with food, lodging, wares, medicine, ship repair, brothels—everything sailors in a foreign port needed.

St. Augustine's buildings also reflected the region's poverty. The colonists typically lived in shacks constructed of rough wooden timbers, their roofs thatched—in a style copied from the Indians—with the abundant fronds of the palmetto. Even the church, usually a resplendent building in Spanish colonies, was made of the same humble materials. The fort that defended the settlement, too, was made of wood, a poor cousin of the imposing stone fortresses going up elsewhere in Spanish America. Such vulnerability welcomed enemy attacks. In 1577, the colony was besieged by Seloy Indians, forcing all residents inside the wooden fortress. In 1585, Francis Drake ransacked the town, burning down nearly every building. In 1668, the pirate John Davis killed sixty inhabitants. In 1696 a Havana-born priest, Luis Sánchez Pacheco, was martyred by Indians he tried to convert to Christianity. Floods and at least one major fire devastated the struggling settlement.

Yet the colonists persisted. In 1640 a certain Redondo Villegas reported to Spain's King Phillip III that there were about 250 soldiers and that "the Governor has planted and put under cultivation many acres of land, which will be a great help in the sustenance of these people, who are mostly married, and whose small wages and rations given them does not suffice for their support."

It was progress, but it was not enough for the colony to be self-sustaining. And precisely because of the shortages of food and just about everything else, a link between Havana and St. Augustine became essential to the survival of Spanish Florida. The colony was almost completely dependent on Havana for goods, government services, religious leadership, and financial support. The colonists built a dock outside the fortress, and there they gathered to unload the supply ships that periodically arrived from Cuba, bringing food and merchandise that offered at least temporary relief from their impoverishment. In truth, St. Augustine was less a colonial town than a military encampment to guard Spain's northern colonial frontier.

The First Cuban Floridian

The historian José Isern says the earliest known record of a Cuban-born individual living in Florida is a letter written in 1644 by the colonial government in Havana to King Phillip IV, "praising the virtues" of one Juan de Hinestrosa, a native of Havana, and recommending he be brought back to Cuba and made bishop for the entire island. At the time, de Hinestrosa was the *provincial* (a religious official) at the mission of Santa Elena, located on modern-day Parris Island, South Carolina.

Recreation of the port of St. Augustine before the construction of the Castillo San Marcos. (St. Augustine Foundation at Flagler College)

CUBANS IN SPANISH FLORIDA

For more than a century after the founding of St. Augustine, the only protection colonists had from attack were rickety wooden forts that offered little security. Over the years, nine forts had been built to replace those washed away by floods, eaten by rot, or burned down by enemies. Finally, in reaction to the establishment of English settlements north of St. Augustine, the Spanish crown authorized the building of a new, stronger system of defense. A Cuban-born military engineer, Ignacio Daza, was brought from Havana to oversee construction.

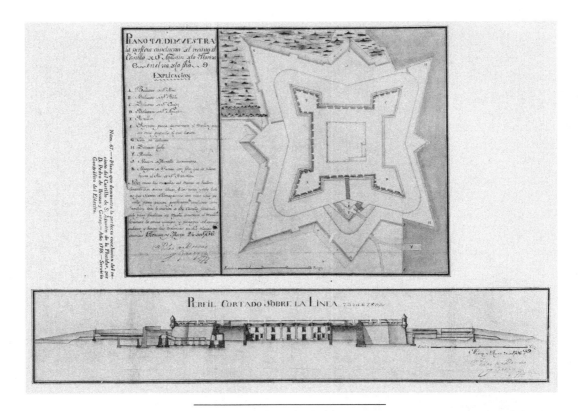

Spanish architectural drawing of Castillo San Marcos, 1756.
(St. Augustine Historical Society)

Daza found that the wooden fortress, as described in his report to authorities in Havana, was "useless, not only for the weakness and poor condition of the beamwork, but also because its lines have been changed by the many repairs that reduced it to a shapeless hulk which violates every rule of fortification." He set out to build an impregnable fortress. As there was no nearby stone suitable for building and not enough money to ship it in, Daza had workers quarry limestone from the coral formations across the bay on Anastasia Island. Skilled masons from Havana cut the blocks of *coquina*, as the material was called, and bonded the stone with mortar made by baking local oyster shells, crushing them to a fine powder, and then adding sand and water. On October 2, 1672, Daza broke ground on the Castillo de San Marcos. Unfortunately, Daza could not fulfill his

Above and below: *Castillo San Marcos, oldest stone fortress in the United States, as it looks today.* (James Quine)

dream of building an impregnable fort. After seven months at work, he unexpectedly died and work on the project soon came to a halt.

It took two decades, and another Cuban, to finish it. The job fell to Laureano Torres de Ayala, the Marqués of Casa Torres, who from 1693 to 1699 was the first of three Cuban-born governors of Spanish Florida. His mandate was to strengthen the colony's ability to defend itself from attack and to project the crown's power in North America. Far as it was from the heart of New Spain in Mexico, Spanish Florida had its own territorial importance, because it bordered on the colonies of Great Britain and France, Spain's geopolitical rivals.

But the St. Augustine where Torres de Ayala went to live 128 years after its founding remained a remote outpost. According to the diary of Jonathan Dickinson, an Englishman who passed through St. Augustine, even in the 1690s the settlement had not grown beyond three-quarters of a mile in length, and was populated by only 300 men and their families. Half the houses were abandoned. To add to the new Cuban governor's woes, the rest of the huge territory—the province also included Georgia and Alabama plus parts of South Carolina and Mississippi—was even more sparsely populated and only nominally Spanish. Englishmen had established colonies in Georgia and the Carolinas, and the handful of villages and missions along the coast north of St. Augustine and west to Tallahassee were constantly threatened by Indians, pirates, and the English.

Torres de Ayala's first priority was the protection of St. Augustine itself. That meant completing Daza's Castillo de San Marcos. With funds collected from the local populace (soldiers' yearly salary was "150 pieces of eight," part of which they "donated" to the construction, according to Dickinson) and contributions from the government of New Spain, Torres de Ayala jump-started the construction of the fortress and expanded plans to include a seawall to protect the town from floods.

In August 1695, two years after the governor's arrival, construction of Castillo de San Marcos—curtains, bastions, living quarters, moat, ravelin, and seawall—was completed.

THE DEFENSE OF SAN MARCOS

The fortress proved indispensable to the defense of St. Augustine in coming years. In November 1702, an English-led force of Indians and colonial American militia under the command of Carolina Governor James Moore sailed south and entered St. Augustine.

Havana-built supply galley of the kind the Cuban Admiral Berroa led to relieve the English siege of Castillo San Marcos in 1702. (St. Augustine Historical Society)

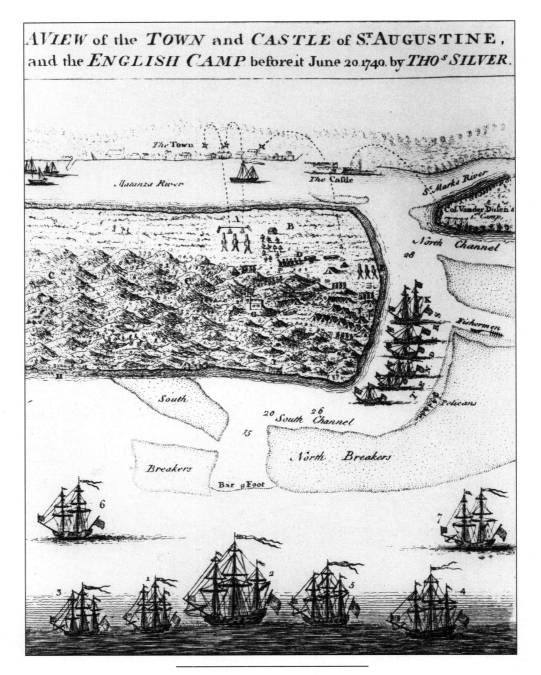

British view of James Oglethorpe's 1740 attack on St. Augustine.
(St. Augustine Historical Society)

All 1,200 inhabitants—every man, woman, and child, whether Spaniard, Cuban, Indian, or black—were ordered to abandon their homes and take refuge inside San Marcos. The English guns were not powerful enough to breach the 12-foot walls Daza had designed, and the settlers were not strong enough to break out. So both sides prepared for a siege.

It was the good fortune of the defenders that the fortress had been built specifically to hold the entire population of the settlement in case of emergency. The St. Augustinians drew their drinking water from a well in one corner of the large open-air parade ground and even had a latrine that used the ocean to flush away the waste that more than a thousand human beings produced each day. Cattle and horses were brought inside. As long as food lasted and morale held, San Marcos was impregnable.

The siege lasted nearly two months. One Cuban officer, Captain Augustín de Ayala, was killed in a sally made to destroy a system of earthworks English soldiers had built "within musket shot" of the castle. San Marcos's defenders held out until Christmas Day, when four warships from Havana under the command of the Cuban-born General Esteban Berroa appeared on the horizon. The English, afraid to find themselves blockaded in the bay, set fire to their small fleet and retreated north by land, but not before torching St. Augustine. Few buildings remained standing outside the walls of Castillo San Marcos. Inside the fort, everyone survived the attack. Shortly thereafter, St. Augustine was rebuilt. It survived another attack in 1740.

Havana to the English

In the summer of 1762 rebuilding came to a halt, as an event unfolded that was to prove of enormous significance to Cuba and its relations with what was to become the United States. That year an armada of 200 ships and 15,000 men, the largest force ever to cross the Atlantic, sailed out of Great Britain for Havana. After a two-month siege, British troops captured Havana, while the rest of Spanish-occupied Cuba was unable to help.

The capital of Cuba was now in English hands. A major port with a population of 75,618, according to the census of 1774, Havana was larger than any city in Spanish America except Lima and Mexico City and had more than twice the population of New York or Philadelphia. It was a walled city, with imposing churches, rich monasteries, a printing press, and a university founded in 1728.

But in a strictly economic sense, it was a closed world. The *criollo* elite—

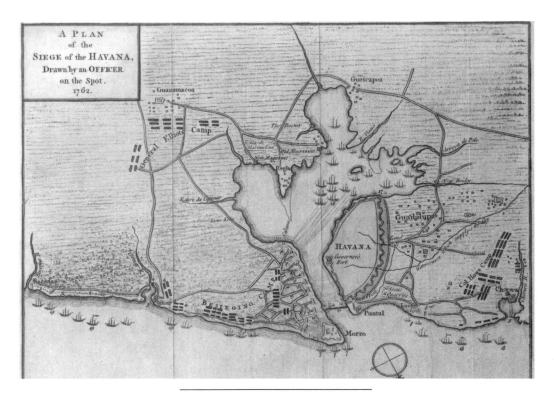

British troops under Lord Albermarle besieged Havana for two months until the garrison at Morro Castle, lower center, *finally fell in the summer of 1762.*
(Cuban Heritage Collection, University of Miami)

wealthy Cuban-born sugar and tobacco planters—were beginning to chafe under the weight of the antiquated Spanish monopolist system, which favored the mother country over its colonies. The crown levied heavy duties to finance the economy in Spain and did not permit its colonies to trade directly with other nations. Edicts promulgated an ocean away, driven more by personal alliances than economic conditions, stifled commerce so that Cuba produced less sugar than French Haiti or English Jamaica, much smaller islands.

This situation ended with British occupation. The British lifted Spain's heavy hand of state and replaced it with the invisible hand of the market—such as it was in those early days of capitalism, at any rate. During the eleven months of British control some 1,000 trade ships docked in Havana. "The British capture of the city was the signal . . . for an immediate descent on the island by English merchants. From North America came food, horses, and grain merchants and, direct from England, linen, cloth and wool sellers, and dealers in sugar equipment," wrote Hugh Thomas in his monumental *Cuba: The Pursuit of Freedom*. So many goods were imported, "they could not be disposed of by Havana shopkeepers for years." Also of great significance, in less than one year under the British, more slaves arrived than in the previous ten years.

The occupation of Havana ended when the British traded the city back to Spain in exchange for Florida. But Havana had mixed feelings about the return of Spanish rule. At first, British troops had looted stores and officers pocketed the public treasury as war booty. Later, a few upper-class *habaneros* collaborated with the English, because the new, less restrictive economic order gave *criollos* a taste of free trade. For the first time, some began to conceive of a political existence outside the dominion of Spain.

Bishop Pedro Agustín Morell de Santa Cruz was persecuted by the British occupiers of Havana and fled to Spanish-held St. Augustine. He thus became one of the first Cuban political exiles in Florida. (Cuban Heritage Collection, University of Miami)

Cuban-born Spaniards would soon begin to think of themselves as "Cuban." It was a first step toward nationhood.

With the signing of the 1763 Treaty of Paris, Great Britain returned Havana to Spain in exchange for Florida. As the British entered St. Augustine, virtually all the Spanish and Cuban colonists evacuated, sailing to Havana. They carted away the records of the local parish, which remained in the archives of the Cathedral of Havana until returned in 1906.

The First Integrated School

The first integrated school in North America was founded at St. Augustine in 1785, and among its first teachers was a Cuban priest, Father Francisco Traconis. The school was open and free to all boys, including black children. It was the first school to teach in Spanish. Father Traconis also became the private tutor to the young grandson of Colonel Bartolomé Morales, commander of Castillo de San Marcos. That child, Félix Varela, would grow up to become the founding father of Cuban national consciousness.

THE AMERICAN REVOLUTION

Thirteen years after Florida passed to the English and Havana back to the Spanish, thirteen Anglo-American colonies issued their Declaration of Independence from Great Britain. It was a daunting task in 1776 to go to war against the largest naval and military power in the world. In the colonies, sentiment was far from united for independence; the Tories opposed it and many others remained neutral. It was only logical, therefore, that after the American Continental Congress declared independence from Great Britain, securing help from foreign powers became of utmost importance.

The Founding Fathers had two countries in mind: The Spain of Charles III and the France of Louis XVI. Ruled by allied branches of the Bourbon dynasty, both had long battled England for world hegemony. Frenchmen and Spaniards were also motivated by revenge and the desire to regain national pride. In 1763, France had lost all her territories on the North American continent to England, and the year before Spain had been forced to give up Florida.

In the end, without the significant military, financial, and naval assistance provided by France and Spain, the American independence movement might well have failed. Every American schoolchild learns about the contribution of the French in the Revolutionary War, but little has been written about Spain's assistance, or about its Cuban colony's commitment to American liberation. Yet it was of great importance. It was a force which included Cuban troops under General Bernardo de Gálvez that drove the Redcoats out of West Florida and the Gulf, opening a second front while Washington's Continental Army prepared the final blow at Yorktown. And it was money raised by Havana residents that helped finance the Yorktown campaign itself.

After the Minutemen fired the first shots of the Revolution at Lexington and Concord, Spain began to prepare for war and to provide vital resources to the American patriots. As far back as 1777 it funneled one million *livres* to the colonists' cause. That same year José Eligio de la Puente, born in St. Augustine of Cuban parents, was sent from Havana to spy on British forces in his native Florida; and that year, too, a Havana merchant named Juan Miralles was sent from Havana on orders from Charles III as liaison with George Washington and the Continental Congress. Miralles, who had arrived in Cuba from Spain as a boy and married into a prominent Cuban family, landed in Charleston, South Carolina, and set out for Williamsburg, Virginia. There he met in secret with Patrick Henry.

The emissary from Cuba and the Virginia leader laid out a strategy that called for Spanish and American troops to take the city of Mobile and the British West Florida capital of Pensacola, sweep through British East Florida and its capital of St. Augustine, and contact American rebels fighting in Georgia. The plan was sent to Madrid, where ministers waited for a formal declaration of hostilities.

Spanish general Bernardo de Gálvez raised an army in Havana and sailed from there in an expedition that ousted British troops from West Florida and the Gulf during the American Revolutionary War. (Louisiana Arts and Science Center)

Miralles befriended George Washington and became such an ardent admirer he sent portraits of the American Founding Father as gifts to authorities in Havana and Madrid, while sending Washington and his wife Martha gifts of Cuban lemons and guava paste. Miralles took up residence in Philadelphia, where he organized the shipment of supplies from Cuba. After Spain's declaration of war in 1779, he spent the winter at Washington's headquarters in Morristown, New Jersey. He died there of pneumonia and was buried with military honors,

Washington marching at the head of a funeral cortege said to be more than one mile long. A requiem mass was held at St. Mary's, Philadelphia, one of the first Catholic services officially attended by the United States government and Congress as a body.

After Miralles's death, the invasion plan he and Patrick Henry had forged was not forgotten in Madrid. The Spanish war ministry was so eager for action—so eager to recapture Florida and humiliate England—it went forward without the American troops. Named as Spanish commander was the governor of Louisiana, General Bernardo de Gálvez.

CUBANS VERSUS REDCOATS

Operating out of New Orleans, Gálvez organized an army. By the fall of 1779 he had taken Baton Rouge and British forts along the Mississippi. The following

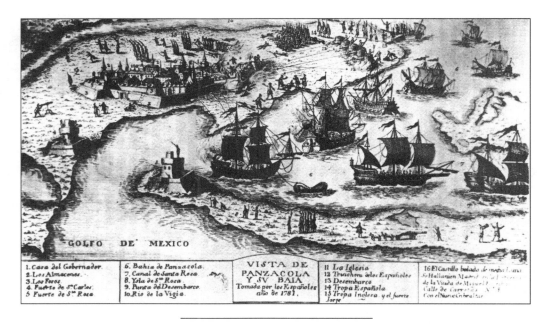

Spanish view of Gálvez's siege of Pensacola in 1781. British troops, left, *defending the fort; the Cuban and Spanish infantry,* right, *and the Armada,* foreground, *led by the Cuban Field Marshal Juan Manuel de Cagigal.* (Pensacola Historical Society)

spring he overwhelmed the British garrison at Mobile with 1,400 troops sent from Havana. There still remained a major objective: the reconquest of Florida. Gálvez did not have enough men or supplies to take on the 2,500 Redcoats and Native American allies that defended Pensacola, so he sailed to Cuba to raise a new army.

The first expedition was forced back by a hurricane. Four months later, on February 28, 1781, Gálvez sailed out of Havana with 1,315 men in 20 ships. The troops landed near Pensacola and began to dig trenches to surround the city for a siege. Reinforcements of militia from Cuba, Mexico, and Puerto Rico arrived by land from Louisiana and extended the trenches ever closer to the British garrison of Fort St. George. But the defenders were also well dug in and would not surrender. The stalemate lasted for two months. Then, one day that May, the besieging troops let out a cheer as they looked toward the sea: Sails appeared on the horizon. Some 1,600 fresh troops had arrived from Havana aboard a 20-ship armada under the command of Field Marshal Juan Manuel de Cagigal, a native of Santiago de Cuba. Now Gálvez had 7,000 men, 4,000 of whom had come from Cuba.

Cagigal's ships bombarded the redoubt. Under cover of the naval artillery, the infantry of Cubans, Mexicans, Puerto Ricans, and Spaniards took the heights just beyond Fort St. George. The decisive moment came when a shell blew up the British powder depot, killing more than 100 soldiers. Surrounded on land and with escape closed by Cagigal's ships, the British raised the white flag. Gálvez, his pan-Hispanic troops, and a Cuban-born field marshal had taken western Florida from England and pinned down Redcoats that could have been mobilized against American rebels to the north.

After the victory, Gálvez was poised for an assault on East Florida and St. Augustine, but British forces soon withdrew and Florida was Spanish once more.

American Florida

In 1783, Britain ceded East Florida back to Spain as part of the same treaty under which it recognized the independence of the United States. Surprisingly, some of St. Augustine's former Cuban residents left Havana and sailed back to their old Florida homes. St. Augustine parish records show 71 children of Cuban-born parents had been born between 1792 and 1799, not an inconsiderable number, given that the total population was perhaps 1,000 residents.

In the early 1800s the young United States maneuvered to acquire Florida from its Revolutionary War ally, Spain. In 1812, an East Florida planter named

Havitantes de la Florida Oriental:

el dia diez proximo se ha de dar posesion de esta Provincia al Señor comisionado de los Estados Unidos legitimamente autorizado para recivirla Coronel Don ROBERTO BUTLER, evacuando el territorio los oficiales y Tropas Españolas, que ocuparan los oficiales y Tropas Americanas, con arreglo al tratado celebrado en Washington en 22 de Febrero de 1819, Real Cedula de 24 de Octubre del año anterior, y demas ordenes con que me hallo, como comisionado para la entrega; en el momento que esta se verifique cesan las autoridades Españolas en el egercicio de sus funciones y entran a desempeñar las suyas las Americanas. De mi deber es participaros esta importante mutacion politica; antes os he hecho saber lo estipulado por nuestro gobierno para aseguraros en el libre egercicio de la Religion Catolica, en vuestras propiedades, y goces que el mismo tratado garantiza; tambien os he manifestado las franquicias, gracias y proteccion que ofrece nuestro gobierno a los que acomode trasladarse a algunos puntos de la Monarquia Española, y en particular a la Ysla de Cuba. Ceso en mandaros, pero aun permanecere entre vosotros el preciso tiempo para concluir algunos particulares de la comision, cuya resolucion espero del superior gobierno, mientras me hallaran pronto a facilitar los auxilios que esten a mi alcance a los que soliciten su traslacion a la Habana, y donde quiera que me halle a daros testimonio del particular concepto y aprecio que me mereceis.

Floridanos, vais a dar la ultima prueba de vuestras virtudes obedeciendo las disposiciones de S. M.; Ojala cesen con este cambio todas las vicisitudes que las circunstancias os han hecho sufrir con resignacion heroica! testigo de ella, y de los sacrificios que habeis hecho por la patria manifestare los que me consten de cada uno si se les ofrece como lo hago en general de todos: me lisongeo con la idea de que sereis felices que es todo lo que os desea vuestro

Amigo y Conciudadano,

EL CORONEL

Jose Coppinger

San Agustin de la Florida 7 de Julio de 1821.

Proclamation to the residents of Spanish Florida from its last governor, the Cuban-born José Coppinger, issued on the eve of the American takeover. Coppinger says the government in Madrid would offer "abatements, graces and protection" to colonists who moved to other "points of the Spanish Monarchy, specially the Island of Cuba."
(Florida Historical Society).

Early twentieth-century postcard view of Charlotte Street, St. Augustine's old commercial district. The buildings on the left, made of coquina *and with overhanging balconies, date from Florida's Second Spanish Period. All burned down in a fire in 1914.*
(Author's collection)

John Houston McIntosh organized an army of several hundred men, took Fernandina and Amelia Islands near Jacksonville, declared an independent "Republic of Florida," and prepared to turn command over to U.S. troops standing by in Georgia. But after two companies of black militia sent from Havana reinforced St. Augustine the Americans desisted.

But not for long: In 1821, an indebted Spain sold Florida to the United States for five million dollars. Cubans and Spaniards living in St. Augustine again sailed to Havana. They found an island where a new era was dawning, during which political upheavals would send thousands of them back north.

After Gálvez's victory, the American states faced a dire problem. While British troops under General Charles Cornwallis massed in Virginia, the Americans were nearly bankrupt. The Comte de Rochambeau—Washington's French ally—calculated there was enough money to pay and supply the men for two months, and no more. Desperate, Washington dashed off an urgent request to American financier

Robert Morris on August 27. "I must entreat you, if possible, to procure one month's pay in specie for the detachment under my command. Part of the troops have not been paid for a long time and have upon several occasions shown marks of great discontent." Morris replied the following day, stating that he could not honor the general's request. Without salaries and sufficient supplies, and cut off by the British control of the sea, the Continental Army of the American Revolution was on the verge of disbanding.

Next, Rochambeau asked Admiral De Grasse—commanding a French fleet in the Caribbean assigned to sail north and provide Washington the sea power he needed—to help raise the money. The admiral first tried French authorities in Haiti, but the colonial treasury there could not meet his needs and local merchants were unwilling or unable to help. So he turned to the Marqués de Saavedra, a Spanish official in Santo Domingo (today's Dominican Republic) the Spanish colony that shared the island of Hispaniola with French Haiti. Saavedra did not think he could raise the funds there, but he believed that in Cuba it was possible.

Arriving in Havana on August 15, 1781, aboard the frigate *Aigrette*, de Saavedra contacted the new governor of Cuba, Juan Manuel de Cagigal, the same military officer who had turned the tide at Pensacola. After learning of the grave situation facing the Americans, de Cagigal went to work. Historians do not agree about exactly what happened next. Some say it was all resolved in six hours, others say it took two days. There is also controversy about what percentage of the money came from the Havana municipal treasury as opposed to private funds. (One story has it that most of the capital was raised by Cuban women who pawned their jewelry.) But De Grasse got the money: 1,200,00 French *livres*, which historian Otto Rodríguez Viamonte has calculated amounts to some $300 million today—enough to support an army of 5,000 for four months. If De Grasse could safely join the American troops, Washington would have the money as well as the ships he needed.

Elated by having raised the funds, de Saavedra left Havana on the *Aigrette* and met De Grasse off Matanzas Bay. Together they raced north, evading the British Navy to reach Chesapeake Bay. There, they met and defeated a British fleet. De Grasse sent an urgent dispatch to George Washington with the good news: Cuban money and French ships were safe and awaiting his orders.

Meanwhile, Washington had been marching south from New York with his army, "distressed beyond expression to know what had become of De Grasse," as he wrote in a letter. That distress eased considerably on September 5th, when a horseman bearing the good news found Washington three miles south of the American encampment at Chester, Pennsylvania, on the Delaware.

Rochambeau had sailed downriver from Philadelphia to meet him there, and as the ship approached, a figure in a blue and buff uniform waited at the dock. Historian Eduardo Tejera quotes the diary of Rochambeau's aide-de-camp, M. Closen: "We saw in the distance, General Washington shaking his hat and a white handkerchief, and showing signs of joy. Rochambeau had scarcely landed when Washington, usually so cool and composed, fell into his arms. The great news had arrived; De Grasse had come."

Financed by the Cuban war chest, Washington's men marched on to Yorktown to defeat the Redcoats, the last great battle of the Revolutionary War. With Cornwallis's capitulation, American independence was assured.

"The million that was supplied to pay the troops . . . may, with truth, be regarded as the 'bottom dollars' of the edifice upon which American independence was erected," says historian Stephen Bonsal.

Help from Cuba arrived in great measure because Spain saw in the American Revolution a chance to strike at Great Britain and win back Florida. That certainly explains the Gálvez expeditions. But there may have been more. Could the Spanish crown's geopolitical strategy alone account for the willingness of Cubans to risk their money to finance a foreign war? Perhaps there was lingering resentment over the British occupation seventeen years earlier. Perhaps among some Cubans there was sympathy for the first nation of the Americas fighting to throw off a European colonial power.

The vigorous young republic that Cubans had helped would serve as a base of operations in exiles' struggle to free the island from Spanish rule. And it would cast a covetous eye on the island and its now rapidly growing, slave-based sugar economy.

CHAPTER 2

Exilios Begin

1789–1868

The independence of the United States from Great Britain was followed shortly by Latin America's own struggles for independence from Spain. Under leaders such as the Venezuelan Simón Bolívar and the Argentinean José de San Martín, nearly all the nations that today make up the Spanish-speaking Americas had by the 1820s defeated Spanish armies and ended Spanish rule.

In Cuba, too, there had been independence movements in the first few decades of the nineteenth century. Even though all of them were broken up by Spanish authorities, an undercurrent of resistance against colonial rule remained as Spain imposed restrictions on the rights and liberties of native-born Cubans. But Cuba was an exception to the rest of Latin America. Despite the growing sentiment in favor of independence it remained a Spanish colony when most of the other former colonies had become sovereign republics. And the principal reason may be summed up in one word: Slavery.

Flag used by the Soles y Rayos conspirators.
(Cuban Heritage Collection, University of Miami)

Conspiracies in Cuba

Even during the brief period of relative democracy permitted in Cuba between 1821 and 1823 by a short-lived liberal government in Madrid, the quest for complete independence gained favor among Cuba's blacks and working-class whites. The first major conspiracy of the period was the *Soles y Rayos de Bolívar* (Suns and Rays of Bolívar). Led by José Francisco Lemus, a delegation traveled to Colombia in early 1823 to ask South American liberator Simón Bolívar for help in sparking revolution on the island. Bolívar, who had ousted the Spanish from Colombia but was in the midst of preparations for fighting for the independence of Perú, declined.

Back in Cuba that April, the conspirators learned Spanish King Fernando VII had reimposed despotic rule. By the summer Lemus and his men were armed and ready to begin the uprising, but Spanish authorities crushed the movement, arresting Lemus and his principal aides. For the times, it was surprising that no one was executed. But Spanish governor Dionisio Vives forced them all to leave Cuba. Lemus went to Mexico, where he died in 1832.

The brief British occupation of Havana in 1762 had brought a taste of free trade that Cubans never forgot. Fifteen years later, under pressure from Havana merchants, the Spanish colonial government finally eased restraints on foreign commerce. The restrictions were reinstated and lifted several times over the next decades but it no longer mattered. The genie was let out of the bottle and officials in a position to enrich themselves turned a blind eye to contraband during the periods of toughened regulations. As a result, Cuba experienced tremendous economic growth. Sugar exports quintupled by the mid-1780s, and a generation later Cuba was the world's largest producer.

The sugar boom enriched Cuba, but extracted a high price. To cut cane in the fields and work machinery in the *ingenios*—the mills that produced the precious commodity—tens of thousands of Africans were captured, brought across the Atlantic and forcibly put to work. The expanding economy demanded more slave labor, and by the beginning of the nineteenth century Cuba's black population was larger than the white. The census of 1827 found 311,051 whites, 286,942 black slaves, and 106,949 free blacks.

The influential Cuban slave owners opposed independence. They feared that a sovereign Cuba would abolish slavery and become a Haiti-style black republic, in which they would lose their fortunes and even their lives. Thus, they set Cuban independence movements decades behind those elsewhere in Latin America.

Some slave owners, fearful that slavery would be abolished even if Cuba remained under Spain, sought annexation to the United States, where they believed slavery had a future. They found support among American followers of expansion through Manifest Destiny, who prized Cuba's riches and strategic position in the Gulf. But most of all they found support among American plantation owners who overcame their reservations about annexing an island of Spanish-speaking Catholics. They understood that making Cuba a slave-owning state meant additional votes in Congress as the South tried to gain an edge in the showdown that would turn to bloodshed in the U.S. Civil War.

America Attempts to Buy Cuba

Several American presidents, beginning with Thomas Jefferson, tried unsuccessfully to buy Cuba from Spain. After one such failure in 1822, Secretary of State John Quincy Adams wrote a letter to the U.S. government minister in Spain. "There are laws of political as well as of physical gravitation," Adams said, "and if an apple severed by the tempest from its native tree cannot choose but to fall to the ground, Cuba, forcibly disjoined from its own unnatural connection with Spain, and incapable of self support, can gravitate only toward the North American Union which by the same law of nature cannot cast her off from its bosom."

The different political factions that would define Cuban history for the rest of the century, on the island and in exile, were taking shape. There were *independentistas*, ready to go to war against Spain for a sovereign republic. More timid were the *reformistas*, who sought increased self-rule for Cuba but as a province under the Spanish crown. And there were *anexionistas*, themselves divided in two camps: those who sought annexation to preserve slavery, and abolitionists who wanted Cuba to join the United States because they preferred American democracy over the decrepit Spanish monarchy. All were opposed by hard-line Spaniards who wanted to rule the island not as a province of Spain but as a colony, excluding native-born Cubans from taking part in government.

Spain itself, however, was in chaos. In the decade following ouster of Napoleon from the Iberian Peninsula, Spain lost most of its empire in the Americas, and control of the government in Madrid switched four times between liberals and reactionaries. Fernando VII aligned himself with liberals when convenient only to go back to his absolutist allies as soon as they were strong enough.

FÉLIX VARELA IN NEW YORK

It was during one of the more liberal periods that Father Félix Varela, the leading light of the first wave of Cubans who sought political refuge in the United States, came to prominence.

Varela, a Catholic priest, was an immensely popular professor of philosophy at Havana's Seminary of San Carlos, where he had taken the radical step of teaching in the vernacular—Spanish—instead of Latin, and insisted that women and men had the same right to an education. He was also the author of *Lecciones de Filosofía*, a textbook on philosophy, logic, and ethics used in universities throughout the Spanish-speaking world. Varela, a disciple wrote after his death, "taught Cubans how to think."

He would also teach Cubans to think of themselves as *Cuban*. In 1821, as a new parliament formed in Spain under a liberal constitution, enthusiastic Cubans voted for deputies to represent them at the Cortes, the Spanish congress. The three men elected, the 33-year-old Varela, Tomás Gener, and Leonardo Santos Suárez, were *refomistas*. In Madrid Varela developed detailed legislation to abolish slavery and establish self-rule for Cuba without demanding outright independence. But in 1823 this relatively democratic period in Spanish history ended with the return of absolutism. Cuba once again was made a voiceless colony rather than the semiautonomous overseas province it had become two years earlier. Parliament was dissolved and the new regime imposed the death sentence on Varela.

Varela and his fellow Cuban deputies fled Madrid and made their way to British-held Gibraltar, where they boarded

Félix Varela, the Catholic priest who founded parishes in New York to help Irish immigrants. He is considered the father of Cuban national consciousness.
(Cuban National Heritage)

JOSE MARIA HEREDIA.

José María Heredia y Campzano. A plaque at Niagara Falls commemorates his poem of heartsickness and longing for the Cuba from which colonial authorities forced him to flee. (Cuban Heritage Collection, University of Miami)

the freighter *Thorndike*, bound for New York. They arrived in December 1823 during a snowstorm. Cristóbal Madan, a former student of the priest who met them at the dock, recalled later how Varela had to hold on to his arm to keep from slipping on the unfamiliar ice during the long walk to a boardinghouse on Broadway. It was the beginning of a cycle that to this day is at the heart of the Cuban-American experience: repression at home followed by exile in the United States.

Literary Exiles

There was intense literary activity among mid-century Cuban exiles. It was while living in New York that Cirillo Villaverde finished writing and first published *Cecilia Valdés*, a classic abolitionist novel about the love affair between the scion of a slave-owning planter family and a *mulata* who turns out to be his half sister. He also helped edit *El laúd del desterrado*, an 1858 anthology of poetry written by Cubans in the United States.

The best known of those poets is José María Heredia y Campuzano. In New York he moved in Varela's exile circles, living daily with the pain of being away from his beloved island.

Heredia traveled on a futile quest to ease his longing for the Cuba he would never see again. Most memorably, he visited Niagara Falls, which inspired his best known poem, "Ode to Niagara." With the deluge of words characteristic of romantic poetry, he wrote of his awe of the falls' majestic power, but even that vision could not erase Cuba from his mind:

Torrente prodigioso, calma, acalla	Prodigious torrent, calm and silence
tu trueno aterrador; disipa un tanto	your terrifying thunder; dispel
las tinieblas que en torno te	the mists that surround you
circundan,	and let me see your placid mien . . .
y déjame mirar tu faz serena . . .	But what do my yearning eyes
Mas, ¿qué en ti busca mi anhelante	search for in you with fruitless anxiety?
vista	Why don't I see encircling your im-
con inútil afán? ¿Por qué no miro	mense cavern
alrededor de tu caverna inmensa	the palms, Oh! the delightful palms
las palmas, ¡ay!, las palmas	that in the plains of my burning home-
deliciosas,	land
que en las llanuras de mi ardiente	are born of the sun to grow into
patria	smiles,
nacen del sol a la sonrisa, y crecen,	and which on uncorrupted soil sway
y al soplo de las brisas del Océano	to the gusts of ocean breezes?
bajo un suelo purísimo se mecen?	

For exiles today, Heredia's poem captures a similar sense of loss, a century and a half after it was written.

The small community of Cuban émigrés, well aware of Varela's reputation, welcomed the philosopher-priest turned politician. But this early *exilios*, like later ones, was not united. Among the expatriates were antislavery *anexionistas*, who believed that Cuba should be annexed by the United States, led by Gaspar Betancourt Cisneros, who decided to stay in the United States after attending college in Philadelphia; *reformistas*, the supporters of an autonomous colony of Spain, whose chief spokesman, José Antonio Saco, had been Varela's student at the University of Havana; and *independentistas*, those who fought for the independent country of Cuba, among whom was the poet José María Heredia, who fled to the United States within days of Varela after being involved in the failed Soles y Rayos de Bolívar conspiracy.

After nearly paying with his life for the intransigence in Madrid, Varela became convinced Spain would never permit genuine reform in Cuba. The former *reformista* became an *independentista*. He stayed in New York briefly and moved

GASPAR BETANCOURT CISNEROS.

JOSE ANTONIO SACO.

Exiled activist Gaspar Betancourt Cisneros (left) was an abolitionist and admirer of American democracy who supported U.S. statehood for Cuba. His friend and political opponent José Antonio Saco (right) was a leader of the exile faction that wanted Cuba to be a Spanish province with local rule. (Cuban Heritage Collection, University of Miami)

to Philadelphia, where he published the first three editions of *El Habanero,* perhaps the first Spanish-language newspaper in the United States. Six months later Varela moved back to New York, where he published the next four editions. He would live in New York nearly the rest of his life.

Varela used *El Habanero* to appeal for Cuban independence. Yet he also worked with the different exile factions. He was so admired he brought together exiles with views as divergent as Saco and Betancourt Cisneros to discuss the pressing Cuban issues of the day. To Varela, the groups had different aims but were united in their desire to end the intolerable status quo on the island.

Under his leadership, *El Habanero,* which was smuggled into Cuba and distributed clandestinely, became the center of intellectual life for Cubans in New York. The exiles that gathered around Varela talked about the issues of the day and debated their different agendas, discussions that made their way to the newspaper. Its pages exploded with exiles' contempt for the greed of slave-owning planters: "On the island of Cuba there is no love for Spain, nor Colombia, nor Mexico, nor anything other than crates of sugar and sacks of coffee," Varela wrote.

El Habanero also kept up with news from Cuba, considered the question of annexation, and examined whether émigrés should ask the new sister republics in Latin America for help in liberating the island. In 1825 a commission sailed from New York to request the aid of Bolívar once again. But like the Soles y Rayos conspirators two years earlier, they received no support. Bolívar was busy in his Peruvian campaign, and the United States let it be known it preferred Cuba under Spain rather than one of the stronger European powers.

Discouraged, Varela ceased publication of *El Habanero* in 1826 and concentrated on scholarly pursuits. He updated *Lecciones de Filosofía* and published *Cartas a Elpidio*, his most important book, in which he urged that Catholicism ought not be divorced from

CARTAS

A

ELPIDIO,

SOBRE

LA IMPIEDAD, LA SUPERSTICION Y EL FANATISMO,

EN

SUS RELACIONES CON LA SOCIEDAD.

Por el Presbitero D. Felix Varela.

TOMO SEGUNDO.

SUPERSTICION.

NUEVA-YORK:
EN LA IMPRENTA DE G. P. SCOTT Y Cª.
ESQUINA DE LA CALLE DE JOHN Y GOLD.

1838.

The 1838 New York edition of Varela's best known work, Cartas a Elpidio
(Cuban National Heritage)

reason. In 1828 he began to write for *El Mensajero Semanal*, another Cuban New York newspaper, founded by his *reformista* friend Saco. Varela remained surrounded by his exile admirers. But he regretfully came to realize that at that point in Cuban history—with planters protecting slavery, South America unable to help, the colonial regime suspending the few freedoms permitted, and the United States interested only in annexation—independence was not attainable.

Frustrated with politics, the priest turned his attention to pastoral duties. As a child, Varela had spent ten years in St. Augustine, where his teacher and mentor was the Irish priest Michael O'Reilly. Forty years later, when Varela arrived in

CHURCH OF THE TRANSFIGURATION,
MOTT STREET,

*Transfiguration Church, founded by
Father Varela in Lower Manhattan. The
parish survives today in Chinatown.*
(Cuban National Heritage)

New York, there were but three parishes to serve the Catholic population, predominantly Irish and concentrated in the notorious Five Points slum. It was to them that Varela dedicated the rest of his life.

In 1827 he arranged for the purchase of the Episcopalian Christ Church, on Ann Street, and became its first pastor. Five years later he founded the School of the Transfiguration of Our Lord, near City Hall, at a time when free public schooling did not exist. The school educated generations of Irish immigrant children. Varela's educational legacy survives today in the Transfiguration School in New York's Chinatown, the direct descendant of the one he established.

In the same busy year of 1832, Varela's priestly devotion was tested by the devastating epidemic that struck New York City. Between July and August, thousands of people came down with cholera, 3,513 of whom died. Contemporary accounts speak of a parade of coffins rumbling through the streets, of tons of uncollected rubbish, of sick men and unburied corpses lying in gutters. Sanitation authorities spread lime and coal dust on the streets and burned fires in a futile effort to cleanse the air. Some 100,000 New Yorkers—half the population—fled to the country. The diary of Philip Hone, a Manhattan notable of the period, records that "the eastern section of the city is nearly deserted, and business of every description appears to be at a standstill."

But not all could afford to escape. Mortality was highest, as Hone put it, "among the wretched population of the Five Points." And through Dantesque alleyways of dust, burning piles of garbage, the dying and the dead, Varela made his way to tend to them. At least one local hospital flatly refused cholera patients, but

The notorious Five Points slum, with a brewery in its very center, where Father Varela ministered to sick Irish immigrants during the cholera epidemic of 1831. (Museum of the City of New York)

Varela helped organize makeshift medical centers for the worst-hit neighborhoods. He practically lived in those temporary infirmaries until the epidemic ran its course, tending to the sick, comforting the bereaved, and risking his own life.

Varela did not get cholera. But he became a beloved figure, "the Vicar of the Irish," as he was called. He opened nurseries and orphanages for children of poor widows, and organized the New York Catholic Temperance Association to battle rampant alcohol abuse. In 1836, after the Christ Church building nearly collapsed, he arranged the purchase of another Protestant house of worship and founded Transfiguration Church, on Chambers Street. It was his base for the next quarter century. For his compassion and organizational vision he was named

Felix Varela in his later years.
(Cuban National Heritage)

Niche at St. Augustine's historic Tolomato Cemetery where Varela was buried until his remains were transferred to Havana in 1911. (Cuban National Heritage)

Vicar General of the New York Archdiocese in 1837. He might have been named archbishop but for the influence that the Spanish church (which had not forgotten his pro-independence activities) had in the Vatican.

Over the next years he continued to help immigrants and defend Catholics, reviled by the Protestant establishment as carriers of "Rum, Romanism, and Rebellion." But there was so much poverty, so much bigotry, so much work to simply keep the school and church financially afloat, that Varela's health broke down. Exhausted and ill, he retired to his childhood home of St. Augustine in 1848 and five years later he died at the age of 64.

A Cuban Priest's American Legacy

Félix Varela left a considerable legacy in the United States as well as Cuba. The priest who risked his health for immigrants and fought anti-Catholic prejudice was finally recognized by Americans with the issue of a U.S. postage stamp in his likeness in 1997. Cubans, however, have always known that he was an early patriot who reformed Cuban intellectual life and became the independence-minded leader of the first wave of exiles. He may be considered, as Pope John Paul II said before Varela's tomb during his visit to Cuba in 1998, "the foundation-stone of the Cuban national identity." The Vatican is considering his candidacy to become his nation's first Catholic saint.

Meanwhile in Cuba things progressively deteriorated. A number of separatist conspiracies had been smashed, and the Spanish government proscribed civil liberties and banned native-born Cubans from holding office or serving in the army. With 40,000 troops brought from Spain to preserve order and the Captain General in Havana ruling by martial law, the island was an armed camp. This gave renewed vigor to anticolonial sentiments, on the island and in exile.

The Rise of *Anexionismo*

Ironically, the most influential exiles favored annexation to the United States, not independence or even autonomy. One of the few dissenters, José Antonio Saco, raised his voice in protest. "Annexation . . . signifies the absorption of Cuba by the United States," he wrote. "I want a Cuba that is not only prosperous, learned, moral and powerful, but that Cuba be Cuban and not Anglo-American."

Saco did not win many converts among fellow exiles. In the middle of the nineteenth century, *anexionistas* held sway.

The group consisted of an uneasy alliance between exiles such as Betancourt Cisneros who sought the freedoms of American democracy, and representatives of rich planters who, paradoxically, wanted that democracy to protect Cuban slavery. The pro-slavery faction proved most active.

With the United States convinced of its "Manifest Destiny" after victory over Mexico, and with North and South spinning toward civil war, the notion of annexing Cuba as a slave state gained renewed strength among Americans also. Several schemes to buy the island played themselves out in 1848 and 1849, including one offer by Cuban planters to reimburse the United States $100 million if it purchased Cuba. In any case, Spain would not consider selling its most prized colony.

NARCISO LÓPEZ

So it had to be tried by force. In 1848, a conspiracy was discovered in Cuba; its leader, Venezuela-born Narciso López, had risen to Field Marshal of the Spanish army during the second of Spain's Carlist civil wars. López escaped to the United States. Thus began the American saga of the most controversial figure in nineteenth-century Cuban history.

Although the plot in which López had participated involved *independentistas*, upon arriving in the United States he began to plan for an invasion backed by *anexionistas*, Cuban as well as American. López traveled between Washington and New York, meeting with leaders of the considerable exile community that by then existed in the United States and—secretly—with Americans who might support the fight, mostly pro-slavery Southerners like the future Confederate President Jefferson Davis.

A key figure in the affair was Ambrosio José Gonzáles, who had been sent by wealthy separatists in Havana to, as he put it in an article for *The Times-Democrat* of New Orleans forty-four years later, "offer General (William Jenkins) Worth, returning home from the Mexican war, $3,000,000, wherewith to raise an expedition of 5,000 men out of the disbanded soldiers of the Mexican war and officered by the best personnel in our army, to land in Cuba in support of a patriot movement to be initiated by General Lopez with a bodyguard of Cubans and Americans."

López had to act with great delicacy: He had to keep the conspiracy secret from the anti-interventionist administration of the newly elected President Zachary Taylor; he had to entice Southerners with the idea of annexing a slave state; he had to play down the slavery issue with antislavery *anexionista* allies like Betancourt Cisneros; and he had to soft-pedal annexation with *independentistas.*

After landing troops in Cárdenas to fight Spanish colonial rule in 1850, Narciso López became the first to fly the Cuban flag on Cuban soil. (Cuban Heritage Collection, University of Miami)

New York's Cuban Flag

The flag of Cuba was created in New York City in 1849, while Narciso López and other exiles planned the invasion of the island. Tradition has it that one hot summer day López took a break from his labors in a park and fell asleep; upon waking, the blue sky and long hazy clouds he saw inspired the idea for a flag his expedition could carry. López told the poet Miguel Teurbe Tolón of his vision and added the red triangle with the lone white star.

Whether or not the legend of the vision in the park is historically accurate, it is documented that at a guest house on Warren Street where exiles gathered Teurbe Tolón made a design based on ideas given him by López, which the poet's wife Emilia stitched together out of silk cloth. The banner was first raised in the balcony of *The New York Sun* ("The star is Cuba—an independent nation," reported the next day's edition) and flew for the first time in Cuba during López's expedition.

MIGUEL TEURBE TOLON.

Along with Narciso López, the poet Miguel Teurbe Tolón designed Cuba's national flag in New York in 1849.
(Cuban Heritage Collection, University of Miami)

The plot progressed in fits and starts. In late 1848, Worth was named commander of federal troops in Texas and dropped out of the intrigue; the promised $3 million dried up. López persisted but in 1849 the U.S. Navy blockaded some 800 followers gathered on Round Island, off the coast of Mississippi. The same year the *"Junta Promovedora de los Intereres Políticos de Cuba,"* which included in its leadership López as well as the abolitionist novelist Cirillo Villaverde and even a future *independentista*, Juan Manuel Macías, began to work in Washington, New Orleans, and New York on plans for invasion. The plan was to land in Cuba, ignite a revolt, then petition for annexation.

COMBAT IN CUBA

The turning point came at a White House reception where Ambrosio González was told by General John Henderson, a former Senator from Mississippi, that "if (González) ever thought of moving in behalf of Cuba, to come to New Orleans and see him." Days later, as González puts it, "some young gentlemen from Kentucky . . . asserted their ability and willingness to raise at their own expense and bring down to New Orleans a regiment of Kentuckians, as fine material as could be found anywhere."

López took up the offer. In New Orleans he assembled three skeleton regiments, one each from Kentucky, Mississippi, and Louisiana. So as not to arouse suspicion, López and his 600 men, with González as second-in-command, de-

Model of the flag designed in New York and flown in Cárdenas during the López landing. It is the same as the modern Cuban flag, except that in the official banner the top "arm" of the star points straight up. (Cuban Heritage Collection, University of Miami)

parted separately in three vessels over twelve days. They met near Contoy Island, off Yucatan, where all boarded the steamer *Creole*. After the transfer of troops at sea, says the diary of Colonel Marion C. Taylor, a young Kentucky officer, "Gen. Lopez deputized Lt. Col. Pickett, of our regiment, to present us the flag of Cuba, as made by the Revolutionists, which was done by a few appropriate remarks, which were responded to by three cheers. It was truly an inspiring scene to behold upon the tossing billows of the ocean two vessels, upon each of which was seen the flags being presented to troops going to fight for the liberty of the oppressed of Cuba."

Landing before sunrise in Cárdenas, on the northern coast, Gonzáles recalls the men "moved in solid column toward the barracks," which they took after a firefight. The Spaniards fell back to the municipal building, which also surrendered. Then, a memorable moment in the history of Cuba: on May 19, 1850, for the first time on Cuban soil, the national flag was raised.

Cirillo Villaverde, author of the classic abolitionist novel Cecilia Valdes *and one of the most active figures in New York's Cuban literary circles in the mid-nineteenth century.* (Cuban Heritage Collection, University of Miami)

The invaders stayed in place. "The town was held the whole of that day. Attacks were made by the Spaniards, of infantry and cavalry from the interior, during the day, but were repulsed," Gonzáles recalled. However, Cárdenas citizens did not join López as he had expected, perhaps because there were hardly any Cubans in the nearly all-American force. When intelligence arrived that 3,000 Spanish reinforcements were on their way, López evacuated the town and under cover of night the *Creole* steamed to Key West, just beating out the pursuing Spanish cruiser *Pizarro*.

Back in New Orleans, López was put on trial for violating the Neutrality Law. The following March, after three hung juries—the last, eleven-to-one for acquittal—charges were dismissed. The same year authorities confiscated the steamer *Cleopatra* in New York, again breaking up a López plot. When President Millard Fillmore (Taylor had died in office) issued arrest warrants, Gonzáles hid in friends' plantations along coastal Georgia and South Carolina. López went undercover in Jacksonville and Savannah; by August he was back fighting in Cuba with yet another expedition out of New Orleans. This time he was captured and on September 1, 1851, he was executed by garrote. Ninety-five Americans who accompanied López were released the following year from prison in Vigo, Spain. When they arrived in New York that March, Cuban refugees there collected $500 to give them "as a token of gratitude for the noble and heroic services that these chivalrous sons and soldiers of Liberty have rendered."

Historians have debated whether Narciso López was a trailblazer of independence as the first patriot to lead an organized military strike against Spanish power and fly the Cuban flag on Cuban soil, or a renegade who nearly wrecked Cuban nationhood by fighting to annex the island to the United States with the expectation of preserving slavery. If his invasion had triumphed, would he have asked for annexation? Did he believe Cubans would go along?

In his manifesto upon entering Cárdenas, López wrote of "the free and independent *patria*" without mentioning annexation. In contrast, the founding declaration of the Junta, which he signed, spoke of the day Cuba could finally "take the place that corresponds to a daughter of the Americas" and then added, echoing John Adams nearly fifty years earlier, "before settling upon the bosom of the great federal family." Yet it remains difficult to believe that a man of López's drive and ambition would risk his life fighting in Cuba only to meekly turn it over to the United States, whose government had even prosecuted him for his military adventures. Antonio de la Cova, professor of Latin American history at Rose-Hulman University, who specializes in this era, believes López's plan was to use American power to make himself *caudillo* of an independent Cuba.

Ambrosio Gonzáles, second-in-command in the Cárdenas expedition. During the U.S. Civil War he became an artillery officer with the Confederacy. (Collection of Antonio de la Cova)

ANEXIONISMO FADES

Anexionismo survived the death of López for a few years. In New York, a new junta led by Betancourt Cisneros lobbied a willing President Franklin Pierce for annexation. But Spain indignantly turned down an offer of $120 million coupled with a threat of "direct action." Politically defeated in Washington, in 1853 the junta offered General John Quitman, a former governor of Mississippi involved with López's failed adventure, $1 million to lead a new invasion. They also arranged for a simultaneous uprising in Oriente province organized, among others, by a planter named Carlos Manuel de Céspedes.

Commissioned by a powerful exile faction, Francisco Estrampes, a teacher in New Orleans, landed in Cuba with a small force. He was captured and executed. (Cuban Heritage Collection, University of Miami)

Two years went by without Quitman taking action. Exasperated, an exile faction led by Domingo de Goicuría and José Elías Hernández took matters in its own hands. In anticipation of the uprising, they sent Francisco Estrampes and a handful of armed followers to land in Baracoa, Oriente. They were captured and garroted. The plotters who awaited disbanded. President Pierce called Quitman to the White House for a confrontation in which the Spanish minister was present. With coconspirators in Cuba routed, and with the antagonism of the Pierce administration, Quitman resigned.

A few months later the junta dissolved itself. Two proclamations in its last days, signed by the *anexionista* helmsman Betancourt Cisneros himself, enigmatically hint that, for some, *anexionismo* had been a ruse: "Annexation was the bait with which to attract the North American public," said one manifesto. Said the other, "The Revolution came to the United States to procure arms, not to assent to premature obligations of impossible incorporation."

Perhaps Betancourt Cisneros and his allies, facing the utter collapse of *anexionismo*, were simply trying to justify themselves before history by making it seem they had favored independence all along. Whatever they truly wanted, never again would *anexionista* exiles play a dominant role in Cuban politics. All their plans had ended in catastrophe. Besides, the United States began to lose interest in Cuba as Americans turned toward a more pressing domestic problem: civil war.

Reform Denied

With a handful of exceptions, Cubans played no major role in the American conflict. But whatever slim hopes *anexionistas* held on to ended with the abolition

EL PUEBLO,

GRATIS PARA LOS CUBANOS.

NEW-YORK, JUNIO 29 DE 1855.   **Num 2.**

FRANCISCO AGUERO ESTRADA,
DIRECTOR-EDITOR, 41 Leonard St.

ADVERTENCIA.

Para evitar en lo posible ciertos abusos, harto comunes en materia de donativos, no se nos ocurre otro medio que publicar todos cuantos nos hagan para el periódico, dando cuenta de ellas; pero como algunos patriotas pueden tener motivos para no aparecer, bastará que elijan un nombre supuesto que no se confunda con otro. El que subscribe les dará un recibo en que se exprese cuantos números exije el donante. Si todos estos números no pudiesen salir, y el periódico terminia, se les devolverá el resto.

Los cubanos que residan fuera de N. York y quieran recibir todos los números de nuestro periódico, lo conseguirán sin mas que enviarnos su direccion con este sobre:

F. AGUERO E.
No. 41 Leonard St.
New-York.

EL PUEBLO.

La abundancia de materiales nos obliga á anticipar este número, á formar con letra menor algunas columnas á pesar del interes de los artículos que contienen. Recomendamos á los amantes de Cuba que mediten sobre ellos.

Cumpliendo con lo que ofrecimos en la *Advertencia*, damos cuenta de los subsidios que se nos han ministrado, i reciban nuestras gracias los favorecedores de "El Pueblo:"

Hemos recibido de *Colatino* $2 para auxilios de "El Pueblo." De *Sagua* 50 cent. i otro tanto por suscripcion de un mes. De *Emiliano* $1 por suscripcion adelantada de dos meses. Ademas se nos han hecho los siguientes ofertas: *Gregorio Joaquin Braco*, $6 en calidad de subsidio i suscripcion por 6 ejemplares de cada número á 5 cent. cada uno. El *Patriota* por suscripcion 50 cent. al mes. El Sr. Casas $1 al mes por suscripcion. El Sr. J. Elias Hernandez i el Sr. *Tabay*, no han espresado cuota.

El apreciable comunicante *Demófilo* merece nuestra gratitud por lo que en favor de nuestras opiniones manifiesta. Por lo demas, él verá en el contenido de nuestros *editoriales* que nos hemos adelantado á sus deseos, i que continuamos hermanados en ideas. Los que están de buena fé no pueden *discrepar* mucho. Las grandes *discrepancias* entre dos, cuando uno es de buena fé, son criterio seguro para calificar al otro de mala.

Una de nuestros compatriotas ha dicho: "Dios i Quitman" Nosotros decimos "Dios i el Pueblo."

ALERTA CUBANOS !!! En las circunstancias dificiles que atravesamos, necesitamos estar armados con el escudo incontrastable de la firmeza, para resistir á los embates i á las torpes combinaciones de la ambicion... Si quereis ser libres, procurad que todo se haga por el pueblo, i para el pueblo, i no por el dinero, ni por los ricos i sus paniaguados; porque acostumbrado el pueblo á tan degradante i arbitrario proceder, esto formará con el tiempo una lei á la cual tendréis que someteros, la república será un nombre vano, i marcharéis inevitablemente al despotismo...

Los hombres pasan ó se cambian; las instituciones quedan i se perpetuan para gloria ó escarmiento de las naciones....

ALERTA CUBANOS!!! Hasta aquí habeis tenido una ciega confianza en ciertos hombres, ya cubanos, ya estranjeros, que no han querido tener otra guia que sus propias luces, ni otra regla que su voluntad, i se os ha dicho que la buena fe, i las rectas intenciones de vuestros jefes revolucionarios respondian de sus operaciones. ¿I qué ha sucedido? Lo que naturalmente debia suceder: que han abusado de las facultades omnímodas que ellos mismos quisieron darse, i que vosotros habíais consentido...

ALERTA CUBANOS !!! Considerad cuanto halaga á los hombres el mando i el poder, i que el que los obtiene, siempre quiere continuar poseyéndolos; i sabed, para que procureis parapetaros i defenderos de las tendencias esclusivistas de los republicanos de nuevo cuño, que mas de una vez ha herido ya mis oidos i mi corazon la osada proposicion de una nueva dictadura... Desconfiad, pues, de los soberbios aristócratas que hablan con énfasis orgulloso en la nobleza de sus antepasados, i que hasta del nombre de la democracia se asustan, porque jamas son los verdaderos amigos del pueblo...

ALERTA CUBANOS !!! Sostened vuestros derechos sin contemplacion alguna, i cual corresponde á hombres libres. La libertad es un bien precioso, que no se obtiene sino combatiendo vigorosamente por ella, ora en la tribuna, ora en el campo de batalla; i si en todos tiempos ha habido pueblos esclavos, aunque valientes en las armas, ha sido ciertamente porque no lo fueron tambien en la tribuna para sostener i hacer respetar sus derechos inalienables.

ALERTA CUBANOS !!! Cerrad los oidos como Ulises para no dejaros seducir por el engañoso canto de las sirenas, que os pretenden encantar con nuevas i soñadas espediciones al mando de jefes improvisados, i de la misma fábrica de la disuelta junta cubana, i no dudeis que se os pretende escluir del derecho de intervenir en la creacion de la nueva junta, diciendo que los cubanos de la Isla son los que deben hacerlo todo, como sucedió ya otra vez para mengua i baldon, i para escarmiento nuestro...

ALERTA CUBANOS !!! No tragueis el anzuelo, porque quedaréis presos cual incautos pececillos, i daréis márjen á que en Cuba se os trate mañana ó luego de la misma manera, i los sagrados derechos del pueblo queden para siempre anonadados... Alerta i siempre alerta, mas que el centinela de una fortaleza sitiada...! Procurad sobretodo que el pueblo de Cuba tanto el que se halla en los Estados Unidos

como el que reside allende de los mares adquiera ideas i hábitos republicanos, marchando, en cuanto sea posible, por la senda segura de la justicia, de la igualdad i la libertad, porque sólo sosteniendo, jeneralizando, i practicando con inalterable constancia, esos saludables principios, puede reformarse un pueblo que por su educacion, costumbres, i carácter contraido desde mucho tiempo, tiene una tendencia fatal ó irresistible al despotismo...

En fin seamos siempre los centinelas avanzados de los derechos del pueblo; miremos en todo á Cuba primero que á nosotros mismos, ó que á cualquiera de nosotros en particular. Para alcanzar la libertad es necesario tener todo el desprendimiento i toda la abnegacion de los héroes... Ejemplos nos ofrece Cuba dignos de eterna recordacion.... Narciso López, Joaquin de Agüero, Estrampes, Pintó, i otros esclarecidos mártires de nuestra revolucion, sean los modelos perennes de nuestra conducta patriótica; i sea nuestra lei suprema la voluntad i los derechos del pueblo libremente congregado, si queremos crear instituciones que lleven el sello de la democracia, que sean una garantía de los derechos comunes, i aseguren la gloria i el porvenir de Cuba....

ERRORES
DE LA REVOLUCION CUBANA.

ARTICULO II

No rememoraremos lo pasado para zaherir, sino para experiencia de lo venidero.

Acostumbrados nosotros los cubanos al régimen español i al abuso que el gabinete de Madrid, i aun los empleados mas insignificantes, hacen impunemente de sus atribuciones, creimos que en los E. Unidos sucederia otro tanto; congratulándonos con la esperanza de que á merced de la patrias que por una fatal ceguedad atramos al pueblo americano, su gobierno se desentenderia de cumplir con los deberes que le impone la Constitucion.

Para alucinarnos hasta el punto de abrazar aquella creencia, fué preciso que olvidasemos una circunstancia característica segun parece, de toda la raza anglo-sajona, i ha sido notada por muchos observadores, á saber: su respeto á la lei. Esta no es como en España i en otros paises en comodin que los tribunales *interpretan*, es decir, amoldan á su antojo en pro de sus intereses ó de sus pasiones; sino una regla fija que no se quebranta sin incurrir en una *efectiva* responsabilidad. Pero la Constitucion de los Estados Unidos (artículo 11, seccion 111) impone al Presidente, entre otros deberes, el de "cuidar de la escrupu-

---

El Pueblo, *published by Cuban exiles in New York in 1855. Even at that low point in the struggle for separatism,* Cubans in the United States *continued to plot and analyze the* "Errors of the Cuban Revolution," *as in the article on the bottom right of the newspaper.* (Collection of Antonio de la Cova) of slavery in America. Instead, changing circumstances in Cuba put *reformismo,* which became known as *autonomismo,* on center stage for the first time since the hopeful days a generation earlier when *reformistas* led by Félix Varela represented Cuba in the Cortes.

The early 1860s in Cuba were a time of improved relations between *criollos* and *peninsulares,* natives of Spain. Under the liberal-minded Captain-Generals Francisco Serrano and Domingo Dulce, the colonial government opened the doors to Cubans and permitted formation of the Reformist Party, dedicated to *autonomismo.* Even a newspaper founded in New York by exile Porfirio Valiente, *El Porvenir,* circulated freely in Cuba. When Serrano went back to Spain as president of the Senate, the emboldened *autonomistas* saw in him an ally at the center of Spanish power. They asked for freer trade, for the end of the contraband slave commerce (although the importation of human beings had been outlawed by international treaty as far back as 1817, Spanish authorities and Cuban slave traders paid little attention), and for representation in the Cortes. Such demands would have earned a prison term just a few months earlier.

Cubans in the Civil War

A small number of Cuban-Americans distinguished themselves in the U.S. Civil War. On the Union side Lieutenant Colonel Julius P. Garesché, chief of staff of Major General William Rosencrans, commander of the Army of the Cumberland, died heroically at the battle of Stones River in 1862. Riding with Rosencrans to rally the men in the face of a Confederate attack, Garesché galloped into the open field in full view of the enemy and was decapitated by a shell.

There was also the Fernández Cavada brothers. Adolfo served on General A. A. Humphreys's staff at the Battle of Gettysburg. At Gettysburg too was Federico, colonel of the 114th Pennsylvania infantry regiment in the vicious fighting at Peach Orchard. Federico was captured and held six months at the notorious Libby Prison. He wrote a book about it, *Libby Life.* At the start of the Ten Years War he volunteered for the Cuban Army and was made Chief of Staff. But in 1871 he was captured and executed despite pleas for mercy from President Grant and Union generals under whom he served. For the South, Ambrosio Gonzáles—Narciso López's second-in-command in the Cárdenas expedition—commanded the artillery at the Battle of Honey Hill as a colonel and served as General P. G. T. Beauregard's chief of artillery.

But the strangest story is that of Loreta Janeta Velázquez. A self-proclaimed descendant of the great seventeenth-century Spanish painter

Diego Velázquez, Havana-born Loreta was educated in New Orleans. When war broke out she saw an opportunity to live her childhood dream of being a soldier.

Velázquez bought a Confederate uniform and had a tailor make "half a dozen fine wire net shields," she wrote in her book, *The Woman in Battle*. "These I wore next to my skin, and they proved very satisfactory in concealing my true form and giving me something of the shape of a man." Wearing a false moustache as "Lieutenant Harry Buford," she says she fought at Bull Run and Ball's Bluff, where she took a prisoner. "I espied a Yankee sergeant reaching for a musket, evidently with the intention of treating me to its contents. Leveling a pistol at him, I cried out, 'No you don't! Drop that, and come up here, you scoundrel!'"

Her disguise was discovered when a doctor, treating a shrapnel wound in her arm, saw the wire mesh contraption under which she hid her breasts. Velázquez says she then became a Confederate spy in the North. After the war, she traveled throughout Latin America, Europe, and the American West. Although historians have challenged the accuracy of her memoirs it remains fascinating reading.

Madrid agreed to elections for Cuban deputies who would discuss political representation with the Spanish government. Still in exile, Betancourt Cisneros wanted nothing to do with the plan—he had no faith in Spanish promises of reform. He died in 1866, the same year the duly elected members of the *Junta de Información* began arguing their cause in Madrid. His old rival José Antonio

Federico Fernández Cavada was colonel of the 114th Pennsylvania Regiment at the Battle of Gettysburg. During the 10 Years War he rose to Chief-of-Staff of the Cuban Army but was captured and executed. (Cuban Heritage Collection, University of Miami)

Saco was one of the deputies. But as in Varela's generation, the hopes Saco and other Cuban reformers had placed in Spanish reformers were blown away in the maelstrom of Spanish politics. Shortly after the arrival of the Cuban *autonomistas*, Serrano found himself on the losing side of a revolt. The new hard-line regime ignored the *Junta* and in 1867 sent to govern Cuba Captain-General Francisco Lersundi, who reimposed dictatorial rule. No autonomy, much less independence.

Loreta Velázquez, born in Cuba but brought up in New Orleans, disguised herself as "Lieutenant Harry T. Buford" and fought for the Confederacy at Bull Run and other battles. (From "The Woman in Battle," Loreta Velasquez, 1876.)

WAR

Saco lived in Europe the remaining twelve years of his life, helplessly watching from afar as *autonomismo* grew in discredit. But one small group of exiles in New York had dissented even at the height of Serrano's popularity. Led by Juan Manuel Macías, a veteran of the Narciso López conspiracies, the "Republican Society of Cuba and Puerto Rico" published the newspaper *La Voz de América,* which called for armed revolt. The paper was regularly smuggled into the island, where it was outlawed.

These New York *independentistas* were allied with Benjamín Vicuña Mackenna, a representative of the government of Chile, then at war fighting a Spanish attempt to regain its former colony. In 1866, Chilean leaders, hoping to open a second front in the Caribbean, authorized Mackenna to tell Macías that Chile would aid a revolution if Cubans took the first step. The old dream of help from Latin America seemed about to come true. But Macías's followers could not manage to raise more than a few hundred dollars. Chile lost interest after Spanish ships withdrew from its ports on the Pacific.

It did not matter. With *anexionismo* dead for a decade, *autonomismo* in tatters after Governor Lersundi's reactionary policies, and abolition made inevitable by Lincoln's Emancipation Proclamation, Cubans began to see independence as the only option. The feeling was particularly strong among the small planters of Oriente in eastern Cuba, who were isolated from the politics of Havana and, with smaller landholdings and fewer slaves than the sugar barons in the west, had less to lose. In Spain the liberal Serrano regained power, but it was too late to stop the avalanche.

On October 10, 1868, Carlos Manuel de Céspedes freed his 37 slaves at La Demajagua, a small sugar plantation near the town of Yara, and rose in arms with little more than 100 men. A month later, Céspedes held the large towns of Bayamo and Holguín with an army of 12,000. The Ten Years War in Cuba had begun.

GENERAL FRANCISCO LERSUNDI.

Captain General Francisco Lersundi, named governor of Cuba in 1867 by a reactionary government in Madrid. He reversed reforms that had given Cubans a measure of self-rule and precipitated the Ten Years War. (Cuban Heritage Collection, University of Miami)

CHAPTER 3

Wars and Independence

1868–1902

Although the rebels lost Bayamo in January of 1869—they torched the town before Spanish authorities reentered—they were by no means ready to give up. The insurgency grew, spreading from Oriente to Camagüey provinces. In Havana, mobs of fanatical anti-independence young Spaniards took to the streets, burning the palaces of wealthy *autonomistas* like Miguel Aldama and terrorizing Cuban citizens. These hard-liners, known as the *Voluntarios,* the "Volunteers," became a law unto themselves, so powerful they forced the resignation of a moderate Captain-General, Domingo Dulce.

The out-of-control *Voluntarios* sparked an exodus. Havana's docks teemed with frantic people attempting to escape. Some turned right around to join the rebellion

Cuban women say good-bye to their husbands on the Havana docks in 1869, when thousands fled the island to escape the unchecked abuses of Spanish vigilantes. (Harper's Weekly)

in the east—it was easier to land there by sea than to cross Spanish lines on land. Others headed to Mexico, Central or South America, and the United States, where they plotted to help the insurgents.

CUBAN NEW YORK DURING THE TEN YEARS WAR

Émigrés who went to New York after *El Grito de Yara,* (the "Cry of Yara," as the start of the war is known in Cuban history) created a small community. The Census of 1870 found 1,565 individuals of Cuban birth living in New York City, a figure that undoubtedly grew in the mid-1870s at the height of the Ten Years War.

Pearl Street in Lower Manhattan, home to dozens of Cuban businesses from the 1860s to the end of the century. (Museum of the City of New York)

Some of those exiles were wealthy merchants such as Aldama, who lived in the best neighborhoods. Others, less affluent, were educated members of Cuba's elite who found employment as translators, editors, or teachers. Ambrosio Gonzáles was in New York in 1876, teaching English "to a very large class of Cuban exiles" at a school on Fifth Street, between First and Second Avenues.

Most working-class exiles lived in immigrant neighborhoods such as the Lower East Side and Chelsea. By the middle of the decade there were enough of them to give birth to a Hispanic, mostly Cuban, commercial district downtown. On Pearl Street was the Polegre restaurant, the Ferrer bookstore, a newspaper called *El Avisador Commercial*. These businesses catered to workers from the dozens of Cuban-owned cigar factories on Pearl Street and Maiden Lane—on just one block of the latter there were ten "segar makers" with Spanish surnames, according to business directories of the era. Further uptown on Third Avenue, a grocer named F. Arteaga owned one of New York's first bodegas.

Cuban-American Population

How many Cubans lived in the United States during the island's wars of independence? Nobody knows for sure. Some Cuban and Spanish historians estimate up to 100,000 people emigrated between the start of the Ten Years War in 1868 and the end of the Cuban–Spanish-American War thirty years later. Many of them moved back and forth between the two countries so regularly that the official figures of the Census Bureau may not give a true picture of the American community. Nevertheless, the Census counts of the Cuban-born population before independence are:

1870: 5,319
1880: 6,917
1890: records destroyed in a fire.
1900: 11,081

EXILES AND U.S. POLITICS

The leaders of the *exilio* of the late 1860s and early 1870s were men like Aldama and the lawyer José Morales Lemus, both from landed families who flirted with *autonomismo*. Indeed, Céspedes's uprising did not initially have their support. Two weeks after the opening shots of the war at Yara, Aldama and Morales Lemus met with Spanish Governor Lersundi in Havana to demand that Cubans be permitted to publicly express grievances. Lersundi said no and dismissed the Cubans brusquely. With Spain shutting the door of reform in their faces, they decided to back the rebellion. They went to where they thought men of money and power like themselves could be most useful—Washington and New York. Morales Lemus became head of the *Junta Central Republicana de Cuba y Puerto Rico*, which represented the insurgency to the U.S. government. His goal was to convince the United States to grant the right of belligerence and recognize independence.

His first contacts proved encouraging. After a White House meeting in 1869, President Ulysses S. Grant hinted that if the rebels in Cuba could "sustain themselves," American help would be forthcoming. Secretary of War John

CARLOS MANUEL DE CÉSPEDES,

Carlos Manuel de Céspedes, one of Cuba's Founding Fathers, freed the slaves at his sugar estate in the town of Yara and rose in arms against Spanish colonial rule in 1868, beginning the Ten Years War.
(Cuban Heritage Collection, University of Miami)

Rawlins promoted a resolution, which awaited passage in the Senate, calling for Grant to recognize independence if the rebels organized a government. Morales Lemus wrote to Céspedes saying he had "received indications about the possibility of arranging that Cuba receive ships, arms and munitions that the (U.S.) government no longer needed and would sell at one fourth of the cost."

That April, Cuban leaders gathered in Guáimaro, Camagüey, to write a constitution and declare the birth of a "Republic in Arms." Céspedes was the first president. This created the entity referred to in the Senate bill. But the legislation stalled. Recognition came from Latin-American capitals, not from Wash-

JOSÉ MORALES LEMUS

José Morales Lemus, a civilian leader of
exiles in New York and Washington tried
to convince the administration of Ulysses
S. Grant to back the Cuban rebels.
(Cuban Heritage Collection, University
of Miami)

ington. And far from selling arms, the federal government intercepted exile supply ships.

The change in American policy was in part due to the death of Rawlins in September 1869. The absence of the exiles' most effective Washington ally created a vacuum into which Secretary of State Hamilton Fish was quick to move.

Fish is a controversial figure in Cuba–U.S. relations. Herminio Portell Vilá argued in his landmark *History of Cuba in its Relations with the United States* (1938) that Fish's policy was to wait for Spain to realize it could not hold on to Cuba, then buy it for the United States. It was an annexationism based on the commercial possibilities Cuba offered, different from the pro-slavery annexationism of *antebellum* Southerners.

The historical record shows that Fish presented Morales Lemus a plan to pay Spain $100 million for the "independence" of the island, a sum guaranteed by American bankers. Fish believed the offer would be accepted by Spanish Prime Minister Juan Prim, a statesman with the foresight to recognize "the manifest course of events in the American continent, and the inevitable termination of all colonial relations."

Morales Lemus and his exile followers had reservations. After so many retractions of Spanish reforms going back to the Varela years, they did not trust Spain to keep its word. And even if Spain did comply with its promise to leave Cuba, there was concern about a purchased independence, about a republic indebted from birth to a foreign power.

But Fish promised the United States would "throw its immense weight" in favor of independence, and reminded exiles he spoke "in the name of the most

poder del partido radical que representais, porque sin el a-
poyo que de ese partido aguardamos, puestos en lucha los cubanos con un enemigo sanguinario, feroz, desesperado y fuerte,
si se consideran nuestros recursos para la guerra, vencerian
si, que siempre vence el que prefiere la muerte á la ser-
vidumbre; pero Cuba quedaria desolada, asesinados nuestros
hijos y nuestras mugeres por el infame gobierno que comba-
timos, y cuando segun el deseo bien manifiesto de nuestro pueblo la estrella solitaria, que hoy nos sirve de bandera, fuera á colocarse entre las que resplandecen en la de los E. U.
seria una estrella pálida y sin valor.

   Si es cierto lo que asegura un perió-
dico de ese pais; si estais autorizado para reconocer nuestra
independencia, apresuraos, General, á prestarnos vuestro va-
lioso, nuestro decisivo apoyo; dando así al mundo un testimonio elocuente de lo que significa con respecto al des-
tino de los pueblos el partido cuya gefatura y repre-
sentacion os estan encomendadas.
   Patria y Libertad.
Camaguey Abril 6 de 1869.
   La Asamblea.
Salvador Cisneros Betancourt

Miguel Betancourt

Antonio Zambrana

To help Morales Lemus in his lobbying efforts in Washington, rebel leaders in Cuba sent President Grant a letter urging him to "recognize our independence . . . [and] . . . lend us your valuable and decisive support." The three dots in the outline of a triangle next to the signatures are a Masonic symbol. These members of the Cuban Constituent Assembly were Masons and hoped to kindle some sort of solidarity in Grant, a fellow Mason. (Library of Congress)

The Cuban exile Junta in New York City during the Ten Years War. (Harper's Weekly)

powerful nation on earth," which would not allow Spain to make a fool of it. Faced with a choice between continuing a devastating war without foreign support, and acceding to foreign support that ostensibly led to independence, the New York junta voted to back Fish's plan. The proposal was presented to the Spanish government.

Prim responded that Spain would accept $125 million for Cuba. He also offered a general amnesty, with one condition: To save Spain's military honor, nothing could proceed until the rebels laid down their arms.

That condition killed the initiative. Cubans would not disarm, because they believed the *Voluntarios* were still beyond the colonial government's control; even if the mobs were tamed, there was no trust in the goodwill of Madrid. Morales Lemus reported to Fish the position of Céspedes: "Patriots . . . will not depose their arms until independence is fully assured; and they will not accept any mediation that does not have as its basis the recognition of that independence."

Fish's plan was dead, but in 1870 Prim contacted the New York junta directly, without the United States as a go-between. He sought to revive *autonomismo* with a proposal that called for "a constitution similar to that of Canada." The poet Juan Clemente Zenea, carrying a safe-conduct pass issued by the Spanish legation in Washington, left New York to present Prim's proposal to Céspedes in Cuba.

That June Morales Lemus died in his Brooklyn home. His funeral was held at New York City Hall, the flag Narciso López had unfurled at Cárdenas draped over the casket. He never knew that the rebels rejected Prim's offer. Only independence would satisfy them. On his way back to New York, Zenea was captured by Spanish troops. In December, while Zenea was held captive, Prim was assassinated in Madrid. And in early 1871 Zenea was executed, his safe conduct a useless relic of Prim's bygone authority.

JUAN CLEMENTE ZENEA

Exiled poet Juan Clemente Zenea traveled from New York to Havana carrying a peace proposal from a liberal Spanish government to rebel Cuban forces. He was executed by conservative Spanish troops and buried in a mass grave, a fate he foretold in poem that tells of a poet's "obscure secret tomb/ without a willow or a cypress." (Cuban Heritage Collection, University of Miami)

FACTIONALISM AND THE END OF FIGHTING

By now exiles in the United States were divided in factions that reflected divisions among rebels on the island. On one side Céspedes wanted a strong military to run the war and for abolition to be gradual. His rival, the young lawyer Ignacio Agramonte, wanted immediate emancipation and a civilian legislature with power over the military.

A Cuban newspaper from New Orleans, a city important for Cuban separatist activities throughout the nineteenth century. (Collection of Antonio de la Cova)

The prison on Gardiner's Island, New York held exiles intercepted by the U.S. while carrying supplies to rebels in Cuba. (Frank Leslie's Illustrated Newspaper)

The war raged on. The year was the best one for the rebels. General Calixto García retook Holguín, Agramonte prepared to take the war west to Las Villas, and a young black general named Antonio Maceo earned a name by defeating Spaniards in Guantánamo. It was not to last.

In May 1873 Agramonte was killed in action. Then the factionalism exploded. In November Céspedes was forced to step down. He was killed the following year in combat. A supporter of Agramonte, Salvador Cisneros Betancourt, was named interim president.

The changes threw exile leadership in New York into chaos. Between their own infighting and the lack of official recognition from the United States, exiles did not accomplish much.

Bonds such as this helped finance the Ten Years War. (Collection of Antonio de la Cova)

Spain, too, was in anarchy, suffering through its Third Carlist War, the deposition of a king, the establishment of a republic, and then the restoration of the Bourbon dynasty in 1875. With Madrid consumed by internal crises and Cubans badly split, the war dragged on. A force of 1,400 under the Dominican General Máximo Gómez did manage to surprise Spaniards in Las Villas, the first time the struggle had been taken to central Cuba. Gómez's "invasion of the west" could have reignited the war. But an anti-Gómez faction detached troops from his command and he had to retreat back to Oriente.

The *Virginius* Incident

The last ship that New York exiles sent to Cuba with arms and men caused an international incident that brought the United States and Spain to the brink of war. After its completion of two successful missions, capturing the *Virginius* had become an obsession of the Spanish navy. The Spanish steamer *Tornado* finally seized the prize in October 1873, off the coast of Jamaica. The Spaniards imprisoned the 103 Cubans aboard as well as the crew of 52

American and British sailors in Santiago. This was illegal under maritime law—the *Virginius* had been caught in British jurisdictional waters, no armaments were found aboard (they had undoubtedly been thrown into the sea during the eight-hour chase), and it was flying the U.S. flag.

In Santiago, *Voluntario* mobs demanded immediate executions. The Spanish governor of the city, Juan Burriel, did not bother to contact the captain general in Havana and on his own authority ordered the firing squads to begin. Secretary of State Fish cabled an angry note. "If Spain cannot redress the outrages perpetrated in her name in Cuba, the United States will." Fifty-three men had been shot to death by the time a British ship threatened to bomb Santiago if the killings did not stop.

Spain agreed to return the *Virginius,* free the survivors, pay an indemnity, and punish Burriel. War between Spain and the United States was postponed for a quarter of a century, until another incident involving an American ship, the *Maine*.

Captain General Arsenio Martínez Campos, a Spanish governor respected by Cubans for his fairness and sense of honor. (Cuban Heritage Collection, University of Miami)

It was the last major convulsion. In 1876, General Arsenio Martínez Campos arrived from Spain as new captain general and began an offensive, both military and political. By the next year, with the rebel army splintered into groups that refused to recognize a central authority, and with newly elected president Tomás Estrada Palma captured by the Spaniards, the Republic in Arms ceased to function. In February of 1878 most rebel leaders accepted the peace proposal of Martínez Campos, offering amnesty, more autonomy, and civil liberties.

The abolition of slavery was not one of the terms. At Mangos de Baraguá, Oriente, Antonio Maceo—whom Cubans call the "Titan of Bronze"—told the Spanish general he did not accept and would continue to fight. But he had almost no

The teenaged José Martí as a political prisoner, wearing ball and chain at the San Lázaro marble quarry in Havana.
(Cuban Heritage Collection, University of Miami)

munitions and only a handful of followers. Under Martínez Campos's orders Spanish soldiers answered rifle volleys with shouts of "Viva Cuba!" Maceo ceased operations in May, ending hostilities.

The Ten Years War shattered Cuba. More than 200,000 Spanish soldiers and 50,000 Cubans died. Nearly every estate in Oriente was in ruins. But the slaughter forged the Cuban identity as a nation willing to shed blood for its independence and ameliorated white Cubans' fears of a race war. Whites, blacks, and mulattos had fought side by side for a decade, at times under the command of nonwhite officers.

JOSÉ MARTÍ

Barely a year had passed after the Peace of Zanjón when Cubans, dissatisfied with the glacial pace at which Spain implemented promised reforms, took up arms again. There were localized uprisings in the countryside, while in the cities revolutionaries were coordinating plans with General Calixto García, the hero of the Ten Years War, who had escaped from a Spanish prison to the U.S.

One conspirator arrested in Havana was a young man of 26, who sought exile in New York City, José Martí. He was physically small and frail. The bushy mustache and luminous balding forehead of his later years would make him instantly recognizable in exile circles, and to later generations who proclaim him, to this day, as Cuba's national hero. Yet he lived all but about two years of his adult life in exile abroad, most of it in the United States.

José Julián Martí y Pérez was born in Havana in 1853, the son of Spanish immigrants. Although his father served as artilleryman and then colonial policeman in the Spanish army, the independence of Cuba became Martí's crusade from an early age. One year after the Ten Years War erupted Martí published a broadside called *La Patria Libre* in which he complained of living under a regime that "negates all liberties, and brings misery to free men." Some weeks later Martí sent a note to a schoolmate who had joined the *Voluntarios*, condemning him as an "apostate." He was condemned to six years at hard labor. He was 16 years old.

As his health deteriorated, relatives convinced authorities to shorten the rebellious teenager's sentence with the condition he leave the country. Martí sailed from Cuba in 1871 and lived as an exile in Spain (he studied law at Zaragoza) and Latin America, continuing to write in favor of independence. Upon returning to Cuba at the end of the Ten Years War, he was arrested again for conspiracy and again deported. This time he went to New York on January 3, 1880.

Martí had spent his adult life fleeing political repression—from colonial authorities in Cuba, from the *caudillos* of the moment during his sojourns in Guatemala and Mexico. New York was different. He immediately recognized that the United States had something the Hispanic world had nowhere achieved. "I am finally in a country where each can be his own master," he wrote. "Here one can breathe freely because liberty is the basis, the shield, the very essence of life." It was in the United States that Martí carried on the political and literary work that became the rallying cry for generations of Cubans.

Martí and son José, to whom he dedicated the poems in Ismaelillo. (Cuban Heritage Collection, University of Miami)

Paradoxically, Martí also feared American ambitions. "I lived in the monster, and know its entrails," he wrote days before his death. He hoped an independent Cuba would stop American expansionism from "falling upon the lands of our America," by which, of course, he meant Latin America. Yet he understood U.S. politics was not monolithically annexionist, that forces supported his dream of independence. Exiles, he wrote, had to win "the sympathy . . . of the North . . . without which independence will be very difficult." He was to spend nearly all of the last fifteen years that remained of his life in that ambivalent "North," writing poems that revolutionized Spanish-language letters and organizing a different kind of revolution—one that was to finally lead, after nearly a century of hope and false starts, to Cuba's independence.

All the more remarkable is that Martí accomplished this in exile, organizing Cuba's war for independence, and while suffering profound anguish in his private life. To the Cuban diaspora of today, he remains the highest model of political commitment and organizational brilliance.

MARTÍ: POET/JOURNALIST

Politics aside, Martí had to find a way to make a living. He improved his English enough to translate a work on Greek and Roman antiquities, novels, and a logic textbook for the publisher Appleton-Century. He taught Spanish at private academies. He became vice-consul of Argentina, Paraguay, and Uruguay. Martí got to know Manhattan, "the theater, the clubs, Fourteenth Street." He became a New Yorker, shopping for books at Brentano's, meeting friends for literary talks at a Broadway bookstore owned by a Cuban named Nestor Ponce de León, going to the opera, dining at Delmonico's or at Polegre, on Pearl Street.

His most financially rewarding work was as a freelance journalist who could write in both English and Spanish. Martí became the New York correspondent for *La Opinión Nacional*, a newspaper in Caracas, Venezuela, and for *La Nación* of Buenos Aires, the leading daily in Latin America. His articles introduced Whitman, Emerson, Longfellow, and other American writers to the Spanish-speaking world, and covered a vast variety of American topics.

He reported on the assassination of President Garfield, on the new commercial sport of boxing, on the political corruption of Tammany Hall, on Buffalo Bill's Wild West shows; he wrote about the inauguration of the Statue of Liberty and its welcoming message to immigrants, and described an event that to his South-American readers must have seemed fantastically exotic: The great, bustling city

The old Delmonico's Steakhouse at the corner of 14th Street and Fifth Avenue. The elite of Hispanic New York gathered there in 1883 to hear Martí speak on the celebration of the 100th anniversary of the birth of South American liberator Simón Bolívar. (Museum of the City of New York)

of New York brought to a standstill by the blizzard of 1888. Martí wrote glowingly of American democracy and economic progress, but also angrily about American injustice. When eleven Italian immigrants acquitted of murder were lynched in New Orleans in 1891, Martí was unsparing: "the city, captained by lawyers and journalists, bankers and judges . . . marched to the prison where a jury had just acquitted the accused . . . and fired upon them until their bodies were in shreds."

Writing in English, he was the art and literature critic for a magazine called *The Hour* and for the New York daily *The Sun*. He also, of course, wrote about Cuba for American readers. "We Cubans are not (a) nation of miserable bums or moral pygmies," he wrote in the *Evening Post* in response to an article published in the Philadelphia newspaper *The Manufacturer*. "Cubans are living everywhere, working as farmers, engineers, artisans, teachers, journalists."

Martí was also a publisher. Working out of offices at 77 William Street,

First issue of La Edad de Oro, *the children's magazine Martí published in New York in 1889.* (Cuban Heritage Collection, University of Miami)

around the corner from the cigar factories of Maiden Lane, in 1889 he published the four issues of *La Edad de Oro*, an illustrated children's magazine with rhymes, stories, and lessons about history, geography, world cultures, and natural science. After moving to larger quarters at 120 Front Street in 1892, he began to publish *Patria*, a fiercely *independentista* newspaper.

It is the poems Martí wrote during his New York years that form his lasting contribution to literature. Martí is a founder of *modernismo*, a literary movement that pushed Spanish-language poetry into the literary mainstream of the nineteenth century. "When nothing flourished other than the residues of pathetic Romanticism or the coldness of the Academics," wrote his biographer Jorge Mañach, "he unchained the most profound voices and called forth a language of great energetic concreteness."

Martí's literary reformation was rich in irony. His "modern" poetry had its foundation in medieval classics, and those medieval classics were from Castile, the heart and soul of the Spain he devoted his life to fighting. Yet Spain was also, as he well understood, his ancestral nation, *la madre patria*. One critic wrote that Martí's most famous work *Versos Sencillos* (*Simple Verses*, which he wrote in 1890 during a doctor-ordered respite in the Catskill Mountains of New York State), suggests the author read medieval Spanish literature deeply until he "unlocked the secrets of the ancient romances" (the deceptively simple form of Spanish popular verse based on the eight-syllable line) and then added his own stamp. As an additional irony, the voice that changed poetry in Spanish issued forth during painful exile in the English-speaking world.

Soon after his arrival, Martí picked up where he left off in Havana before his

Corner of Maiden and William Streets in Lower Manhattan, a center of Cuban revolutionary fervor in the 1880s and 1890s. On Maiden, left, *were Cuban-owned businesses and cigar factories; up the block on William was Martí's first New York office.*
(Museum of the City of New York)

Patria, *the newspaper Martí founded and published out of his Front Street office in Manhattan.* (Cuban Heritage Collection, University of Miami)

deportation, continuing to plan support for the insurrection with García. The two lived in a Manhattan boardinghouse, at 51 East 29th Street.

Martí made his first political speech in New York just three weeks after his arrival. With García in attendance, he spoke in support of a new uprising. It must not have been easy for the young Martí. The leaders of Cuban New York were veterans of the Ten Years War, who carried great prestige and authority and looked down upon the younger generation of civilians.

That summer Calixto García landed in Cuba with arms and men. With 2,000 Cuban soldiers in the field, it seemed that the dogs of war were about to be let loose again. But the nation was exhausted from a decade of combat and the fighters poorly armed. Inside six months, García was captured.

With García in prison, his second-in-command Emilio Nuñez (who gave up a dental practice in Philadelphia to go fight in Cuba) sent an emissary to New York to ascertain whether exiles wished him to lay down arms. The *Guerra Chiquita,* or "Small War," was fizzling out.

The entire affair would have been a minor chapter in the history of Cubans in the United States, except that its end marked the rise of José Martí. In an atmosphere dominated by the old warhorses, the young Martí, who had never seen combat, realized that it had been a mistake to begin a new war. He dared write Nuñez back, "I advise, as a revolutionary and a man who admires and envies your energy, and as a dear friend, that you don't uselessly remain in the field of battle, since those you fight to defend are now unable to send help." Martí was taking the first steps of his long journey to earn the trust of the older warriors.

He continued his campaign for respect the following year, 1882, when he wrote to the most veteran of veterans, General Máximo Gómez, then running

One of the giants of Cuban history is General Antonio Maceo, who overcame racial misgivings to become the most successful Cuban battlefield commander in the War of Independence. (Cuban Heritage Collection, University of Miami)

a farm in Honduras and considering whether to start a new rebellion in Cuba. Martí had the delicate task of advising the stern Gómez that the younger exiles did not believe the time was right. Martí began the letter with great deference, introducing himself as someone who did not want to "appear as a vulgar agitator . . . whose name you have never heard." Soon enough he got to his point: "Our nation is not yet strong enough for war, and it is just and prudent . . . to announce we do not intend to carry out, against its will, a premature war." Gómez did not pursue further war planning, but the patriarchs of '68 continued to treat Martí and his generation like upstarts.

Martí pressed on. In 1884, Gómez and Antonio Maceo finally came to New York to see the persistent young revolutionary. They met for the first time at the hotel owned by a Madame Griffou, at 21 West Ninth Street in Manhattan. Gómez was 49, the haughty general who nearly a decade earlier marched his 1,400 men into central Cuba and shocked the Spanish army; Maceo, at 36, was the dashing cavalry leader who had so many times in the Ten Years War routed Spanish infantry with his *machete*-wielding charges, an undying rebel who refused what he considered a dishonorable peace at Zanjón. Martí was only eight years younger, but his lack of military glory created a huge gap between the men.

The Expatriate Middle Class in New York

Cuban visitors who could afford it stayed at the Hotel Español e Hispano-Americano on 14th Street or the Hotel Americano on 13th. Martí's newspaper *Patria* carried ads for attorneys, accountants, and bilingual private schools. One issue listed twenty-eight "Cuban or Puerto Rican" physicians. Some Cuban New Yorkers had time and money for a vacation—the Everett House Hotel in Saratoga Springs advertised regularly in Spanish-language newspapers, billing itself as "The Hotel Most Favored by Hispanic Americans."

A GENERATION GAP

The purpose of the meetings was to bring together the prestigious veterans of 1868 with the new generation to prepare another uprising. But they quarreled about the character of leadership. Martí believed civilian control of the military was essential if a future Cuban republic was to be born a democracy. Gómez and Maceo demanded military control.

After the uncomfortable first meetings, Gómez and Maceo invited Martí to Gómez's suite. As Martí biographer Jorge Mañach reconstructs the scene, an aide was preparing a bath for Gómez when Martí arrived. Gómez told Martí he was to move to Mexico City immediately and organize exiles there. Martí was taken aback by the command, but he had lived in Mexico and had fond memories, so he accepted the order and began to speak enthusiastically of all he could do there. Gómez stopped him cold. "Limit yourself to follow instructions. As for anything else, attend to what Gen. Maceo may dispose," Mañach quotes Gómez as saying. Then he turned and stepped into his steam bath, a towel draped over his shoulders. According to Mañach, Maceo smiled knowingly and said to Martí, "The old man considers the war in Cuba his private property and will permit no one to interfere."

Martí was in no way soothed by Maceo's attempt at lightheartedness. He walked out. He waited two days to re-spond, to make sure the heat of the mo-ment did not cloud his judgement.

"What anguish it causes me to have to say this! . . . But something goes be-yond the personal sympathies you in-spire in me and even beyond the opportunities [for an uprising] that pre-sent themselves: And that is my de-termination to not contribute an iota—despite my blind love for the cause to which I am giving my life—to bring to my homeland a regime of personal despo-tism, which would be more shameful and deplorable than the political despotism it must now endure," he wrote to Gómez. "One cannot found a nation, General, the way one commands an army camp."

The incident was a catastrophic set-back. The men went their separate ways, Maceo and Gómez back to plan-ning a war they could not spark, Martí to face painful accusations from fellow exiles that he had impeded the struggle. What he saw as courage in standing up to a looming military dictatorship, other exiles saw as lack of respect.

It was an excruciating time in Martí's

Martí and María, the little girl who, most historians say, he fathered in New York with Carmita Mantilla. (Cuban Heritage Collection, University of Miami)

life. An attempt to reconcile with his wife had failed. And, with gossip about his private life spreading through Cuban New York, a distraught Martí withdrew from political activity, putting aside the cause of Cuban independence that had been dear to him since the age of sixteen. He concentrated on writing the news-paper articles that afforded him a living.

A SECRET LIFE

José Martí is such a revered figure that Cuban historians hesitate to write about his most conspicuous character flaw. Martí had a string of affairs in

Mexico and Guatemala, even while courting his future wife Carmen Zayas Bazán. The two were unsuited for each other. Carmen wanted a "normal" husband, not a political firebrand. His forced absence following deportation in 1880, with their son barely a year old, added a physical dimension to the emotional and intellectual distance between the couple.

After arriving in New York, Martí lived in boardinghouses owned by Manuel Mantilla, a fellow Cuban émigré, at 243 Grand Avenue and 324 Classon Avenue, both in Brooklyn. His wife and son joined him that March, but stayed for only five months before returning to Havana.

Martí had come to know Manuel's wife, Carmen "Carmita" Mantilla. In her, Martí found the soulmate his wife could not be. Eleven months after meeting Martí, Carmita had a daughter, María. Most historians agree her father was Martí. Carmita and Martí remained close for years even when Manuel lived in the same house.

Martí adored his little girl, and loved to spend time with her at the family's cottage in Bath Beach, Brooklyn. He also deeply loved his legitimate son, José. When Carmen took young José back to Cuba, a heartbroken Martí left for Venezuela, where he lived for a few months.

Birth certificate of María Mantilla. Although the father is listed as being Manuel Mantilla—Carmita's husband—it is widely believed the real father was José Martí.
(Collection of Antonio de la Cova)

Martí's despair poured forth in *Ismaelillo,* a book of poetry published in 1882 after his return to New York and dedicated to his boy, now back in Havana. In one of the poems, "Mi Caballero," or "My Knight," Martí reminisced with great tenderness of the bygone mornings when the three-year-old José would climb on his father's bed, wake him with a kiss and sit on his chest pretending to ride a horse:

¡Que suave espuela	What soft spurs
Sus dos pies frescos!	His two bare feet!
¡Como reía	How my small horseman
Mi jinetuelo!	Would giggle!
Y yo besaba	And I would kiss
Sus pies pequeños,	His tiny feet,
¡Dos pies que caben	Two feet that fit
En un solo beso!	In a single kiss!

Carmen Zayas Bazán, Martí's long-suffering wife. (Cuban Heritage Collection, University of Miami)

Carmen "Carmita" Mantilla, was she Martí's longtime lover? (Cuban Heritage Collection, University of Miami)

Morally conflicted, Martí well understood the gravity of adultery. In December of 1882 Martí and Carmen decided to give their marriage another try. This time they rented their own apartment, a brownstone in Brooklyn within sight of the bridge. They even brought Martí's aging father, Mariano, for a visit from Cuba, perhaps in an attempt to recreate a traditional home with an extended family. Carmen and Martí lived together for two years. But they lived in incompatible universes. While he obsessed about independence, she complained that her husband refused to settle down in Cuba.

Shortly after Don Mariano returned to Havana, Carmen did too. Don Mariano died in 1887 in Havana, filling Martí with grief even though he and the old Spaniard were political antagonists. Martí wrote, "I thought of the poor artilleryman/Lying in his tomb, quietly./I thought of my father, the soldier/I thought of my father, the worker."

In 1891 there would be one last attempt to reconcile. But by then his relationship with Carmita was a decade old, and Martí was so deeply involved in the revolution there was no chance of reconciliation. Carmen sought permission from the Spanish consulate to return to Cuba without the knowledge of her spouse.

Four years later, two days before embarking to fight in the war he had organized, Martí wrote María a letter, urging her to study hard and not forget the Spanish language. He knew he was facing death. "If you never see me again, place a book over my tomb. Or upon your heart, because there I will be buried if I die in a place unseen by men. Work. A kiss. And await me." María grew up and married a *Mambí* officer. One of their children was the actor César Romero.

MARTÍ'S REVOLUTION IN CUBAN NEW YORK

After two years of public silence, Martí made his comeback in a speech at Manhattan's Masonic Temple, in front of Cubans gathered to commemorate the *Grito de Yara*. He defended his ideas about democracy, but did not attack Gómez or Maceo. One year later, at the 1888 commemoration of the twentieth anniversary of the Yara rising, again at the Masons' hall, hecklers drove him off stage demanding a political rival, Ramón de Armas, speak first. Martí acceded even though de Armas was not even scheduled. Then he took the podium and waited for silence. "Why point out errors?" he said. "We should instead unite all Cubans. We are unity. We unite what others separate. We are the reserves of the *patria!*" The crowd, even those who had heckled him, "applauded deliriously," according to biographer Manuel Márquez Sterling.

The speech marked a turning point. Martí wrote to the old *caudillos,* seeking to patch up differences, and published a stream of newspaper articles calling for unity. With black émigré Rafael Serra he founded "La Liga de Instrucción," a school where the children of black Cuban New Yorkers learned to read and write. He continued to triumph in patriotic speeches at the public meeting rooms that dotted the New York of the 1880s: the Masonic Temple, and Steck, Clarendon, Hardman, and Steinway halls. "The voice came from the middle of the crowd but I could not see who it was," recalled one listener. "A tenor-baritone, a warm and emotive voice that seemed to come from the heart without passing the lips . . . when he finished, a unanimous applause and a roar of enthusiasm . . . my friends ran over to me waving their arms, 'Come, come, it's Martí!'"

By 1891 he had resigned his consulships and stopped doing translations for

Manhattan's Union Square. In the center, Steinway Hall, one of the public meeting places where Cuban exiles gathered to hear Martí speak in the 1880s and 1890s.
(Museum of the City of New York)

Oil portrait of Martí, painted by Herman Norman in New York, 1891. It hung behind Martí's desk at his Front Street office in Manhattan. (Cuban Heritage Collection, University of Miami)

publishing houses and articles for Latin American newspapers. He dedicated himself full time to organizing what was to be the War of Cuban Independence.

Martí became a celebrity in Cuban New York. Members of the Latin-American intelligentsia visiting the United States would head to his fourth floor headquarters at 120 Front Street to pay tribute to the famous man. The small office was crowded with exile admirers, fellow plotters, intellectuals from the Spanish-speaking world—much like Varela's home had been the heart of the Cuban community seventy-five years earlier. Cigar workers would drop by from Agüero cigar factory around the corner on Fulton Street or walk the few blocks from Maiden Lane or Pearl Street. Martí would also visit them at their jobs. Contributions from cigar workers' Artisans League paid for the startup of his newspaper *Patria* in 1892.

Martí had spoken at Cuban political clubs in Philadelphia, New Orleans, Chicago, and Boston. But there was still Florida to conquer. New York had been the center of exile activity during the Ten Years War and right through the late 1880s. Now, Martí realized that the unity he sought required the participation of the booming cigar-making communities of Tampa and Key West.

MARTÍ IN FLORIDA

Perhaps 10,000 Cubans lived in Florida by the mid-1890s, some 2.3 percent of the state's population. They centered on Tampa's Ybor City and Key West, where they had established cultural institutions and, more significantly, pro-independence clubs and newspapers like *El Yara*. It was a fount of political activism Martí could not ignore.

At the invitation of Nestor Leonelo Carbonell, president of the revolutionary Club Ignacio Agramonte, Martí arrived at the Hotel Cherokee in Tampa in November 1891. He was to speak at ceremonies commemorating the twentieth anniversary of the execution of eight medical students in Havana, who had been accused by Spanish authorities of desecrating the tomb of an anti-independence journalist. Martí spoke at the Cuban Lyceum, the heart of Ybor's Cuban community. There, Cubans held dances and concerts, they put on plays, they formed a medical aid society, and held classes for the children of exiles. And there would Martí forge unity.

Para informes, acúdase al DEPARTAMENTO HISPANO-AMERICANO, 346 y 348 Broadway, Salones 18 y 19; ó á las Oficinas, Sucursales y Agencias que tiene establecidos en todas las capitales, ciudades y pueblos importantes de los países hispano-americanos.

HOTEL AMÉRICA

Cable: "BERUTICH."
Teléfono: 334, 18th Street.

Sucursal en París:
HOTEL AMÉRICA,
56 Rue Lafayette.

Irving Place, Cor. 15th St.
—— NUEVA YORK. ——

HOTEL DE PRIMER ORDEN.

Ultimamente reformado y decorado como los mejores de la ciudad. Está situado en el punto más céntrico. Cuenta con 125 habitaciones para familias, con salas y baños particulares y luz eléctrica. Hay ascensor para todos los pisos. La mesa y servicio nada dejan que desear. Todos los empleados hablan, además del inglés, el español, francés é italiano. El Agente del Hotel siempre se encentrará á la llegada de todos los vapores y en los paraderos de los ferrocarriles, avisando anticipadamente por telégrafo.

Precios:—Cuarto solo, desde **$1.00** — Con comida, **$2.50** al día, según las habitaciones

ARTURO T. BERUTICH, ⎫
E. SPINETTI, ⎬ **Propietarios**

Advertisement in the exile newspaper El Porvenir *provides a glimpse into the small but cosmopolitan world of Cuban New York in the 1890s.* (Cuban Heritage Collection, University of Miami)

Outside the Martínez Ybor factory in Tampa, Martí center, just to the right of the open doorway with local Cuban leaders and tobacco workers in 1892. (Cuban Heritage Collection, University of Miami)

Early Key West

Cubans were living in Key West as early as 1831, when 50 Havana tobacco workers opened a cigar factory. But the big influx came at the start of the Ten Years War. While exile leadership remained in New York, Key West's working class émigrés also conspired for independence and were influential in local politics. Carlos Manuel de Céspedes, son of the rebel leader, became mayor in 1875, and in the 1880s Fernando Figueredo and Manuel Patricio Delgado were elected to Florida's state assembly. Three Cubans were appointed Justice of the Peace of Monroe County in the 1870s. After the war exiles returned to Cuba but within a couple of years many headed back to Key West, dissatisfied with the reform Spain had permitted. This began a new boom. Key West's first

The original San Carlos building, built 1871, burned down 1886. (Cuban Heritage Collection, University of Miami)

Spanish-language newspaper, *El Yara,* was founded by José Dolores Poyo and in 1883 there were more than 80 cigar factories employing 3,000 workers. Another Cuban, Eduardo Hidalgo Gato owned not only one of the largest cigar factories, but also the largest bank. Martí's men trained for war on his property. Cubans were also responsible for founding the municipal fire department, building the first trolley, and installing a system of gas lamps to light the streets at night. By the time Martí arrived, Key West, with a population of 18,000, was practically a province of Cuba.

The lasting legacy of the period is the San Carlos Institute. White and black Cubans and their children attended bilingual classes on the history and culture of Cuba and the United States at San Carlos, making it one of the first racially integrated schools of the postwar South. The institute was founded in 1871 in a small wooden house on Ann Street and moved to a larger building three years later, which burned down in the great fire of 1886 that destroyed much of Key West. A local Cuban named Martín Herrera raised enough money to buy a new building on Duval Street, Key West's main thoroughfare, and it was there that Martí made some of his most famous speeches. He fondly called the San Carlos "La Casa Cuba."

The Founding of Ybor City

One of the men who fled *Voluntario* abuses in 1869 was Vicente Martínez Ybor, a Spaniard brought up in Cuba. Facing arrest for his pro-independence activities, he boarded a ship to Key West and founded a cigar factory there. Seventeen years later, unhappy with labor problems and the island's inaccessibility (it was only reachable by ship), the now successful cigar maker bought a 49-acre swamp two miles northeast of downtown Tampa. It was his idea to open a new factory with subsidized housing for workers—a company town.

It was the birth of Ybor City. An account of its early days tells of swarms of insects in such large numbers that residents "were forced to go around with goggles to keep the gnats from their eyes." Nevertheless, it had a magnificent harbor and a railroad. More cigar makers moved in and thousands of Cuban cigar workers arrived over the next decade. Additional factories opened in West Tampa, a newly incorporated and also largely Cuban city. State assemblyman Fernando Figueredo, who had moved from Key West to West Tampa, was elected its first mayor. By 1895—the year Cuba's war started—West Tampa and Ybor City together accounted for 120 factories with some 5,000 workers, the majority Cuban. More than 20 percent of Tampa's population was Cuban-born according to the 1900 census.

Another town founded by exiles was Martí City, near Ocala. It depended on tobacco and citrus crops. In 1894 a freeze destroyed its orange groves, and the war in Cuba prevented new tobacco leaf from reaching its factories (stockpiles allowed factories in Key West and Tampa to stay in business). Workers moved back to Tampa. By 1896 Martí City was a ghost town.

The San Carlos Club, heart of Key West's Cuban community in the early 1890s. (Cuban Heritage Collection, University of Miami)

Tobacco workers at an Ybor City cigar factory, about 1900. (Cuban Heritage Collection, University of Miami)

Martí with black and white Cubans in Key West, 1892. Martí made sure to include the large community of black Cubans in his struggle for independence. (Cuban Heritage Collection, University of Miami)

Ybor City in 1902, with homes, businesses, and two cigar factories in the distance.
(Tony Pizzo Collection, University of South Florida)

In his first Florida speech Martí proclaimed the duty of his generation to inherit the struggle, yet insisted it could not succeed without "Cubans who bore arms" a generation earlier. He also reached out to Spaniards who might choose to stay in Cuba after independence, and spoke on the still touchy subject of racial unity: "Should we fear the black man, the generous black man, the black brother? . . . I know he has risen nobly as a column, firmly on the side of liberty . . . let others fear him. I love him."

Conditions in Cuba

While Martí and his fellow exiles conspired in the United States, *autonomismo* was again on the rise in Cuba. Some of the reforms promised at Zanjón had been instituted. There was more freedom of speech and of the press than Cuba had ever experienced. Slavery was abolished in 1880. The judiciary became more independent. All this gave impetus to the Liberal Autonomist Party, made up of Cubans who sought self-rule under the Spanish crown.

However, the government in Madrid favored the rival Party of Constitutional Union, which sought to keep Cuba a voiceless colony. A poll tax of 25 pesos kept many Cubans from voting, giving an electoral edge to the Constitutional Unionists. But in mid-1893 Antonio Maura, the new, progressive Minister of Colonies in Madrid, presented a plan to the Cortes that would have given Cuba most of the rights of a Spanish province. Maura understood that without real autonomy Cubans would again take up arms and the island would be lost to Spain.

But hard-liners in Spain opposed autonomy. Martí and his followers disapproved of Maura's plan too, but for the opposite reason: They wanted full independence. Maura was forced to resign. *Autonomismo* had failed again. By 1894 Cuba was ripe for revolt.

Workers at Key West's Gato Cigar Factory enthusiastically contributed funds to the War of Independence. (Cuban Heritage Collection, University of Miami)

The effect was electrifying. In future visits, businesses in Tampa would close shop to let workers hear Martí speak. The story was similar in Key West, where he arrived Christmas Day. With its dozens of political clubs, pro-independence feeling was strong. But precisely because there existed so many different groups and so much racial diversity—a fifth of the tobacco workers were black—Martí was concerned.

At the dock, a marching band played *La Bayamesa,* the anthem written during the Ten Years War. One of the old veterans, José Francisco Lamadriz, stepped out to welcome him. The two men embraced.

"An *abrazo* for the past revolution," said Martí.

"An *abrazo* for the new revolution," responded the old warrior.

A large crowd lined the route between the dock and the Hotel Duval, waving Cuban flags and shouting *"¡Viva!"* to Martí. He was sick and a doctor ordered bed rest for a week, but on January 5 the San Carlos Institute was packed with exiles who heard Martí once again call for unity among the generations and the races. Key West, like Tampa, had embraced him.

Martí and Máximo Gómez in Patria's *Manhattan office, 1894.* (Cuban Heritage Collection, University of Miami)

From then on Martí shifted his energies to Florida. It was in New York that he founded his newspaper, *Patria,* but it was in Key West that he started his Cuban Revolutionary Party, which finally brought about the unity he desired (62 pro-independence clubs in Key West alone joined).

Martí had convinced everyday Cuban émigrés to trust him. For instance, cigar workers in Tampa, Key West, and New York donated 10 percent of their salaries to the cause of Cuban independence.

Still, the patriarchs of '68 living outside the United States—the men he had quarreled with a decade earlier, Máximo Gómez and Antonio Maceo—remained to be persuaded. Martí visited their farms in the Dominican Republic and Costa Rica, respectively, and finally won them over. With money raised from tobacco workers and support from the old generals, all was ready.

In 1894 Martí's Cuban Revolutionary Party spent $75,000 to charter three steamships and buy arms. The expeditionary leaders came together secretly at Fernandina, on Amelia Island, some 25 miles north of St. Augustine, to await Martí's arrival from New York. The *Lagonda* was to proceed to Key West and pick up the rest of the conspirators there. The *Amadis* was to get Maceo in Costa Rica. Martí himself would board the *Baracoa* and pick up Gómez in the Dominican Republic. The several hundred men and their leaders were to land in different places in Cuba, where Martí had arranged for a simultaneous uprising.

But federal authorities, alerted to the expedition, annulled the sailing charters and confiscated the weapons before Martí arrived. Martí was shattered, his work seemingly gone to waste. All was not lost, however. The exiles' American attorney, Horatio Rubens, was able to procure the release of most of the war material. Guns and munitions—though not the ships—were returned to the exiles. Martí planned another landing.

On January 29, 1895, Martí issued an order out of his Front Street office in Manhattan. Then he left the United States for good, heading out to meet Gómez in the Dominican Republic. Martí's order was transported to Tampa, where a cigar factory owner named Blas Fernández personally wrapped it inside a box of cigars destined for Cuba. It contained secret instructions authorizing Martí's agent in Havana, Juan Gual-

General Máximo Gómez, the old fox of Cuba's wars for independence. (Cuban Heritage Collection, University of Miami)

berto Gómez, to order the start of a new rebellion on February 24. Beginning that day (known in Cuba as the *Grito de Baire* for the first town to rise in arms) Cubans throughout the island grabbed their guns and machetes and stormed Spanish army installations. On April 1 Maceo, following Marti's plan, landed in Baracoa. On the 11th, aboard a small rowboat launched from the steamship *Norstrand* and in a driving tropical downpour, Gómez, Marti, and four aides landed on the rocky coast of Playitas, near the southeastern tip of the island. Marti had finally brought the War of Independence to Cuban soil.

THE WAR OF INDEPENDENCE

Shortly after arriving, the expeditionaries joined Cuban forces already fighting. Cuban troops became known as the *Mambises*, a term of scorn first used by the Spaniards but adopted by Cubans, much like the "Yankees" of the U.S. Revolutionary War took their name from a word used pejoratively by the British. Marti, Maceo, and Gómez met at a farmhouse called "La Mejorana." The three were together for the first time since that awful day at Madame Griffou's New York hotel eleven years earlier.

It was their last meeting. On May 19 a Spanish column surprised Gómez's men at a place in the Cuban countryside called Dos Rios. Marti, conspicuous on a white horse, ignoring the general's pleas, charged the Spanish infantry. He was shot and killed.

"He was a man of genius, of imagination, of hope and of courage, one of those descendants of the Spanish race whose American birth and instincts seem to have added to the revolutionary tincture all modern Spaniards inherit," said an obituary written by Marti's friend Charles Dana, publisher of the New York *Sun*. "His heart was warm and affectionate, his opinions ardent and aspiring, and he died as such a man might wish to die, battling for liberty and democracy."

The death of Cuba's leader was a blow from which the nation has not yet recovered. With Marti alive, would he have consented to American intervention? Would an independent Cuba with Marti as president have fallen into the morass of political corruption and U.S. interference that characterized the early years of the republic? With a cleaner, more democratic, and more independent government, would the conditions that led to the Castro dictatorship have been created in the first place?

The Cuban military continued to fight, but the civilian leadership changed direction. Marti's successor as head of the Cuban Revolutionary Party was Tomás

The Mambí *army in a machete charge during the War of Independence.*
(Cuban Heritage Collection, University of Miami)

Estrada Palma, who had briefly been president of the "Republic in Arms" late in the Ten Years War. Estrada Palma lived in New York State's Central Valley, where he ran a boarding school for the children of well-to-do Hispanic families. He was a U.S. citizen, unlike Martí, and lived in the United States uninterruptedly from the time he went into exile at the end of the Ten Years War until he became Cuba's first president in 1902.

Estrada Palma was more trusting of American politicians than Martí had been. Working out of the *Patria* office, his objective was to rouse American sympathy. Estrada Palma organized "Cuban Fairs" that featured Cuban produce, marching bands, and photo exhibits of the war. The New York "Yellow Press," led by William Randolph Hearst's *Journal* and Joseph Pulitzer's *World,* took up the cause with glee, exaggerating rebel triumphs and Spanish atrocities.

New Yorkers outside the office of the Journal *reading news bulletins of the Spanish-American War.* (Museum of the City of New York)

Not that there weren't real triumphs, as well as real atrocities. This *exilio*, unlike earlier ones, was ready to help, because Martí's efforts in raising funds and volunteers paid off: In 1896 alone, fifteen expeditions landed in Cuba from the United States carrying thousands of rifles and munitions boxes (including those confiscated and returned to exiles at Fernandina), even light artillery. By comparison, just twelve supply ships landed in the entire course of the Ten Years War. This, together with the "war taxes" rebels imposed on landowners in Cuba, made for a much better armed force than in 1868. In 1896 Maceo went so far as to carry the war to Mantua, the westernmost town in Cuba, hundreds of miles beyond where Gómez had been twenty years earlier. But near Havana, Maceo was killed in action. It was a tremendous blow to the military leadership.

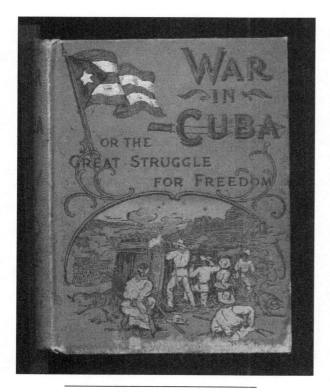

Book about the war in Cuba written by Gonzalo de Quesada in 1896 as part of exiles' drive to win the sympathy of the American public. (Author's collection)

Spain's response to the Cuban advance was to send more troops—there were 200,000 Spanish soldiers in Cuba in 1896—and bring home Captain General Martínez Campos, the respected officer who had made the Peace of Zanjón. His replacement was the ruthless Valeriano Weyler, a man reviled by Cubans to this day. To isolate rebels from supporters in the populace, he decreed the entire citizenry of the countryside "reconcentrate within towns occupied by [Spanish] forces. . . . Anyone outside the towns shall be considered a rebel." Knowing that rebels were summarily executed, tens of thousands of panicked peasant families overwhelmed small towns, leaving behind unharvested crops and unattended livestock. Soon streets were filled with emaciated Cubans. Famine killed thousands. Weyler had organized the world's first concentration camps.

Although the *Mambí* army continued fighting in eastern Cuba, Weyler's tactics pacified western provinces. However, his larger strategy, to end the war altogether, backfired badly. The concentration camps produced more atrocities for exiles and the New York press to denounce.

COME THE AMERICANS

There was a groundswell of protest about Weyler's savagery, and calls for U.S. intervention—not only in the yellow newspapers, but also in exile circles. Although some Cubans worried that if the United States went in, the Americans would not permit Cuba to become a fully sovereign republic, others foresaw a quick end to the war if the United States entered. Without Martí—who would

The Cuban exile leadership in New York after the death of Martí. Tomás Estrada Palma, his successor as head of the Cuban Revolutionary Party and future Cuban president, is sitting second from right. (Cuban Heritage Collection, University of Miami)

have surely opposed intervention—Estrada Palma failed to take a strong stance. "The Cuban people do not now desire annexation . . . they are desirous that the American government in some manner manage to provide a guarantee for the internal peace of our country," he wrote in 1898.

The aging Estrada Palma preferred to emulate Morales Lemus's policy of the 1870s. Once again, exiles sought to purchase Cuban independence with money from U.S. banks and tried to convince a U.S. administration to recognize the rebels. The plan to buy Cuba did not progress. As to recognition, Secretary of State Richard P. Olney told Estrada Palma he would not consider it until Máximo Gómez stopped burning down American-owned plantations that did not pay "war tax." Estrada Palma's response was that the Constitution of the Cuban Republic in Arms exempted from payment those plantations that belonged to citizens of nations that had granted Cubans the right of belligerency.

Disagreements became moot the night of February 15, 1898, when the battle-

Cuban General Calixto García, left, *and U.S. General Rufus Shafter during their uneasy meeting.* (Cuban Heritage Collection, University of Miami)

ship *Maine* (which had been sent as a diplomatic show of force to protect American interests in Cuba) blew up in Havana harbor. The New York newspapers redoubled their call for the United States to declare war on Spain. In late April, a Joint Congressional Resolution authorized President McKinley to use force to move Spain out of Cuba, Puerto Rico, and the Philippines. Cuba "is and by right ought to be free," it said.

In Cuba a new autonomous government, permitted to take power as a last minute concession by Spain, sought a negotiated settlement. The rebels would not hear of it. They had so grown in confidence that the cautious Gómez offered a prediction: "This war cannot last more than a year . . . this is the first time that I have put a limit to it." In fact, it lasted but a few weeks once the Americans entered.

The main American force landed in Cuba at Daiquirí that June, at the time and place General Calixto García had suggested. Some 1,000 of his troops engaged the Spanish force, enabling the Americans to land with hardly a casualty. But hard feelings quickly built up between the Cuban and American allies—the correspondence of American officers makes it clear they were disturbed to see that blacks in ragged clothes made up more than half of the *Mambí* army.

After the Americans took Santiago, hard feelings broke out in the open. The U.S. commander, General Rufus Shafter, informed García he had accepted the surrender terms of Spanish General Juan José Toral, which prohibited Cuban troops from entering the city. The Spanish feared *Mambises* would go on a killing rampage—indeed, they had committed some atrocities in the course of the war. But García wrote an angry letter to Shafter, insisting his men were not "savages who don't know the principles of civilized war." Neither did Cubans participate in talks to negotiate the Treaty of Paris, which formally ended hostilities. It was signed by Spain and the United States, but not by any Cuban. What had started in 1895 as the Cuban War of Independence ended three years later as a war between Spaniards and Americans, with Cuban participation put aside.

American occupation followed. The Cuban Constitutional Convention, writing the charter for independence, was told that for occupation to end Cuba had to accept as part of its constitution the Platt Amendment, offered by Connecticut Senator Orville Platt as a rider on an appropriations bill. It turned over to the United States territory near Guantánamo for a naval base, and gave it the right to intervene "for the preservation of Cuban independence." Of course, the provision thwarted the same Cuban independence it was supposed to protect.

A Cuban commission led by Calixto García visited Washington to protest. They left with an ultimatum: No Platt Amendment, no independence. Convention delegates voted 13–12 to accept it.

There was still the matter of a presidential election. Of the major figures who survived the war, Calixto García died while on his Washington mission and Máximo Gómez refused to run,

Calixto García, one of the leading generals of the Cuban wars of independence. The scar on his forehead is from a suicide attempt when he was captured by Spanish troops near the end of the Ten Years War. He shot himself under the chin, and the bullet came out his forehead. (Cuban Heritage Collection, University of Miami)

saying "Men of war for war . . . and men of peace for peace." The candidates were two former presidents of the "Republic in Arms" during the war years: Bartolomé Masó, who campaigned against the Platt Amendment; and Estrada Palma, who resigned himself to what seemed a *fait accompli.* When the American governor, General Leonard Wood, appointed only supporters of Estrada Palma to the five-member board that was to oversee the voting, Masó withdrew his candidacy. On the last day of 1901, Estrada Palma, who remained in the United States for the whole of the campaign, was elected president without opposition.

Carlos Finlay

One sure benefit of U.S. occupation was the eradication of yellow fever, a scourge of the tropics since the first epidemic in Mexico in 1648. There was no treatment, and no way to prevent it—no one knew how the disease was transmitted, excepting one lone Cuban doctor.

In 1881 Dr. Carlos Finlay, an 1855 graduate of Jefferson Medical College, Philadelphia, presented a paper at the International Sanitary Conference in Washington claiming yellow fever was caused by the *Aedes aegypti* mosquito. No one listened—the medical community considered Finlay's contention an untested theory. The idea lay forgotten until 1901, when Finlay convinced Dr. Walter Reed, a U.S. Army surgeon given the job of ending yellow fever on the island (U.S. forces suffered more casualties from the disease than from combat), that the 20-year-old theory had merit. Reed, controversially, performed experiments with human subjects who exposed themselves to *Aedes aegypti.* Nearly all contracted the fever; most died. But Finlay was proven right. After a sanitation campaign to eliminate the stagnant water that was the mosquito's breeding ground, yellow fever disappeared.

Traditional Cuban and American perspectives on the Finlay-Reed relationship differ. To Cubans Finlay is the hero of the tale—the inspired scientist whose insight, considered foolish for two decades, resulted in the elimination of his country's most serious health problem. To Americans, the hero is Reed—the practical, hardheaded scientist who converted a theory into fact and eliminated the most serious health problem of an exotic tropical island.

Carlos Finlay, the Cuban doctor who first said yellow fever was transmitted by mosquitoes. (Cuban Heritage Collection, University of Miami)

The republic born with its sovereignty mortgaged to the United States was not what Martí had envisioned. But it appeared to be all that Cubans could get without going to war against the Americans. On May 20, 1902, at the baroque palace of the Captain Generals, where Spanish governors had ruled the island with an iron hand, Governor Wood officially turned over the government to Estrada Palma. Crowds gathered at the plaza outside and at Morro Castle, the fortress lighthouse that for four centuries has guarded the entrance to Havana harbor, to witness the lowering of the American flag and the raising of the banner of the new Cuban Republic.

At the Morro, the ancient patriarch Máximo Gómez must have thought of his thirty-four years of struggle as he watched Cuba's flag ascend the mast, blowing in the wind. He was only partly right when he muttered, "I believe we have arrived."

Plaque at the Panama Canal honoring Finlay for the discovery that "made possible . . . the great work of the Canal."
(Author's collection)

SECTION II

REPUBLIC TO REVOLUTION

CHAPTER 4

Immigrant Years

1902–1952

Many exiles returned to Cuba after the end of Spanish rule, and emigration to the United States slowed to a trickle during the first decades of independence. The federal census counted 11,081 Cuban-born residents in 1900 (undoubtedly fewer than in the 1890s during the fighting in Cuba) and 15,133 in 1910. A decade later the number had declined to 14,782. Over the next twenty tears it grew by barely 3,000.

On the island, political and economic life was recovering from the war, but the times were still turbulent. President Tomás Estrada Palma's second term was cut short by an armed uprising of members of the rival Liberal Party, which led to a second U.S. intervention that lasted from 1906 to 1909. It was followed by the terms of Presidents José Miguel Gómez, Mario García Menocal, and Alfredo Zayas. They respected civil liberties, but ran scandalously corrupt administrations. There were also a number of small-scale uprisings, which were put down with the threat of American intervention—the Platt Amendment continued to hamper Cuban sovereignty.

The sugar-dependent economy suffered dramatic boom-and-bust periods between 1902 and the Great Depression. At one point during the so-called Dance of the Millions in early 1920, the price of raw sugar climbed to 22 1/2 cents per pound, a wild bonanza to a country that once believed a price of 6 cents was enough to guarantee prosperity. By Christmas, it was down to 3 3/4 cents. Investors lost fortunes, working Cubans lost jobs.

Yet few Cubans chose to leave. Of those who did, most settled in New York, Tampa, or Key West. In particular, it seems a number of longtime Florida Cubans returned to the state. But things were different now. They were no longer exiles eager to return to their homeland after it was freed, but immigrants in search of economic opportunities.

CUBAN NEW YORK AFTER INDEPENDENCE

A few wealthy upper class Cubans lived in the New York area in the years after independence, such as the members of the Rionda clan of sugar magnates. There were also working class Cubans, who continued to live in the old neighborhoods of Chelsea and the Lower East Side. In the 1920s some were moving to what was to become East Harlem. But they were soon vastly outnumbered by Puerto Rican immigrants. In 1920 the New York Cuban and Puerto Rican populations were roughly the same size, but by 1930 there were 44,908 Puerto Ricans compared to 19,774 individuals classified by the U.S. census as making up the "white, foreign-born population from Cuba and the West Indies."

Small though it was, the New York Cuban community of those years enjoyed a short time in the limelight with the arrival from Havana of a boxer named Eligio Sardiñas, better known as "Kid Chocolate." He began to establish his American reputation in down-and-dirty arenas in the rapidly Hispanizing East Harlem, where he won sixteen fights between August and December of

Kid Chocolate training by lifting horseshoes in New York's Central Park, 1930.
(Associated Press)

1928—nearly a match a week. American promoters took note of the wiry featherweight with the superb boxing technique, and the following year he worked his way up to a match against Al Singer, who was wildly popular in the Jewish community of New York. In a sold-out Polo Grounds, Kid Chocolate won by decision and earned $49,000, a huge purse in those years for a boxer in the lighter weight categories.

The victory made the Cuban fighter famous not only among New York's Hispanics, but throughout the entire city. Two years later he finally won a world championship with a seventh round TKO against Benny Bass for the junior Lightweight title.

But Kid Chocolate had always loved New York nightlife, and now that he was recognized everywhere and treated like a celebrity he loved it even more. Unable

New Jersey's Sugar Barons

One of the wealthiest towns in the United States, Alpine, New Jersey, was developed in the years following independence by Manuel Rionda, a Cubanized Spaniard who made a fortune in sugar.

When his cane fields were torched during the War of Independence, Rionda and his family moved to New York, where he founded Cuban Cane Sugar Co. In 1909 he became president and chairman of the board—a position he held until his death in 1943—of the Wall Street brokerage firm Czarnikew-Rionda and Co. It owned six plantations in Cuba, which accounted for 10 percent of the country's sugar exports in the half-century prior to the revolution, and controlled more than 20 percent of Cuban raw sugar exports to the United States Rionda's cousin Bernardo Braga became mayor of Alpine in 1929; Rionda succeeded him two years later—they are probably the first Hispanics elected in New Jersey.

In the early 1900s Rionda bought hundreds of acres in Alpine, with commanding views of the Hudson River and the New York City skyline. He built a palatial estate called "Rio Vista," Spanish for "River View." According to Alpine's history book, it had bridle paths, gardens, "a huge fountain that flowed into a stone-bordered pool," and a 100-foot tall stone clock tower.

Rionda and his family wanted to share their New Jersey *hacienda,* so over the next few decades they periodically brought in busloads of Cuban immigrants from New York City for picnics and swimming in the estate's two-acre lake.

With the arrival of Fidel Castro in 1959 the Riondas lost their fortune, and sold Rio Vista tract by tract to developers who built the luxurious homes that stand on the old Cuban property today.

The Rionda mansion, razed in the 1960s. (Alpine Historical Society)

to stay out of the clubs, he lost interest in training and his career quickly went downhill. Boxing experts, however, have not forgotten that in his prime Kid Chocolate was dazzling, and consider him one of the best pound-for-pound boxers in the history of the sport. Cuban fans also remember him as the man who, even for a brief time, turned the New York spotlight on their community in New York during the era of Babe Ruth and Lou Gehrig.

Still, the Cubans of New York in the few decades after independence were absorbed into the larger Hispanic or even non-Hispanic New York. They left no tradition to shape a Cuban community with a sense of having links to the exile past—although certainly a handful of families must have carried traditions on for a while—and no historic landmarks were left, such as can be found in Tampa and Key West.

In Florida, the story was different. Although immigration did not increase greatly after independence, the distinctively Cuban communities that had grown up in Key West and Tampa managed to thrive. They survive to this day, with third- and even fourth-generation Cuban-Americans who regard themselves as the heirs of those exiles from the nineteenth century. No counterpart exists in New York.

CUBAN FLORIDA AFTER INDEPENDENCE

The cigar industry continued to thrive in Key West in the first few decades after Cuban independence, and its Cuban community grew prosperous. A "Cuban Club" was built on Duval Street in 1917 for cigar makers and their families to socialize, and soon became a prominent center of Key West Cuban life. The San

A cigar box label from one of the factories in Lower Manhattan shows an American Rough Rider and a Cuban Mambí *shaking hands.* (Cuban National Heritage)

Key West's San Carlos Club in the 1920s. (Historical Association of South Florida)

Primary schoolbook used at the San Carlos, 1942. (Cuban Heritage Collection, University of Miami)

Carlos was more oriented toward education. After independence it continued to hold bilingual classes for high school students during the day and adults at night. The Cuban government paid the salary of the Spanish teacher and the state of Florida paid the English teacher. On the ground floor, the Cuban consulate had its office.

The arrangement lasted sixty years, until the Castro revolution. After that the building deteriorated throughout the 1960s and 1970s and shut down. But in 1992 it was restored and reopened as a cultural center. The restoration was an echo of what had happened six decades earlier: In 1919 the original Duval Street building, the one Martí had known, burned down. But with community support led by Dr. José Renedo and directors José Fernández and Ramón Perdomo, construction of the new San Carlos was completed in 1924. That building, designed by the Cuban architect Francisco Centurión in the Cuban neo-baroque style, is the one that stands today, a reminder of the prosperity of the postindependence Cuban communities that helped shape the culture and history of Key West.

Tampa's Cuban community was perhaps even stronger. There was a mass return to Cuba at the end of the war in 1898 but many *Tampeños* eventually went back to the more stable political climate and better paying jobs in Ybor City's thriving cigar industry.

In 1900 three-quarters of Ybor City's population was made up of immigrant cigar workers, and by the 1920s there were more than 200 factories employing more than 12,000 workers. Most were Cuban, although there were smaller numbers of Spaniards and more recently arrived Italian immigrants. The factories operated along traditional Cuban lines.

R. Testar,
Photographer.

1411 7th Avenue,
IBOR CITY, FLA.

Late nineteenth-century patriotic photo, with woman in traditional Cuban dress and man in Mambí *uniform.* (Historical Association of Southern Florida)

The skilled workers cut tobacco and rolled *panetelas* or *coronas* on long, narrow tables. Entertainment was provided by a "lector," who read aloud the news of the day, poetry, the novels of Cervantes or Victor Hugo.

The old center of the Cuban community, the Lyceum, where Martí spoke in the 1890s, was housed in a rambling wooden structure that had once been a cigar factory. Now, the tobacco boom fueled a building boom. Aside from more factories, Cubans in the first three decades of the twentieth century put up the Baldomero F. Marcos and the Llanos buildings, and social clubs expanded old headquarters or built new centers. These social clubs were central to life in Ybor

Typical cigar workers' homes in Ybor City. (Tony Pizzo Collection, University of South Florida)

Cigar factory work floor, with lector, upper right, *gesturing as he reads to his audience.*
(Tony Pizzo Collection, University of South Florida)

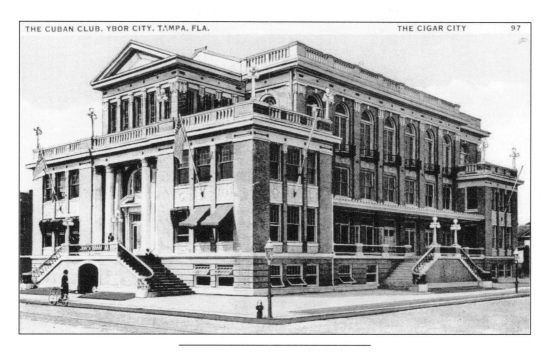

THE CUBAN CLUB, YBOR CITY, TAMPA, FLA.   THE CIGAR CITY   97

1920s view of the Círculo Cubano, Tampa's leading Cuban club.
(Historical Association of Southern Florida)

City. They functioned like mutual aid societies, providing medical care and prescriptions to members, and also helped preserve Cuban culture among immigrants. With independence achieved, politics no longer galvanized the community, so it was the dances, sports activities, and classes sponsored by the clubs that reinforced Cuban identity. The grandest new structure of the boom years belonged to the Círculo Cubano, built in 1917 at a cost of $60,000, with a theater, ballroom, pharmacy, library, and cantina. It is now on the list of National Historic Places.

With so many Cubans, Ybor City was like a city within a city. Outside, in Tampa itself, the population of mostly white Southerners—"Crackers," as they were called—stayed aloof. Inside Ybor City, Cubans, Spaniards, and Italians sometimes banded together in a common identity as "Latins" in reaction to "Anglo" hostility. The Círculo Cubano would attract large crowds with boxing matches featuring a "Latin" against a "Cracker." But all was not harmonious among the "Latins." Among Spaniards and Cubans there were lingering resent-

The Círculo Cubano sponsored many social and cultural activities for the Cuban community. (Tony Pizzo Collection, University of South Florida)

ments stemming from the war. Yet even the Spaniards had Cuban connections—most had lived on the island and their clubs maintained links with Spanish clubs in Havana. Italians tended to look down on Cubans. They lived in "Little Italy," on east Ybor City; Spanish speakers lived in the west.

Cuban blacks, too, enjoyed the years of Ybor City's boom. Black Cubans made up 13 percent of the Cuban population, and 10 percent of Tampa's overall black population. Inside Ybor City they were spared much of the segregation that was the law in those years. José Martí had done a great deal to unite Cubans of all races during his speeches in Tampa in the mid-1890s, and after independence black and white Cubans continued to work side by side at the cigar factories, attend the same Catholic schools, and live in racially integrated Ybor City. Yet pressure from Southern segregationists eventually changed it all:

Allegories of Cuban-American friendship were a common theme of cigar-box labels at the turn of the century, such as this one from Ybor City's Good Friends Cigars.
(Cuban National Heritage)

Right around the time of Cuban independence the state government in Tallahassee told the then-racially mixed Cuban clubs they were required by law to segregate. This resulted in the creation of two black Cuban clubs: The Freethinkers of Martí and Maceo and the Marti-Maceo Union Club. They built new buildings in 1904 and 1909, respectively.

The Martí-Maceo Union Club owned the largest dance hall available to blacks—Cuban or American—in segregated Tampa, and would frequently rent the facility to American blacks. But the two groups did not mix for many years. The two black Cuban clubs' charters restricted membership to Cubans, and no American blacks joined until the 1920s, under the pressure of a new Florida law that—ironically, given that the state at the same time enforced racial segregation—made it unlawful for a social club to exclude Americans.

Among teenagers on the street, too, there were tensions "We attended St. Peter

Afro-Cubans dance in Tampa's Martí-Maceo Club, about 1940. (Tony Pizzo Collection, University of South Florida)

Claver's, a Catholic School, located two blocks on the 'other' side of Nebraska Avenue, the psychological boundary between the black American and the black Cuban ghettoes," a black Cuban *Tampeño* named Evelio Grillo wrote in his memoirs. "While some black Americans lived in Ybor City, no black Cubans lived outside Ybor City and West Tampa." There were street fights between Cuban and American blacks, too, just as there were between non-black "Latins" and Southern whites. "The fact that we spoke Spanish set us apart and made us subject to the derision and the abuse which all language minorities experience in all societies," Grillo recalls. "When they wanted to tease us, our black American schoolmates called us 'tally wops,' a combination of two terms of derision applied to Italians, 'tally,' and 'wop.'"

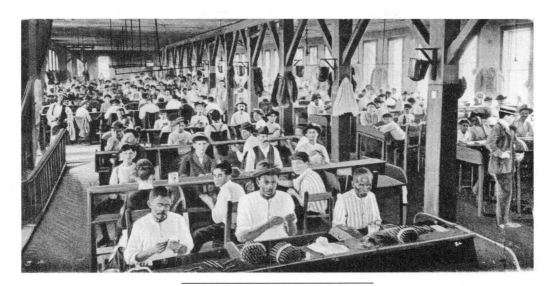

Racially integrated cigar factory in Ybor City, 1906. By then, segregation had forced the creation of separate black and white social clubs for Cubans. (Historical Association of Southern Florida)

By the 1930s Ybor City's black Cuban population had declined by half, and made up less than 3 percent of the overall black population of the area. Many went back to Cuba or, like so many Southern blacks, moved to northern cities. It was but one sign of the end of the Tampa cigar's heyday. The Great Depression crippled the hand-rolled cigar industry that so many Cubans, black and white, had depended on since the 1880s. Mechanization added a further blow in the late 1940s. Dozens of factories closed, and at the Círculo Cubano membership fell from its high of 5,000 in 1930 to less than half that number.

The Chess Master

One of the legendary grandmasters of chess was José Raúl Capablanca, a Cuban who won some of his greatest triumphs while he lived in New York City. A graduate of Columbia University, he made his first mark in chess circles in 1909, when at the age of twenty he defeated U.S. champion Frank Marshall at the Manhattan Chess Club, in New York. Over the next few years he lived in Cuba and New York, where he won several tournaments between 1913 and 1919. Beginning in 1916, he went eight straight years without losing a game.

He won the World Championship in Havana in 1921, when he defeated Emmanuel Lasker of Germany, and lost it eight years later in Buenos Aires to Alexander Alekhine, of France. He continued to win tournaments, but was never given another chance at the title. Capablanca died in 1942 of a stroke he suffered at the Manhattan Chess Club. Chess players today continue to study the games of the Cuban master, who has been called the greatest natural chess genius of all time.

THE *MACHADATO*

While immigrants in Tampa and Key West enjoyed the years of the cigar boom, Cuba held on precariously to its democracy. For all the corruption and misgovernment, civil liberties were by and large respected. There was a vigorous free press and voters could choose between competing political parties. Yet the electorate was weary of corruption, and in 1925 voted into office a former officer in the old *Mambí* army who promised to clean things up. His name was Gerardo Machado and he ruled for an eight-year period known as the *Machadato*.

José Raúl Capablanca the year he won the world's chess championship. (Cuban Heritage Collection, University of Miami)

In his first term Machado won great popularity by embarking on a program of public works on a grand scale. Machado's government built the Carretera Central, which for the first time connected eastern and western Cuba with a modern highway, and changed the face of Havana by building some of its best known symbols: the opulent Capitolio, its dome modeled on the U.S. Capitol; the laurel-tree lined Paseo del Prado, a majestic boulevard that led from Central

Cuban dictator Gerardo Machado visiting President Calvin Coolidge in the White House. Mrs. Coolidge is holding Machado's arm, Señora de Machado is holding Coolidge's. (Bohemia)

Park to the sea; and the famous *escalinata,* the monumental stairway leading up the main entrance of the University of Havana, the site of student revolts in years to come.

But Machado forced through constitutional changes to make sure of his re-election without opposition. This, of course, drew opposition. Then Machado opponents began to turn up dead. The press was muzzled. The police continued murdering political opponents. Cubans realized that for the first time since the birth of the republic the nation was in the grasp of a vicious dictator. And by 1931 the Cuban elite, as it had during colonial days, found itself back in exile. They headed to New York and also to a newer city in Florida: Miami. For the first

Former Cuban President Mario García Menocal, second from left, taken prisoner after the failure of the Rio Verde expedition to oust Machado. (Bohemia)

time, Miami began to play a role in the history of Cubans in America. The anti-Machado exiles walked the same political paths their forebears had trod the previous century, attempting to gain the favor of American public opinion and swing the American government to their side. And, just in case, they secretly prepared an armed landing.

From exile in Miami the former president Mario García Menocal joined forces with his political rival Carlos Mendieta to arrange for exiles in New York to acquire arms and the ship *Ilse Volmaner*. Mendieta and Menocal then secretly went back to Havana; from there they drove to a marshy area named Rio Verde, in Pinar del Rio province. They were supposed to contact the captain of the Cuban Navy cruiser *Patria* and coordinate internal risings with the landing of the *Ilse Volmaner* expedition in Oriente province, the traditional cradle of Cuban rebellions.

While anchored near New York Harbor, waiting for the rest of the party, the thirty-seven men aboard the *Ilse Volmaner* received a radio message that "the Revolution had exploded all across Cuba." They steamed to the island and on August 17 landed at Gibara, in Oriente. Emilio Laurent, the military leader of the group, had his men occupy the telephone and telegraph exchanges and block the roads. "Then I realized the calamitous picture that awaited us," he would write in an article for the Havana news magazine *Bohemia*. "There was no such revolution that the radio had informed us; neither in Oriente nor in Camagüey had anyone risen, and the handful of bands in the rest of the island had been annihilated by the government."

This included the group in Rio Verde. Hunted down in the marshes, Mendieta and Menocal were imprisoned. *Patria*, the very ship that the rebels thought would take their side, instead blockaded Laurent's exit at sea. Machado's airforce bombed Gibara, which gave it the distinction of being the first town of the Americas to be bombed from the air. Laurent's men tried to escape, but were defeated in a shootout fought in a palm grove a few miles out of town.

By the end of 1932 Menocal was back in Miami. The number of Cubans there had grown from a few hundred to more than a thousand. There were two main political groups. One faction, Florida historian Francis J. Sicius notes, consisted of wealthy older men who "formed a colony on the beach near Menocal's stone mansion with a tiled roof on Collins Avenue at Lincoln." The other group, more radical, was led by a student named Carlos Prío Socarrás who would be elected president of Cuba in 1948.

The older men continued to press from exile, invited by the American envoy Sumner Welles to join a united opposition front to hold talks with Machado. But an organization in Cuba called ABC proved the key. Their view of how to get Machado out of office was new: Rather than take to the backwoods—the *manigua* in which the generation of '95 had forged its reputation—ABC fought in the cities, with a campaign of bombings to which Machado's police responded with great brutality. In August 1933, with Cuba caught in a vicious spiral of violence, Machado gave in to Sumner Welles's ultimatum to leave office. Some of his followers fled to Miami where, as they got off their airplane, a crowd of exiles angrily shouted them down as "murderers" and "butchers." Machado himself first flew to safety in the Bahamas. Eventually he settled in Miami, where he died.

The post-Machado years in Cuba were chaotic. There were no less than nine changes of government between 1933 and 1936. It was during this period that a sergeant named Fulgencio Batista rose to become Cuba's de facto leader; until 1940 he proposed and deposed presidents at will. But good things happened, too. In 1933 Franklin Delano Roosevelt inaugurated his "Good Neighbor Policy" and

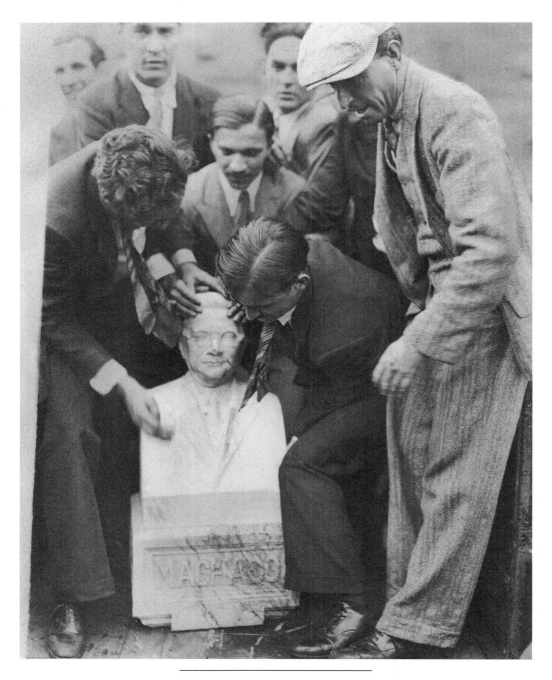

Exiles deface a bust of Machado, which they removed from the Cuban consulate in New York when he fell from power. (New York Times Pictures)

the following year abolished the Platt Amendment. In 1940 a Cuban Constitutional Convention wrote a new charter that guaranteed liberties and provided European-style social-democratic benefits. Batista was voted in as president in a fair election. For the next decade, as presidents Ramón Grau and Carlos Prío followed Batista in office, corruption persisted as the endemic evil of Cuban political life. But the nation was freer and more prosperous than it had ever been. It was Cuba's decade of democracy. Once again, as in the years before the *Machadato*, it sent to the United States immigrants rather than exiles.

The 1940s witnessed the largest migration since the wars of independence—the U.S. census counted 18,000 foreign-born Cubans in 1940 and 33,700 in 1950. Instead of the traditional strongholds in Florida, many headed to New York. By 1950 there were 13,295 "foreign-born white Cubans" in New York, nearly twice the number in Florida (non-white Cubans were apparently not counted by the Census Bureau). However, Florida, with the old settlements in Tampa and Key West, probably had a larger number of U.S.-born Cubans.

With no political crises and with fairly secure jobs in the strong economy of the period following World War II, Cubans in the United States for the first time began to leave a cultural imprint not just locally—as they had in Florida for more than seventy years—but on the national scene.

BÉISBOL

The first Cubans to become celebrities in the United States were baseball players. *Béisbol* had been played on the island since the nineteenth century, when it became a symbol of nationalism and was even banned by Spanish authorities for its links with independence movements. Baseball was brought to Cuba by three Cuban students from Alabama's Springhill College, Enrique Porto and the brothers Nemesio and Ernesto Guilló, who brought balls and bats to Havana in 1864. On the eve of the Ten Years War they founded the Habana baseball club. A decade later, Almendares—Habana's storied rival for nearly a hundred years until the Castro revolution dismantled the traditional ball clubs—was founded by a group that included Teodoro and Carlos de Zaldo, another set of brothers who learned the game while students in the United States, at Fordham.

Cubans émigrés in the United States played baseball too. In the early 1890s the Cuban cigar factories of Florida sponsored baseball teams for the workers, and proceeds from games were donated to José Martí's revolutionary cause. After independence two racially mixed but predominantly black Cuban ball clubs called

Wenceslao Gálvez, who lived in Tampa during the War of Independence, became one of the early Cuban baseball stars as shortstop for Almendares in the 1880s. In 1889 he wrote El baseball en Cuba, *the first history of Cuban baseball, and also a book on Ybor City.* (Collection of Roberto González Echevarría)

the Cuban Stars East and the Cuban Stars West barnstormed the states with top players such as pitcher José de la Caridad Méndez (who famously struck out Babe Ruth three times when the Yankees played an exhibition game in Havana) and the slugging outfielder Cristóbal Torriente. A few years later Alejandro Oms and Martín Dihigo played with the New York Cubans (winners of the 1947 Negro World Series) of the Negro National League. Dihigo was in a category by himself; he excelled at hitting, pitching, and every fielding position during a career that stretched from the 1920s to the late 1940s. An idol in his native land, Dihigo played in the Cuban league during the winter and in Negro leagues in the summer. He is the first Cuban elected to baseball's Hall of Fame in Cooperstown.

Before Jackie Robinson, there was Estalella

When Rafael Almeida and Armando Marsans, the first Cubans to play major league baseball in the modern era, opened the 1911 season with the Cincinnati Reds, the local press made sure fans understood the two were

The Cubano Baseball Club of Key West in the 1900–1901 season. (Collection of Roberto González Echevarría)

white. "Two of the purest bars of Castilian soap ever to wash upon our shores," the Cincinnati *Enquirer* assured readers. Adolfo Luque, the first Cuban star, was white, too, as were a handful of Cuban major leaguers in the first decades of the century. Cubans who were black played in the Negro Leagues.

Then things got complicated. In 1935 the Washington Senators signed a Cuban outfielder named Roberto Estalella. He was a slugger, powerfully built— and not white. In Cuba Estalella would have been termed a *mulato*, a word that refers to people of mixed black and white ancestry. Like the majority of the Cuban population, Estalella descended from Spanish colonists and black slaves. But he was so light skinned he was not unequivocally "black." And even though an American of a similar complexion might have been considered black and forbidden to play in the majors, Senators' management decided Estalella's race was not "black" but "Cuban." Estalella played for fourteen years, hitting a lifetime .282.

Yet no American "*mulatos*," and certainly no American blacks, played in a

Major League ball club before Jackie Robinson in 1947. Although both Estalella and Robinson had African ancestry, the Cuban was able to play before the American because fans and the baseball establishment accepted the absurd notion that Estalella was Cuban, not black. As a result of America's confused views about race, foreigners of African ancestry played major league baseball in a time when Americans of African ancestry could not.

Estalella had broken the color barrier, and nobody even knew it.

There was also at least one team of white Cubans playing in the United States during the first decades of independence. According to *The Pride of Havana*, by Yale Spanish literature professor and baseball fan Roberto González Echevarría, in 1913 a wealthy Cuban from New York named Antonio Hernández founded an

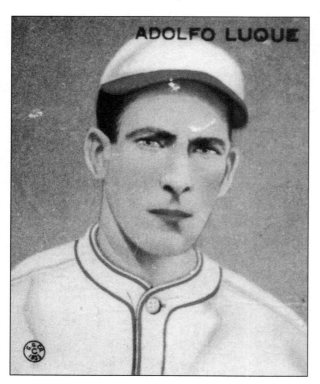

1920s baseball card of pitcher Adolfo Luque, first Cuban-born star in the major leagues. (Collection of Roberto González Echevarría)

all-Cuban baseball club in the Jersey shore resort of Long Branch. The Long Branch Cubans played that season and the next in the New Jersey–New York State League, one of the many professional minors that served as feeders to the majors. Long Branch featured as their pitching ace the great Adolfo Luque, who in 1914 began a 21-year major league career during which he won 193 games for the Cincinnati Reds, Boston Braves, Brooklyn Dodgers, and New York Giants.

Luque was the first Cuban Major League star, so it can be said he was the first Cuban famous to the general American public. He was not the first to play in the majors, though. Esteban Bellán, a catcher, played in 1871 for the Troy Haymakers of the old American Association, which baseball historians consider a major league. In the "modern" era the first Cubans were third baseman Rafael Almeida and outfielder Armando Marsans, who had decent though unspectacular careers 1913–1919. They were

Outfielders for the New York Cubans of the Negro National League before a game in 1935, the year the club was founded, at Belmar, New Jersey. From left, José Perez, Alejandro Oms, Martín Dihigo, and Cando López. (The Coast Advertiser)

followed by a handful of players that included Luque and Miguel Angel González, who in a scouting report would describe a prospect with the now classic "Good field, no hit." González in 1938 with the St. Louis Cardinals became the first Hispanic Major League manager (years later, Luque as the Almendares manager and González as the Habana manager had a famous rivalry in the Cuban league).

After them, in the 1930s, three more Cubans arrived. One was Roberto Estalella, who actually preceded Jackie Robinson as the first player of African ancestry in the major leagues. The number of Cuban big-leaguers increased as time went on. In 1946 the Havana Cubans began playing in the minors as part of the Florida International League—the first team based in Cuba to play in American organized baseball. By the end of the decade, a total of 43 Cubans had appeared on Major League rosters.

Estalella in the uniform of the old Cuban League club Marianao, from a series of photos of baseball stars that appeared in the Havana magazine Alerta. (Collection of Roberto González Echevarría)

THE MUSICAL EXPLOSION

Another way émigrés influenced American culture was through Cuban music, that multiform blend of African rhythms and Spanish melodies with the occasional and unexpected classical allusion. It had achieved a measure of popularity in the United States by the 1930s, when Xavier Cugat, a bandleader who was born in Spain and spent his youth in Cuba, played to American audiences at the Waldorf Astoria and the Palace Theater, in New York. He recorded more than 200 songs in the next ten years. Another Cuban bandleader, Don Azpiazu, had one of the biggest hits of 1931 with his version of Moises Simon's Cuban classic "El Manisero." The following year, an all-sister group known as the Anaconda Septet toured the United States.

But Cugat and Azpiazu played Americanized Cuban music, not the real thing. Both bandleaders well understood they were playing for Americans who, as Cugat once put it, "know nothing of Latin music, they do not understand it or feel it."

Something closer to the real thing had to wait for the emergence in the 1940s of three Cuban musicians from the Puerto Rican neighborhood of Spanish Harlem: Luciano "Chano" Pozo, Mario Bauzá, and Frank Grillo, better known as "Machito." Their music was different from what their contemporaries were playing back on the island, because they were influenced by American musicians such as Chick Webb and Cab Calloway. In turn, the three Cubans influenced American music right back. And precisely because the American influence came from swing, jazz, and bebop, which shared an African heritage with traditional Cuban music, the Cuban New York sound was more than merely a watered-down version of the real thing. Latin jazz and "Cubop" were new forms of Cuban music, in touch with its deepest roots in Cuba yet distinctively American. It was, in short, the authentic music of Cubans in the United States.

The first of the three to play in the United States was Machito. He was born in Ybor City in 1912, during the heyday of the cigar, but his family moved back to Cuba when he was a teenager. In 1937 he returned to the United States, but settled in New York instead of his native Tampa, where the tobacco industry was in decline. In 1940 he founded the orchestra he was to lead until his death in 1976, the first to blend jazz and Cuban music.

Machito was the lead singer and conductor. The man responsible for the innovative new arrangements was another Florida-born Cuban, his brother-in-law Mario Bauzá, born one year before Machito in Key West. He joined Machito's orchestra one year after its founding and hired the American jazz soloists who gave

Mario Bauzá, born in Key West when it had a large Cuban community at the turn of the century, moved to New York and with his brother-in-law Machito founded the foremost Cuban music orchestra in the states. (Associated Press)

the orchestra its special sound, improvising Afro-American riffs on top of driving Afro-Cuban polyrhythms. By the end of the decade Machito and Bauzá were regularly playing the Palladium, on Broadway and 53rd, where great instrumentalists like Dizzy Gillespie, Charlie Parker, and Woody Herman popped in to jam with the Cubans. It was a time of great musical ferment, when the African musical traditions of the United States fused with the African musical traditions of Cuba.

One day in 1947 Gillespie asked Bauzá to recommend a drummer to play the *tumbadora,* the central percussion instrument in Cuban bands. Bauzá introduced him to Chano Pozo, who unlike Machito and Bauzá himself had no history in the United States, having recently arrived from Havana. Pozo first played with Gillespie at a September 1947 Carnegie Hall concert that has become legendary among jazz fans. The collaboration between Pozo and Gillespie was a sensation.

Their seminal hit, "Manteca," has had enormous influence on jazz musicians, enticing them to explore the complex rhythms they heard from Pozo's *tumbadora*. But the partnership lasted just fourteen months. Pozo was shot dead outside Harlem's Rio Café in an argument over a woman. He was only 33 years old. Fans wonder to this day how Pozo would have changed Cuban and American music had he lived.

Unrest at Home

Back on the island, though, Cubans were worried about more than music. The prosperity and respect for civil liberties that characterized the 1940s was marred by corruption and "political gangsters," armed bands that took it upon themselves to settle partisan differences by killing opponents. Sick of violence and corruption, Cuban voters got ready to elect a new president in June 1952 from a slate of candidates who campaigned on platforms of fighting corruption and *gangsterismo*.

But Fulgencio Batista got there first. The former strongman, who had lived in semiretirement in Daytona Beach from 1944 to 1948, staged a coup d'état on March 10. Batista ordered tanks to surround the Presidential Palace. President Carlos Prío took refuge in the Mexican Embassy, flew to Mexico, and then went to exile in Miami just as he had done in his days as a student activist during the *Machadato*. His supporters followed.

Once again, political turbulence in Cuba was sending exiles to the United States. They had no way of knowing that democracy would still not be reestablished in Cuba even by the end of the twentieth century.

CHAPTER 5

Fighting the Sergeant

1952–1958

Batista, the former army sergeant who for twenty years had hung like a shadow over Cuba had come back to destroy the fragile constitutional order. His rule would be marked by brutality and theft. Former president Prío, Cubans complained, had given in too easily. Conscious of his place in history, the former president would spend most of the rest of the decade in the United States trying to overthrow the man who overthrew him.

The Miami where Prío went to live was familiar to Cubans. Its Cuban population was between three and five thousand at the time, much less than Tampa, Key West, or New York City. They were concentrated around Southwest Eighth Street and Flagler, an area that would in the coming years become known as "Little Havana." In any case, Miami's overall Hispanic population was already large enough in 1953 for Horacio Aguirre, a Nicaraguan immigrant, to open *Diario Las Americas,* a Spanish-language newspaper still in existence.

But Miami's real importance to Cubans during the early 1950s was as a vacation spot. With round trip fares between Havana and Miami under $40, the short hop north was affordable to working class Cubans. An estimated 40,000 to 50,000 tourists a year visited Miami out of Havana in the early 1950s.

Their habit was to come during the summer, when American vacationers would not think of braving South Florida's semitropical heat. So it was no won-

Nearly the entire Cuban population of Union City and West New York in 1956 fit inside this Hudson County catering hall for a dinner honoring a local Italian-American politician. Two decades later, the community was the largest in the United States outside of South Florida. (Courtesy Roberto "Figurín" León)

der that at hotels, restaurants, and shops throughout Miami Beach signs went up proclaiming, "Se habla español." Local businessmen realized Cuban summer visitors provided an opportunity to make money year-round rather than just in the traditional winter season when American tourists arrived to get away from cold northern cities.

A Milkman's "Second Capital of Exile"

The Miami of the late 1940s and early 1950s was a favored Cuban honeymoon spot. Two newlyweds who arrived in the summer of 1949, Manuel and Lydia Rodriguez, changed the course of Cuban-American history. The *Star Ledger* of New Jersey told the story in 1999. At the Somerset Hotel, where they stayed that summer, Manuel and Lyda befriended an Italian-American woman named Florence Colarusso who had temporarily left her New Jersey home to take a summer job waitressing in sunny Florida. At the end of their vacation, the Rodriguezes did not return to Cuba. Instead, they took the long drive to New Jersey with their new American friend.

They first lived in New York City like so many other Cuban émigrés of the period, but after a short while they moved to Hudson County, where Florence lived in the town of North Bergen. They learned English and found jobs. Manuel (Manolito, everyone called him), 23-years-old, had been a shoemaker and found a job in a shoe factory; Lydia, a year younger, worked at a chicken-packing plant. The two legalized their immigration status and saved their money. Two other Rodriguez brothers, Raúl and Silvio, arrived in the mid-1950s. They all began a milk delivery business in Union City and West New York, which are also in Hudson County. The business prospered, and the success story of *el lechero*, the milkman, got back to the couple's hometown of Fomento, in Las Villas province.

Fomenteros began to follow Manuel, his brothers, and Lydia to Union City and West New York, finding work in the famed embroidery factories there. Slowly, Cubans made their presence felt. Gilberto Labrada, another *fomentero*, opened one of the area's first Cuban bodegas. The Spanish-American Grocery, on Bergenline Avenue near 25th Street. By November 1955 enough Cubans lived in Union City that a young Fidel Castro thought it worthwhile to visit the town while on a U.S. tour to raise funds for the revolution. Castro attracted a large crowd that spilled into the street outside a bar called El Molino Rojo, one block away from Labrada's bodega. Nobody had a demonstration permit, so local police ordered the Cubans to break it up.

By the time Castro took power in 1959, perhaps 3,000 Cubans, largely from Fomento, were living in Union City and West New York. They founded a "Cuban Lyceum" to keep the culture alive. It was only the beginning. Close to 100,000 Cuban exiles, from Fomento and throughout the island, would settle in the area during the Castro years. It was the largest Cuban population in the United States outside of Miami. With its anti-Castro activism, and with just about every store on Bergenline Avenue operated by Cubans, the North Hudson County area would in the 1970s become known as the "Second Capital of Exile." It would not have happened but for a milkman from Fomento who vacationed in Miami in 1949.

CONSPIRACIES

But after the fall of Prío, Miami became for Cubans something other than a vacation spot. It became, like Tampa and Key West in the previous century, a place of exile.

Prío landed in Miami near dawn on March 17, and within a week he was holding a news conference to announce he did not wish to form a government-in-exile. Indeed, Prío had different plans.

That October, near Fort Worth, Texas, an ex-convict named Floyd Hill was arrested in a vacant field as he dug up a thermos jug stuffed with $128,000. As it turned out, the loot was part of $248,000 Hill had stolen from two Cubans at a hotel a month earlier. Police and the FBI learned that the Cubans had ties to Prío, and that the money had been intended to buy weapons for an anti-Batista uprising in Cuba. Another incident took place days before Christmas, when authorities broke into a Mamaroneck, New York, gasoline station and confiscated more than a thousand rifle grenades, 1,800 clips for M-1 rifles, and nearly one thousand bazooka shells. Three men were arrested. One of them confessed that the munitions were meant for Prío's fight against Batista.

American Mambo, Cuban Guaguancó

In the early 1950s a dance craze swept the United States: The mambo. Its popularizer was a Cuban band leader named Dámaso Pérez Prado who had made his reputation in Mexico before going to the United States. Compositions like "Mambo No. 5" and "Mambo No. 8" climbed the American charts, and all of New York was dancing the mambo at the Palladium.

Ironically, Pérez Prado was more famous and successful in the United States than in his native land. Cuban music fans believed the mambo played by Cuba-based musicians—such as the great Beny Moré—was more authentic.

The reverse was true for another Cuban musician at the time, Arsenio Rodríguez. Blind since being kicked by a horse at age three, Rodríguez became one of the best players of the *tres*, the Cuban guitar. Yet his fame rests upon adding two trumpets and the conga drum to the traditional Cuban septet, creating the *son guaguancó* rhythm that is the basis of much Cuban music.

In 1953 Rodríguez left trumpet player Félix Chapotín in charge of his hugely successful orchestra and immigrated to the United States in hopes of having an operation that would restore his sight. The surgery failed, but Rodríguez stayed in New York City, continuing to influence Cuban music in Cuba more than Cuban music in the United States.

Soon enough there was fighting in Cuba. On the 26th of July, 1953, some 160 opponents of Batista staged an unsuccessful attack on the Moncada army barracks in Santiago, and the Rural Guard barracks in Bayamo, both in Oriente. About 61 men were killed in action or murdered by Batista's henchmen after being captured. Their leader, a young man named Fidel Castro, escaped to hide in the mountains, but within a few days he was captured. His life was spared through the intercession of an old friend of the family, Bishop Enrique Pérez Serantes, and instead he was sent to prison.

Back in the United States, authorities were on to Prío's plans to fight Batista. In December, the former president was arrested in Miami and charged with conspiracy to smuggle guns to Cuba. He pleaded not guilty. But the conspiracies did not end. Another large arsenal was discovered in Manhattan in March 1954. "Anti-tank guns, hand grenades, semi-automatic rifles, and considerable amounts of ammunition were piled almost ceiling-high in two rooms of an apparently abandoned store at 173 West 99th Street," reported the *New York Times*. Eight Cuban exiles were taken into custody.

Investigators came to believe that at least three other large shipments of arms had made their way to Cuba from the same address. FBI agents spread through Miami and New York, questioning exiles suspected of involvement in gunrunning. Late that spring another exiled former president of Cuba, Prío ally Carlos Hevia, was arrested in his Coral Gables home.

"(We) have successfully fought communism and dictatorship in Cuba and have shown our love and support of America and democracy," Prío told reporters the day he and Hevia were indicted in New York. The indictment, he said, was "an endorsement of a man who is now ruling Cuba as a police state." In September the defendants plead *nolo contendere*. The maximum penalty amounted to a $9,000 fine, not much for the wealthy Prío. "I am glad that American justice has recognized the exceptional circumstances of this case," he said.

ENTER CASTRO

It was now 1955. His enemies either in prison or with their hands tied in exile, Batista felt strong enough to grant Prío political amnesty. He left his Miami estate, Casa Reposada, and returned to Havana to undertake "non-violent civic opposition." Another of Batista's foes, Fidel Castro, was released from prison in May the same year.

Castro left for Mexico, where he began to conspire again. Short of money, he decided to ask for help from émigré Cubans in the United States. He got a tourist visa at the embassy in Mexico City, borrowed money for train fare and crossed the Texas border that autumn.

Castro first spoke to Cubans in the Northeast—in New York, Philadelphia, Bridgeport, Elizabeth (New Jersey), and Union City. In New York, before 800 people at Palm Garden Hall on 52nd Street and Eighth Avenue, Castro spoke of "thousands of families thrown into exile by misery and oppression, who arrive by the hundreds each month, filled with sadness and sorrow, people exiled from a land where no one speaks out."

The del Valle family holding a birthday party in New York City. There may have been 15,000 Cuban immigrants in New York when the del Valles moved there in the mid-1950s. (Courtesy Emilio del Valle)

Castro left the Northeast and, in a conscious effort to echo the footsteps of José Martí in the 1890s, headed to Florida. Castro spoke to Cubans in Key West, Tampa, and Miami, a city that was barely on the map when Martí was in the state. Speaking to a thousand people at Flagler Theater, Castro sought to impress them with his moderation by urging Batista to transfer power to Cosme de la Torriente. *Don* Cosme, as Castro called him in that speech (a rare use of the Spanish honorific by a Cuban), was a respected member of an old Cuban family who since the Machado years had managed to keep his dignity and reputation for honesty through the worst of the bloodshed and political thievery. Castro spent seven weeks in the United States before heading back to Mexico with about $9,000 in contributions and, just as important, a reputation among exiles as a man of action who could take on the hated Batista regime.

Not that Batista was hated everywhere. When he took a two-day vacation in Daytona Beach, where he had lived in the late 1940s, the mayor proclaimed an official "Batista Day" and received him with a welcoming ceremony at the airport. Ironically, early spring 1956 would find the Cuban dictator in Florida and the president he had deposed in Havana. Batista believed his grip on power was secure enough to be in the United States and Prío believed the amnesty gave him enough political maneuvering room to be in Cuba.

"Loooo-see, I'm home!"

No Cuban is more famous in American popular culture than Desi Arnaz—unless one counts Ricky Ricardo, the character he played for six years on "I Love Lucy."

Desiderio Alberto Arnaz y de Archa was born in Santiago de Cuba in 1917 to a wealthy family that in the 1930s supported the regime of Gerardo Machado. With Machado's ouster, the family fled to Miami, where 17-year-old Desi attended high school and organized his first musical group, the Siboney Quartet.

His first big break came when he sang for Xavier Cugat's popular orchestra in 1937. Three years later he starred in the Broadway and movie versions of "Too Many Girls," on the set of which he met Lucille Ball. They married a few months later.

For the next ten years Lucy and Desi traveled the country, separately most of the time, playing in theaters and nightclubs. In order to spend more time together, they proposed to CBS a situation comedy starring themselves. Executives said no. They did not think audiences would accept a Cuban man married to an American woman. But Lucy and Desi did not give up. They risked their $5,000 savings shooting a pilot. CBS liked it, and hesitantly gave the couple the go-ahead.

"I Love Lucy" was first broadcast on October 15, 1951. It was fantastically successful, as Americans made a habit of tuning in at 9 PM Monday nights. The episode in which Little Ricky was born drew a record audience of 44 million viewers. The show was produced until the end of the 1956–1957 season, and then CBS aired reruns in prime time until 1961.

"I Love Lucy" revolutionized television. It was the first program to be filmed using a three-camera-technique Arnaz helped develop, which remains the industry standard to this day. Arnaz was a sharp businessman, too. The deal he worked with CBS called for a lower salary than normal in exchange for ownership of the show. It paid off—he made millions, and his Desilu Productions produced several major television shows of the era.

Desi and Lucy divorced in 1960. Three years later he sold his share of Desilu and practically retired from show business, spending most of his time with his horses at his California ranch. He died in 1986.

Desi Arnaz and Lucille Ball receiving the Order of Carlos Manuel de Céspedes, Cuba's highest civilian honor, from Consul General Eduardo Hernández in July 1959.
(Courtesy *Miami Herald*)

BATISTA OPPOSITION GROWS

This quickly changed. Batista had been back in Havana barely a few days when Colonel Ramón Barquín, who had been Cuban military attaché in Washington, led a group of progressive young officers of the Cuban army in a coup attempt. They failed and went to prison, but the regime was shaken. It was the most serious challenge since the attack on Moncada nearly three years earlier. Later the same April, a group allegedly connected to Prío attacked the Goicuría barracks in Matanzas. They failed too, and fourteen young men were massacred. But Batista was forced to realize that his hold over Cuba was not as tight as he had believed. He cracked down even further on basic liberties and forced Prío and Carlos Hevia (who had also gone back to Havana under the amnesty) out of the country. Prío was actually dragged out of his home, thrown in a car, and put on a plane to Miami. "It was a matter of going to the airport or to his grave," Prío's American lawyer told the *New York Times*.

The two former Cuban presidents were initially refused political asylum by immigration authorities on grounds that their previous convictions for arms-smuggling made their presence on American soil "prejudicial to the public interest, safety and security." After a one-month court battle, they were granted permission to remain. Prío signed an agreement not to engage in "any activity which may be prejudicial to the public interest of the country or in violation of its laws."

But he continued to work against Batista. In September of 1956 Prío attended a meeting on American soil that was to prove fateful in the history of the Cuban nation.

Prío had known of Fidel Castro while he was president. At the time of Batista's coup, Castro had been nominated to run for Congress by a fraction of the Ortodoxo Party, the mainstream opposition to Prío's Auténtico Party. He had a reputedly violent past in his days as a law student at the University of Havana, but was a minor figure, until the Moncada assault brought him national prominence.

Now, three years after Moncada, Castro needed money and Prío needed action. Emissaries arranged a meeting in Texas. Prío flew in from his base in Miami. Castro, operating out of Mexico City, made his way to the American border. Lacking official permission to enter the United States, he fell in with a group of Mexican laborers and waded across the Rio Grande to Reynoso, where he changed into dry clothes. Castro then headed out to meet Prío at the Hotel Casa de Palmas, in McAllen.

Protestors demand the release from jail of former Cuban President Carlos Prío, who was briefly imprisoned in the United States in 1958 on charges of smuggling arms to aid the uprising against Fulgencio Batista. (Courtesy *Miami Herald)*

Historians have different versions of exactly what happened next. Some say Prío immediately gave Castro $50,000 to fund a military attack against Batista and another $50,000 later. Some say Castro received only $50,000 altogether. Whatever the case, Prío certainly agreed to turn over to his rival a substantial sum of money.

With guns and ammunition paid for in large part by the money Prío agreed to put up in Texas, an expedition mounted by Fidel Castro left Mexico on a boat named *Granma,* purchased from an American living in Mexico, and landed in eastern Cuba on December 2, 1956. Although no one knew it at the time, Prío had funded a movement destined to end his reign as Batista's foremost enemy and begin a tragic new era in Cuban history.

PRÍO ECLIPSED

At first, most of Cuba believed Castro's 82 *Granma* expeditionaries had been wiped out by Batista's forces shortly after landing. Castro, Batista insisted, was probably dead. But Herbert Matthews of the *New York Times* climbed the mountains of the Sierra Maestra and found Castro alive with what remained of his group of supporters. On February 24th the *Times* published the first installment of the now famous three-part series that made Castro into a mythical figure worldwide. "Fidel Castro, the rebel leader of Cuba's youth, is alive and fighting hard and successfully in the almost impenetrable fastness of the Sierra Maestra at the southern tip of the island," read Matthews's lead in the first article. "President Fulgencio Batista has the cream of his Army around the area, but the Army men are fighting a thus-far losing battle to destroy the most dangerous enemy General Batista has yet faced."

It was nothing of the sort, at least not until Matthews intervened. At the time of Matthews's visit, Castro had fewer than 20 men, ragged, hungry, and low in munitions. To trick the American reporter, Castro ordered his handful of followers to march past over and over again, making it appear there were many more fighters than there actually were. And with Matthews characterizing Castro's program as "a new deal for Cuba, radical, democratic and therefore anti-Communist," Cubans of all classes began to see in the rebel leader a new hope in the struggle against the despised Batista.

Other armed groups were active too. On March 13 the Directorio Revolucionario, composed largely of university students, assaulted the Presidential Palace to assassinate Batista. Some 40 youths were killed including the leader, José Antonio Echevarría, a charismatic rival of Castro. Prío's Auténticos tried to get in on the action also. That May, a boat with 27 expeditionaries set off near Key Biscayne. Upon landing in Oriente they were captured by Batista's troops and all but one summarily shot dead.

The fiasco was a setback not only in Cubans' fight against Bastista, but also in Prío's own fight with his rival Castro, who was growing stronger in the Sierra. Yet Batista continued to focus on Prío as his main enemy. In an interview with Associated Press, Batista dismissed Castro as having no more than "a handful of supporters" while complaining that Prío had spent $5 to $6 million buying arms to overthrow him.

Castro's exiled friends in the United States continued to press. Sign-carrying picketers became a fixture at the United Nations and at Cuban consulates. One time they demonstrated in front of the New York Times building, but not in protest—they left "a signed album in tribute to Matthews," reported the newspaper. The exiles began to sell bonds, though they were merely non-redeemable receipts for contributions to the cause. "It is just for your own pride," claimed an activist for the *26th of July Movement*, Castro's organization named for the date of the assault on Moncada. It was not their only way to raise money. A 20-year old American named Charles Ryan appeared in New York after spending time fighting for "liberty and democracy" in the Sierra with Castro. After one speaking engagement at the Manhattan Towers Hotel, he reportedly raised more than $1,000 for the revolution.

By now the *26th of July Movement* had its own leadership in exile, separate from the exiles of the Ortodoxo Party to which Castro had belonged. Far from being bearded, wild-eyed revolutionaries, its leading representatives in the United States were distinguished members of the Cuban establishment such as Felipe Pazos, former president of the National Bank, and young moderates like Ernesto Betancourt, the movement's registered agent in Washington. Both would eventually break with Castro and head to exile again, Betancourt becoming the first chief of Radio Martí.

In the fall of 1957, the various exile opposition groups agreed in Miami to form a new Council for Cuban Liberation. The pact was formally signed by Pazos for Castro's *26th of July Movement*, Prío for the Auténtico Party, the respected academician Roberto Agramonte for the Ortodoxos, and young Faure Chaumón for the Directorio. Finally, it appeared that every major opposition group in exile had joined together in a united front to overthrow Batista and hold free elections.

But Castro did not want to share the stage. From the Sierra Maestra he issued an angry 34-page handwritten letter withdrawing his group from the pact. "The *26th of July Movement* . . . claims for itself the function of maintaining public order and reorganizing the armed forces of the republic," Castro wrote. He denied giving Pazos permission to sign the pact and insisted that Manuel Urrutia Lleó—a moderate judge hounded by Batista into Miami exile after voting to acquit the revolutionaries captured in Castro's *Granma* landing—should be the interim post-Batista president. Prío and the other members of the pact agreed to Urrutia. But they did not agree to let the *26th of July* assume what amounted to absolute power.

With that, the alliance dissipated. It was now clear that Castro's *26th of July* had become the leading anti-Batista force, in Cuba as well as in exile circles.

Brooklyn's Own

Nearly as many Cubans played Major League baseball during the 1950s as had played in all the years up to that time. There were more impact players, too. Camilo Pascual used his wicked curveball to win 174 games, mostly with the Washington Senators. Orestes "Minnie" Miñoso, quickly signed by the Cleveland Indians after Jackie Robinson broke the color barrier and became an all-star outfielder after being traded to the Chicago White Sox. Future MVP Zoilo Versalles and future multiple 20-game winner Mike Cuellar made their debuts in this decade.

Then there were the Sugar Kings, a Havana-based Class AAA International League team that won the minor league's "Little World Series" in 1959. Team owner Bobby Maduro, as well as many Cuban fans, viewed the club as an audition for a major league expansion franchise in Havana, a dream that never came to be. After taking power, Fidel Castro banned professional baseball. The best Cuban players escaped; the Sugar Kings moved to Jersey City.

And fans of the Brooklyn Dodgers will always have a fond memory of Sandy Amoros in left field in the seventh game of the 1955 World Series. Bottom of the sixth, with Brooklyn up 2–0, the hated Yankees had two runners on base and Yogi Berra at bat. Berra hit a fly deep to left field that looked like it was going to drop in for a two-run triple. But Amoros reached the ball just inside the foul line and fired a relay to shortstop Pee Wee Reese, who fired to first for a double play. That killed the Yankee rally, and the Dodgers held on to win—their first Series victory over the Yankees in five attempts.

El 26 IN THE UNITED STATES

Prío had additional problems. He was indicted again by the federal government in February 1958, charged once more with conspiracy to smuggle. The former Cuban president even spent a day in jail in Miami when he chose to join codefendants who could not raise the $3,000 bail. It was largely a symbolic act, since Prío was a millionaire with more than enough cash to post bail for his friends.

With Prío facing legal troubles, the *26th of July* seemed to step up its activities in the United States. Urrutia left Miami for a tour of New York, speaking at the Palm Garden in the Belvedere Hotel and calling for the United Nations to declare Cuba in violation of the 1948 Universal Declaration of Human Rights. "In the most clear and absolute terms, we want to express our group's rejection of Com-

Prío confers with lawyers in federal court in New York during legal proceedings in his indictment for gunrunning. (Courtesy *Miami Herald*)

munist cooperation," he told reporters in April. That same month the anti-Batista forces won a significant victory when the United States imposed an arms embargo on the Cuban regime.

The movement's rank and file seemed to be everywhere, too. They put up a Cuban flag on the 86th floor observation deck of the Empire State Building. At Rockefeller Center, exiles took the Cuban flag down from its pole and raised the red and black banner of the *26th of July*. There were street protests in Miami, New York, and Los Angeles. Gun smuggling continued. In Los Angeles, five Cubans were arrested for manufacturing machine guns. Arms for Castro's movement were intercepted in Miami, Fort Lauderdale, and Ocala, and even as far from all things Cuban as Morgantown, West Virginia.

Supporters and the press mob Prío upon his release from prison in Miami.
(Courtesy *Miami Herald*)

One of the most publicized busts took place at the end of March in Brownsville, Texas, where 35 members of the *26th of July Movement* were intercepted as they departed for Cuba with a shipload of arms. The men went on a hunger strike. Cuban exiles in Miami, New York, and Los Angeles joined in solidarity. They did not eat for seven days, and publicity in American newspapers gained public sympathy for the anti-Batista cause. Two months after their arrests, 33 of the group were given three to five years probation; the other two were acquitted.

There was more. Later that year 31 exiles aboard the cabin cruiser *Harpoon* were arrested north of Miami with more than $10,000 in military equipment; in Fort Lauderdale, a plane was seized with rifles and submachine guns in crates stamped "Fidel"; off Key Biscayne, the 80-foot yacht *Restless II* was seized in

Members of Prío's Organización Autentica imprisoned at the Broward County jail after U.S. authorities arrested them in 1958 while attempting to sail to Cuba to fight Batista.
(Associated Press)

what customs agents called "the biggest haul yet." Overall, federal authorities seized nearly 20 arms shipments in 1958; many others (90 percent, claimed exile figures) made it through.

South Florida at the end of the Batista era had become home to somewhere between 20,000 and 40,000 Cubans who gave it a new image. "In the past two years, gaudy, gritty-Greater Miami has become revolutionary headquarters of the Americas, with guns, boats, planes and men to man them," reported *Time* Magazine in 1958. "Financed by ex-President Carlos Prío Socarrás . . . by rich ex-patriates, and by wealthy Havana sympathizers who donate as much as $50,000 apiece at clandestine rallies, the rebels trade with arms dealers all along the Gulf and East Coast." The Batista regime, in an echo of a charge the Castro regime would make decades later, protested that Miami had become a center of "gangster activities" by its political enemies.

SOME COME, SOME GO

That things were coming to a head in Miami was but a sign that things were also coming to a head in Cuba. In November, another rigged election was won by the Batista-backed candidate. In the field the Batista army, led by corrupt, incompetent officers and fighting for a regime nearly all Cubans hated, was falling apart. Castro in the Sierra was growing in power. As the end of the year neared, the eastern capital of Santiago was cut off by rebel troops. Santa Clara, where there was house-to-house fighting, was bombed by Batista's airforce. In Havana,

A Border Patrol agent displays a howitzer, rifles, and grenades taken in the raid against Prío's expeditionary force.
(Associated Press)

bombs planted by the *26th of July* underground went off almost daily. And, as if to seal Batista's fate, U.S. Ambassador Earl Smith notified Batista in mid-December that Washington would no longer support his government.

On December 30 Batista's two sons flew to New York "for the New Year holiday." It was the dictator's attempt to spirit his children out of a country he now realized he might no longer control. Shortly after the New Year struck Fulgencio Batista gave up. He boarded a plane at Camp Columbia and flew to the Dominican Republic. Castro's forces seized power in key spots throughout the island. At the airport in Miami there were fistfights between members of the old regime fleeing the new order and jubilant former exiles flying back to their beloved island. They thought a new age of freedom, honesty, and justice had arrived for the not quite fifty-seven-year-old Republic of Cuba.

SECTION III

REVOLUTION

TO

EXILE

CHAPTER 6

Castro's Takeover

1959–1965

Batista's departure caught everyone by surprise. Despite the deteriorating political and economic situation in Cuba, few were expecting his dictatorial regime to fall that New Year's Eve. "The sudden news that Batista was gone jolted all of us," recalls José Martínez, a Miami resident who was in his early thirties when Batista fell. "It was surreal. I was overwhelmed with emotion to hear that, at long last, the tyrant had been deposed." The entire country rejoiced. People spilled out into the streets shouting "¡Viva Cuba Libre!" with patriotic fervor. It was the dawn of a new era. Justice, freedom, and democracy had finally arrived, or so it seemed.

Fidel Castro entered Havana January 8, after a 600-mile journey with the victorious Rebel Army from Santiago, on the western end of Cuba. Alongside Castro were his brother Raúl, Ché Guevara, Huber Matos, Camilo Cienfuegos and many other heroic figures who had fought against the Batista dictatorship. Church bells pealed and factory whistles blew as a column of tanks and jeeps bristling with bearded rebels waving rifles—and, famously, flaunting rosaries or religious medals—paraded through the seaside Malecón boulevard and broad Twenty-third Street. More than a million people lined the route, celebrating in ecstasy. Fathers lifted young children up on their shoulders so they could see Cuba's new saviors above the heads of the crowd. People sang and danced, waved Cuban flags, held up homemade signs with patriotic slogans, and chanted "¡Viva Fidel!"

A young Fidel Castro in his triumphant arrival in Havana in January of 1959.
(Courtesy *Miami Herald*)

And no wonder. Castro had chased away the hated Batista, and was not linked to the discredited politics of the corrupt pre-Batista democracy. The Revolution, it seemed to nearly every Cuban, was destined to finally carry out José Martí's dream of a sovereign, just, and democratic Cuba. Thousands of exiles returned from the United States including Carlos Prío, free on bail after his second arrest for arms smuggling. "My duty at present is to be in Havana," he told reporters as he prepared to fly out of Miami in the days following the triumph of the revolution. He knew leadership has passed from his hands.

The new government was composed of well-known and respected figures. The new president of Cuba was Manuel Urrutia, a well regarded judge from Santiago. "We have come to govern . . . but the sovereign people of Cuba will govern us," he proclaimed shortly after being sworn in as president. His cabinet was pluralistic and represented a wide political spectrum. José Miró Cardona, dean of the law school, was named prime minister; Felipe Pazos, a highly respected economist, took over as head of the national bank; Roberto Agramonte, a prominent figure of the Ortodoxo party, became foreign minister; and the charismatic leader of the *26th of July Movement*, Fidel Castro, was named commander in chief of the armed forces.

DISSENT AMONG THE REVOLUTIONARIES

By the summer of 1959, there were major rifts within the Cuban government. At issue was the ideological soul of the revolution. At the beginning, Castro adamantly argued that his revolution followed a humanistic democratic model, rather than a Marxist-Leninist approach. In fact, during a visit to Washington, D.C., during the spring he addressed the issue directly at a televised press conference. Speaking in heavily accented English, Castro said, "I know you are worried . . . first of all if we are Communist. And of course . . . I have said very clearly that we are not communist."

However, by the end of the year his actions would contradict his public pronouncements. With overwhelming popular support, Castro managed to discredit and oust his potential adversaries in a short period of time. In February he replaced Miró Cardona as prime minister. Then he took on President Urrutia. Urrutia had made statements denouncing the role of the Communist Party in Cuban history, reminding the Cuban people that the Communists had forged an alliance with Batista—and that sealed his fate. Castro was incensed by Urrutia's charge. He went on the offensive and berated Urrutia on national television, accusing the president of betraying the revolution for his attacks on communist infiltration. Sensing his days were numbered, President Urrutia sought political asylum in the Venezuelan embassy in Havana. Castro named Osvaldo Dorticós president of Cuba. Dorticós had close ties to the Communist Party.

By the winter of 1959, all of the country's moderate cabinet leaders had been forced out and replaced by communist sympathizers. It did not take Castro long to go after his own trusted military leaders of the *26th of July Movement*.

Among the first was Huber Matos. "I recall going to visit Fidel after I had written him a long letter outlining to him why I wished to resign from the armed forces," Matos remembers. "At the meeting, I argued with him about the increased communist presence among the revolutionary ranks. I flatly told him we had not fought a revolution to establish a communist regime. He told me I was undermining his heroic efforts to bring social justice to Cuba and concluded by telling me my remarks were counter-revolutionary and for that I would pay the ultimate price." Shortly thereafter, Commander Matos was arrested and sentenced to twenty years in prison.

In the following months, Castro was able to emerge as "Maximum Leader," bringing under his complete control all of the island: Independent mass media were abolished, practically all foreign and domestic businesses were expropriated by the government, the Catholic Church was shut down, firing squads continued their executions of the regime's enemies, the number of political prisoners mounted, and scheduled elections were canceled. In December 1961, Castro proclaimed on national television, "I was and will always be a Marxist-Leninist until my last dying breath."

THE FIRST EXILES

The first Cubans to flee the island under Castro were intimately associated with the Batista regime. Some 3,000 government officials, businessmen with links to the regime, soldiers and police personnel escaped to Miami the first few weeks of 1959. However, by the end of the year, there was a drastic change in the kind of people fleeing Cuba.

Now *Batistianos* who arrived in Miami months before were joined by professionals who supported Castro at first but had grown disenchanted. All told, 26,527 refugees were admitted that first year.

In 1960 the Cuban-born population of the United States was 79,150 with an additional 45,266 classified as having Cuban ancestry, according to the census. The vast majority of the foreign born had arrived between 1959 and the few months of 1960 that were included in the census, a direct result of the Cuban Revolution. The number would grow through the rest of 1960—60,224 total. *El exilio* had begun.

Cuba's highly educated and mostly white elite—wealthy landowners, sugar barons, industrialists, entrepreneurs, and professionals—was disproportionately represented in this first wave of exiles. A 1963 study by Stanford University found that 7.8 percent had been lawyers or judges in Cuba, compared to one half of one percent of the Cuban population in the last census, taken in 1953. Another 34 percent were "professional and semi-professional" or "managerial and executive," compared to 9 percent of all Cuba. And 36 percent had completed high school or had some college, compared to 4 percent on the island.

Still, a substantial number of exiles wore blue collars, even in the early years. According to the study, 20 percent were "skilled, semi-skilled and unskilled" workers, more comparable to the 27 percent that fit those same categories in the Cuba of 1953.

These men and women had an outlook different from that of the European immigrants over the last century who saw America as the Promised Land. "We did not come as immigrants pulled by the American economic dream, but as refugees pushed by the Cuban political nightmare," wrote Nestor Carbonell, who left Cuba in 1960 at the age of 24 and later became a top executive for Pepsi Cola.

Miami's new Cuban residents devoted little time to putting back together their shattered business or professional lives. The focus was political—getting rid of Castro, something they were convinced could be accomplished in a matter of months. The move to Miami was temporary, they thought.

One of the greatest pianists and composers of both popular and "classical" Cuban music was Ernesto Lecuona. He is to Cuba what George Gershwin is to the United States. Lecuona composed nearly 700 musical works in his lifetime, including popular songs and pieces for piano, violin, and orchestra. His best known works include "Malagueña," "Maria la O," "Siboney" and "La Comparsa." Lecuona left Cuba shortly after the revolution, and died in exile in 1963 at the age of 68. (Cuban Heritage Collection, University of Miami)

Miami's landmark Torre de la Libertad, or Tower of Liberty, the old reception center for Cuban refugees.
(Courtesy Olivia de Diego)

The Cuban Ellis Island

Just like immigrants of previous generations had Ellis Island, Cuban exiles had Freedom Tower, *la Torre de la Libertad*. Modeled on Seville's twelfth-century Giralda tower, it was built in the mid 1920s on Biscayne Boulevard as Miami's first skyscraper. It became the Cuban Refugee Program's reception center for half a million exiles between 1961 and 1974.

Upon arriving the exiles submitted to X-rays and inoculations. They were given a "Red Cross Personal Kit" and government surplus food such as cheese and canned peanut butter. The *Torre* of those days was a hotel-like facility. Families would sleep, eat, and even watch movies at the *Torre* until arrangements were made to stay with a relative, rent an apartment or go out of state as part of the Refugee Resettlement Program.

Freedom Tower is being renovated by the Jorge Mas Canosa Freedom Foundation. The Mas family bought it to make it a museum for historical exhibits that reflect the sentimental and symbolic value that *la Torre de la Libertad* holds for Cuban exiles. It is scheduled to open on Cuba's centennial in 2002.

"All we had in mind was to return to Cuba," recalled Luis Botifoll, who had been a leading banker in Havana before going into exile in 1960. "I had American clients that I had represented in Cuba and they offered me a permanent job, but I did not accept it. Nobody wanted to commit themselves to a job. We all lived day-to-day."

Botifoll arrived in Miami before the first nationalization laws took effect in Cuba. "When I left the government had not yet confiscated my business," he said. "But I realized that the regime was becoming totalitarian, that sooner or later it would end all private initiative. And I expected that in Miami there would be a revolutionary movement to overthrow it."

He was right on both counts. In July 1960 most exile groups united in a Frente Revolucionario Democrático (FRD), led by veteran Auténtico politician Antonio Varona. Unsurprisingly given the century-old history of factious Cuban exiles, one key rival group stayed out, the more liberal Movimiento de Revolucionario del Pueblo (MRP) led by former Castro minister Manuel Ray. Yet aside from their infighting, it was these early activists and their sense of feeling like victims of communism that gave the Cuban community in the United States its lasting political character.

THE BREAKING OF RELATIONS

Also in 1960 began the open confrontation between Castro and the United States. That year Cuba resumed diplomatic relations with the Soviet Union, seized foreign and domestic businesses, and continued to institute a totalitarian state. In response, the Dwight Eisenhower Administration suspended its quota of Cuban sugar in July, and in October slapped on the initial sanctions of what would become a total embargo.

Just one month before that Castro came to New York City for a meeting of world leaders at the United Nations. He and his followers lodged at the Theresa Hotel in Harlem after walking out of Midtown's Shelburne Hotel in a fight over the bill. It was at the Theresa that he met Soviet Premier Nikita Krushchev, the two men embracing warmly. Castro returned the visit at the Soviet Consulate on Park Avenue. That bear hug in which the Soviet leader held the Cuban revolutionary would have enormous consequences not just for the Cuban nation, but for the ongoing Cold War.

What irritated and alarmed the U.S. government the most was Castro's shift toward the Soviet Union. Castro's turn to the Soviet was strategically very important to him. He had not fought his revolution just to implement domestic programs, but instead wanted to expand his revolution beyond Cuba's borders. In a very real sense, Castro's foreign policy objectives outweighed all domestic consid-

Fidel Castro surrounded by New York City policemen during his first visit to the United States as head of the revolutionary government. (Courtesy *Miami Herald*)

erations. His ultimate goal was the "liberation" of Latin America, a goal symbolized in his slogan: "The Andes will become the Sierra Maestra of South America."

Castro understood from the beginning that his vision for Latin America, sooner or later, would cause a major confrontation with the United States. It would undermine U.S. economic interests and challenge U.S. hegemony in the hemisphere. Therefore, he needed a shield against U.S. power. Obviously, only the Soviet Union had the power and the will to serve as such a shield. Consequently, on May 7, 1960, Castro established diplomatic relations with the U.S.S.R., which immediately began supplying most of Cuba's petroleum needs. By the time the United States reduced importation of Cuban sugar in July 1960, Cuba was also receiving large quantities of weapons from Russia or her satellites. For the Soviets, their newfound relationship with the Cubans opened up the door to an area previously dominated by the United States. In response, the United States in January 1961 broke diplomatic relations with Cuba.

Rebirth of the Bat

A little over a year and a half after the Cuban revolution triumphed, Castro ordered all large and mid-size Cuban businesses to be confiscated by the government without compensation to their rightful owners. That included Bacardí, the rum maker that had become the best known Cuban-owned firm in the world.

Juan Prado, then the sales manger for Bacardí in Havana, witnessed the take-over. "Some milicianos (militiamen), showed up with a copy of a decree, believe it or not with misspellings . . . a one page paper where they wrote in the words "Ron Bacardí" with our address . . . and that was it." The regime confiscated $76 million in assets and tried to appropriate Bacardi's trademark symbol of a flying bat.

The company had a long history. It had been founded in 1862 in Santiago de Cuba, Oriente province, by a Catalan immigrant named Facundo Bacardí Massó. At the time, rum was considered a crude, cheap spirit, "something once reserved for Caribbean pirates. It was not consumed by polite society or served in fine establishments," says the company in telling its own history.

Don Facundo set out to create a "civilized rum." He experimented with different raw materials, with new techniques of fermentation and distillation. "He then added a step never tried before: mellowing the rum through charcoal filtration to remove impurities," the company says. "Continuing his experimenta-

Bacardí's famous bat symbol, a stylized reminder of the live bats that gathered around the rum company's tower in Santiago de Cuba.
(Courtesy Bacardí)

tion with oak barrel aging and blending techniques . . . at last he produced the type of spirit that met his standards. His rums were mellower and more refined than other rums."

The secret formula was passed down through generations. When the Castro government took over Bacardí's facilities in Cuba, executives working out of the United States began to rebuild the company outside of the island. They also won the right to retain the trademark "bat." In later years, under company President Manuel Jorge Cutillas—a direct descendant of Don Facundo—Bacardí grew to become one of the world's largest privately held companies, with sales in 170 nations and revenues exceeding $2.5 billion.

THE BAY OF PIGS

Fleeing from a communist-leaning regime, the exiles saw themselves caught in an international conflict. Thus they were embraced as freedom fighters by the United States, and they would become pawns in the global struggle between the superpowers.

As early as the spring of 1960, the United States began to consider military options to overthrow Castro. In meetings with exile leaders, the Eisenhower Administration outlined its plan to land small groups of exiles trained by American experts in guerrilla warfare. They were to join up with insurgents already fighting in the Escambray Mountains and in Castro's old haunts, the Sierra Maestra.

But that fall, as Cuba began to receive Soviet arms, the strategy changed "in favor of a massive landing by a conventional expeditionary force also composed of exiles," as sociologist Juan Clark put it. The force, named Brigade 2506 for the serial number of the first of its members to die during training, was to have air support from exiles flying American B-26 bombers. Plans were accelerating when Eisenhower, in his last days of his presidency, broke diplomatic relations with Havana.

After much debate within the cabinet of the newly sworn in John F. Kennedy, the decision was made to go ahead with the invasion, as long as American participation was kept covert. Kennedy insisted the operation needed to be seen as entirely an exile affair.

This took a lot of negotiations between the CIA and exiles and among the exiles themselves. There was disagreement between the rival groups and there were Cuban complaints of CIA high-handedness. Eventually the MRP and the FRD merged into the Cuban Revolutionary Council, nominally the civilian leadership of the invasion. It was also supposed to form the provisional government of Cuba had the invasion triumphed, with Miró Cardona as the first post-Castro president. For direct leadership of the Brigade, the choice was Manuel Artime, a former officer in Castro's army who broke with the regime. Richard Bissel, deputy director of the CIA, oversaw the entire operation.

It was Americans who planned everything, including the choice of a landing site at Bay of Pigs—a swampy, isolated region on the south of Cuba. Originally the landing was to be near Trinidad, a superior location because it was close to guerrillas fighting in the Escambray. But the Kennedy Administration killed the idea in the belief a "too spectacular" landing in Trinidad would reveal American backing. Kennedy also reduced the initial air strike from sixteen to six planes, according to historian Antonio de la Cova. The exiles, trusting American military know-how, went along.

By March of 1961 the number of exiles training at bases in Guatemala reached 1,500. Cuban Miami was abuzz. Everyone knew where the recruiting offices were. The invasion was an open secret.

From its inception, the success of the invasion depended on two premises: first, that Brigade 2506 would take control of Cuba's airspace, and second, that the invaders would have the backing of the Cuban people, particularly rural guerrillas and the urban resistance. Neither materialized.

At dawn on April 15 six B-26s flown by exiles bombed Campamento Columbia and airfields at Santiago and San Antonio de los Baños. They destroyed only half of Castro's airforce. The exile B-26s had been painted with the colors of the FAR, the Revolutionary Air Force, to give the impression that the attacks were part of an uprising by Castro's own military. But nobody was fooled—United Nations Ambassador Adlai Stevenson, given that fabrication by his bosses in the Administration, was embarrassed when his story fell apart in front of the world body. Because of the international uproar, the Kennedy Administration canceled the two remaining air sorties in a last minute decision that proved fatal to the invaders. Enough FAR planes remained to control the airspace.

Another effect of the air raids was to tip off Castro to the impending invasion. Since the underground had not been notified, the regime was able to move quickly and launch "the most massive preemptive roundup of actual or potential enemies in Cuban history," according to Juan Clark. Historians estimate that no fewer than 100,000 citizens were detained and interrogated. This shut down whatever support Brigade 2506 would have had in the cities. In the countryside, too, guerrillas were blind. They had not been notified either.

So when the 1,400 heavily armed men of Brigade 2506 steamed to the Bay of Pigs on April 17 they were already doomed—bad landing site, no air support, no contact with the internal resistance. They did not even know Kennedy had canceled the remaining air strikes. For three days, men on both sides fought bravely. After a small advance under withering fire from 122mm. howitzers, 22mm. cannon and tanks, the Brigade was forced to retreat to the landing zone. Their cumbersome B-26 bombers, with no fighter cover, were shot down by Castro's faster T-33 jets and Sea Fury craft. With aerial supremacy assured, the FAR sank two ships that carried nearly all supplies for the invaders.

Horrified CIA agents monitoring the disaster felt helpless when they heard the final radio message from the invading exiles. "We are out of ammo and fighting on the beach. Please send help. . . . In water. Out of ammo. Enemy closing in. Help must arrive in next hour."

It never did. Outnumbered, surrounded, and with no hope of getting fresh ammunition or food, Brigade 2506 was defeated after inflicting 1,800 casualties. Of its members, 114 were killed in action, and 1,189 taken prisoner including the commanders, Manuel Artime, José Pérez San Román, and Erneido Oliva. Of those prisoners, 36 would die in Castro's jails. Most of the rest were ransomed in December 1962 for $53 million in food and medicine. Eight were held back. The last Bay of Pigs prisoner, Ramón Conte Hernández, was not released until October 1986.

Meanwhile Miró Cardona and the Cuban Revolutionary Council leadership had been told by the CIA to confer in New York City. The day before the invasion, they were flown to a base in Opalocka. There, they were kept in the dark about what was happening at the Bay of Pigs. They heard the news on a portable radio they found at the base.

When the exile community heard about the disaster, they were furious. They came to believe Kennedy's fear of showing open American support was naïve—the world would believe there was United States backing no matter what, they

Manuel Artime, leader of the exile force defeated at the Bay of Pigs, with President Kennedy at the Orange Bowl ceremony held after the members of Brigade 2506 were freed. (Courtesy *Miami Herald*)

correctly assumed. More important, they believed that same refusal to acknowledge the obvious prevented the Administration from ordering the air support Brigade 2506 needed to gain a toehold. Thus began the rift between Cubans in America and the Democratic Party.

Battle for the Flag

Brigade 2506 may have lost the battle, but it saved its colors. The Brigade's official flag was presented to President Kennedy in a ceremony at an Orange Bowl packed with exiles days after the majority of the invaders had been ransomed from Cuban prison in December 1962.

"I can assure you this flag will be returned to this brigade in a free Havana," said the President. The banner eventually made its way to the John F. Kennedy Library in Waltham, Massachusetts.

But as invasion veterans came to believe Kennedy's decision to call off the air strikes was responsible for their defeat, they demanded it back.

It took a lawsuit and long negotiations with the federal government, which considered the banner its property. Just two days before the 15th anniversary of the invasion the Brigade got its flag back, glued to a wooden frame and encased in glass. It is on display today at the Brigade 2506 museum in Miami.

CUBAN MIAMI IN THE EARLY 1960s

In between conspiracies and denunciations of the Castro regime, the 260,000 exiles who arrived in Miami between 1959 and 1962 had to find a way to put food on the table and pay the rent. Most left everything they owned in Cuba. They arrived with very little beyond their education and middle-class know-how. But even their business expertise and professional preparation meant nothing, at least not when they first arrived.

Carlos Arboleya will never forget his first days in Miami in 1960, after having resigned his position as chief auditor of Banco Continental Cubano when the Castro regime expropriated private banks. He arrived in the midst of a strike by transportation workers, and had to hitchhike through an unfamiliar city, his family in tow, as he looked for a job and a place to live. "I came with my wife, my one-year-old son and $40," he recalls. "We stayed in a room in a little old lady's home for $5 a week. Banks wouldn't hire me even though I had 16 years of experience in the business." His first steady job was at the Allure shoe factory, earning $45 a week. More than three decades later, he was a vice chairman at Barnett Bank, one of South Florida's largest.

But in the early 1960s success for Arboleya and other exiles was still a long way off. For now, the sudden appearance of 1,500 to 2,000 new refugees each week strained the resources of local government in South Florida. The federal government came to believe it had a responsibility to help the refugees, so in January 1961 it began to fund the Cuban Refugee Program, which would remain in existence until 1981. Through twenty years, it provided $1.4 billion in money, food, medical care, and social services to nearly one million Cubans. Exiles of that era and their children who came of age in the United States like to point out that the money was more than paid back over the years through taxes paid by successful Cubans.

Many Cuban exiles, penniless and prohibited by the Castro government from taking more than three changes of clothes when they left the island, had to make do with clothing donated to charitable institutions when they first arrived in the United States.
(Courtesy *Miami Herald*)

By the mid-1960s enough exiles had opened mom-and-pop shops around Southwest Eighth Street to give the neighborhood an unmistakably Cuban flavor. It became known as the *Sagüesera*, a playful Cuban mispronunciation of "Southwest." Eighth Street would become universally known as Calle Ocho. Little Havana began to take shape. It was a similar story in neighboring Hialeah, a semirural community that began to be populated mainly by working class Cubans. Soon, a Cuban in Dade County would be able to live immersed in a Spanish-speaking Cuban environment.

Banker Carlos Arboleya, left, *one of the earliest of Cuban business success stories, with his family in Miami in the early 1960s.* (Courtesy Arboleya family)

If Not Cuba, Then Miami

In an effort to lessen the impact that a large number of new Spanish-speaking residents would have on South Florida, federal authorities instituted a "Resettlement" program for Cuban refugees. Upon arrival in Miami, exiles were asked whether they were willing to live and work away from the Miami area. For those interested, job interviews were set up and free out-of-state transportation provided. Families who moved away received $100 in pocket money to get started, and singles got $60.

The program resettled more than a quarter million refugees until its end. The largest number, 80,483, went to New York. Another 58,791 went to New Jersey, which also had a large Cuban community. A few ended up in states with no Cuban tradition or community—110 in Mississippi, 46 in North Dakota, 29 in Maine, and one single individual in frigid Alaska. In places like Leavenworth, Kansas, the local high school marching band would welcome arriving refugees at the airport.

In the long run the program failed, as "resettled" Cubans eventually found their way back to where other Cubans lived. A *Miami Herald* poll taken in 1978 found that fully 40 percent of Cubans in Miami had once lived out of the region as part of the resettlement program.

As they had against the Spanish colonial regime, against Machado, and against Batista, Cuban exiles made plans in the United States to overthrow the dictatorial government ruling their island. Even after the Bay of Pigs fiasco, exiles trained in secret bases in the Florida Keys and the Everglades.

In fact, the very day the Cuban Missile Crisis shook the world one group was taking small-scale action. "Six rebels in a 22-foot boat with a 90 horsepower inboard engine, slipping into Cárdenas Bay on the north coast of Cuba to blow up Arechabala Distillery there, ran unexpectedly upon a patrol boat about the same size as their own," reported the *Miami Herald* on October 15, 1962. "They exchanged fire. The rebels' 20 millimeter cannon came out best. The Cuban boat sank. Two men aboard swam away in the dark. The rebels fished the other two out of the water and took them prisoner." One of the prisoners, the story said, asked for political asylum.

Members of Brigade 2506 on Cuban state television after their capture. (Cuban Heritage Collection, University of Miami)

Exiles also scored a major political coup when the Cuban Revolutionary Council under Miró Cardona convinced the Washington-based Organization of American States to expel Cuba.

But the unofficial U.S. policy of turning a blind eye to anti-Castro paramilitaries, as well as the explosive growth of the Cuban exile community, came to an end with the Missile Crisis. In October of 1962, U.S. reconnaissance aircraft photographed intermediate-range missile sites being constructed by the Soviet Union in Cuba. President Kennedy demanded the withdrawal of the missiles and ordered a naval blockade of the island. For the next two weeks the world was on the brink of nuclear war.

Then the Soviets announced they would dismantle the bases and take away the missiles. The Americans, for their part, agreed to remove Jupiter missiles from Turkey and promised not to invade Cuba or permit exiles to do so from American soil.

MILITANTS

Given the direct American involvement in Bay of Pigs, Cuban exiles saw the pledge as a betrayal. No longer could they count on the United States as a military ally in their fight against the Castro regime. The new policy quickly made itself felt. "Thirteen anti-Castro fighters, including 10 Americans accused of planning a pocket-size expedition against Cuba, were arrested in the Florida Keys Tuesday. The big question was why?" reported the *Miami Herald* of December 5, 1962. "Existence of the group has been known for the last several months by federal officials. But until their arrest, members of the cadre had not been interfered with by U.S. agents. Cuban exile leaders speculated that the crackdown indicates a stiffened U.S. policy toward anti-Castro resistance forces operating in Florida."

The Children of Peter Pan

One of the most remarkable episodes of the Cuban drama is Operation Peter Pan, under which 14,000 children became exiles in the United States—alone, without their parents.

With parents in Cuba worried that the Castro regime would abolish parental rights, a Miami priest named Bryan O. Walsh (he would become a monsignor and Episcopal Vicar for the Spanish-Speaking Peoples of the Catholic Archdiocese of Miami) decided to help get Cuban children to the United States and provide for their care.

His main contacts in Havana were Ramón and Polita Grau Alsina, who used the home of their uncle, former president Ramón Grau San Martín, to secretly distribute American visas to desperate parents. They spent nearly twenty years in prison for their role in the scheme.

The first Peter Pan children arrived December of 1960. By 1962, about 300 unaccompanied Cuban children arrived per month.

The children were greeted by a representative from one of the voluntary agencies. They were then transported to one of the receiving centers in Miami, according to their gender and age. Florida City, Kendall, Matacumbe, and Opalocka were large receiving camps that initially housed most of the children. Two group-care facilities, St. Raphael's House for Boys and the Cuban Boys Home, were smaller. From there, they went to live in foster homes to await the arrival of their parents. But the Cuban Missile Crisis in October 1962 ended all flights out of Cuba.

One of the 14,000 Peter Pan children, who left Cuba alone without their parents, bravely clutches her doll. (Courtesy *Miami Herald*)

Operation Peter Pan ended. No one knew when or if the children would ever see their parents again.

When the Freedom Flights began in December 1965, parents of Peter Pan children were given priority. Some five thousand were reunited within the first six months.

Many of these children of Peter Pan went on to become successful professionals and businessmen. "Because their parents made the tremendous sacrifice of sending their children alone to this country," says the Peter Pan website, "it is estimated conservatively that over 150,000 Peter Pan relatives were eventually able to leave Cuba and enter the United States.

In 1963, when it was obvious there had been a change in American policy, Miró Cardona resigned as president of the Cuban Revolutionary Council.

Shortly thereafter the group dissolved, its dream of governing a post-Castro Cuba no longer tenable. Yet exile groups continued to raid coastal installations in Cuba, and exiles continued to be arrested by American authorities on arms charges.

The best known of the paramilitary organizations was Alpha 66, founded by Eloy Gutiérrez Menoyo and Andrés Nazario Sargén, both of whom had fought against Batista before turning against Castro. Gutiérrez Menoyo in late 1964 staged a small armed landing in Oriente province. He was captured and spent twenty-two years in prison. Upon his release he became a controversial figure in exile circles because of the "soft line" he advocated in relations with the Castro dictatorship (see Chapter 10). Sargén, in contrast, carried on into the new century with his militant approach. His Alpha 66 continues paramilitary training.

There were targets outside Cuba, too. Most notably, exiles fired a bazooka at the United Nations building in 1964, as Ernesto "Che" Guevara gave a speech denouncing the United States. The shell did not hit its target, falling into the East River.

ONE EXODUS ENDS, ANOTHER BEGINS

One immediate effect of the Missile Crisis on Cubans was that flights between Havana and the United States came to a halt. Cubans who wanted to leave now had to apply to the regime for permission to go to a third country—most chose Spain or Mexico—and once there, apply for an American visa.

Leaving Cuba in those years became an ordeal in itself. Armed soldiers would come to the homes of Cubans seeking exit visas to make an inventory of possessions, which had to be left behind. Families were permitted to take only what they wore plus two changes of clothes. Once in the third country, the process of obtaining an American visa could take a year. Men who had worked for the Castro government before turning against it were sometimes denied entry to the United States on the suspicion of being communist sympathizers. In all, only about 15,000 Cubans came to the United States each year during this period, compared to a high of 78,611 in 1962.

On the island, more Cubans questioned the course the revolution had taken. The imposition of a totalitarian state that deprived the people of fundamental human rights, along with the rapidly deteriorating economy, brewed discontent.

As an escape valve to release the pressure, Fidel Castro announced on September 28, 1965, that those who wished to leave could do so by boat, through the port of Camarioca in the province of Matanzas.

Thousands of Cuban Miamians headed there to pick up relatives. It was the beginning of a new exodus.

CHAPTER 7

Freedom Flights

1965–1973

El exilio reacted to Castro's Camarioca announcement with a mixture of surprise and skepticism. It was so unexpected after nearly three years of no direct flights, and people had so little trust in the Cuban regime (like others in the communist bloc, its citizens needed official government permission to leave) that they didn't know what to make of it.

Nevertheless, thousands took the risk and sailed across the Straits of Florida to claim relatives waiting in Camarioca. During the first days, most of the vessels were seaworthy and manned by captains who knew their way around the treacherous currents of the Gulf Stream. After the first few boats came back safely exiles realized the journey was possible. They *would* be able to reunite their families, torn apart by Castro and exile. Thousands of people pooled their resources to rent sailboats, tugboats, yachts—just about anything that floated—and headed to Camarioca to pick up loved ones. While many made it back safely, other vessels broke down, ran out of fuel, or got lost and had to be rescued by the U.S. Coast Guard.

Those who made it across were deeply moved by the prospect of a new life in America.

"It was at sunrise when from a distance we spotted a Coast Guard ship in the horizon," recalled María Rodríguez, a retired nurse, one day years later. "The

Some of the nearly 3,000 refugees who arrived in 1965 as part of the Camarioca exodus. (Courtesy *Miami Herald*)

journey had been very treacherous. Our water supply ran out, we had no more food. Some began to curse the darkness, while others pleaded to God for mercy. . . . When we were rescued, I opened a small box I was carrying inside my pocket and took out a tiny American flag my mother had given me. I cried quietly while kissing the flag and said a prayer. . . . For the first time in my life I felt free."

The Castro government found itself embarrassed by the spectacle of thousands of its citizens massing at Camarioca ready to risk their lives to get away. The American government desired to end the chaos that was overwhelming the Coast Guard in the Florida Straits and what in fact was an illegal immigration.

Some 150 vessels carrying 2,979 refugees had reached American shores when the port of Camarioca was shut down on November 15. The 2,014 others who were in the exit compound when the boatlift was halted arrived in Miami later on

About 150 boats of all kinds made the trip between Cuba and South Florida during Camarioca. (Courtesy *Miami Herald*)

specially chartered, safer boats. All told, 4,993 Cubans arrived in the United States as part of the one-month Camarioca boatlift of 1965.

It was but a beginning. The Johnson Administration negotiated with the Castro government to bring about a safe, orderly, and legal way to solve the crisis. From those negotiations, the "Freedom Flights" were born.

The Cuban regime agreed to allow citizens to leave, except for those who worked in what were deemed "critical occupations"—doctors, engineers, and other professional or skilled workers. They had to stay. For its part, the administration of Lyndon Johnson agreed to welcome close relatives of Cubans already in the United States and political prisoners. The Cuban government, however, did not agree to release the latter.

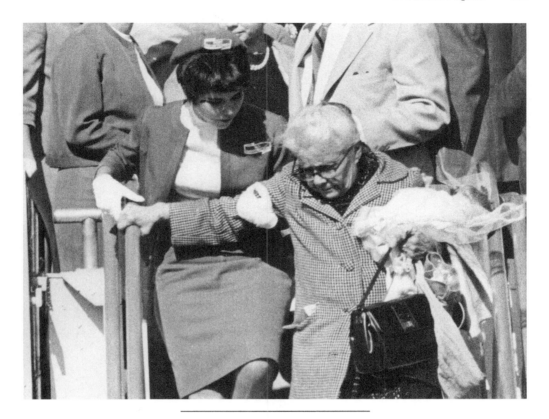

The Freedom Flights brought many elderly parents to reunite with their grown children.
(Courtesy *Miami Herald*)

Nevertheless, America had opened its door to those who could get away. Standing in front of the Statue of Liberty, President Johnson stated, "I declare this afternoon to the people of Cuba that those who seek refuge here in America will find it . . . Our tradition as an asylum for the oppressed is going to be upheld."

The first Freedom Flight took off from Varadero, the famous beach resort east of Havana, on December 2, 1965. The last one was on April 6, 1973. Texas A&M professor Maria Cristina García, in her book *Havana USA*, cites a total of 3,048 Freedom Flights bearing 297,318 refugees. Other figures range from the 260,561 Lorrin Philipson and Rafael Llerena give in *Freedom Flights* to the 340,000 cited by Alejandro Portes and Alex Stepick in *City on the Edge: The Transformation of Miami*.

Young couples arrived on the Freedom Flights also, most of them having endured months or even years of forced labor in farm fields before being allowed to depart.
(Courtesy *Miami Herald*)

A Golden Age of Baseball

While most Cubans in America were obsessing over the liberation of the homeland or simply trying to make a living in a new country, some were playing baseball.

Waiting at Miami International Airport for a Freedom Flight. (Courtesy *Miami Herald*)

The generation of *peloteros* that escaped from the island in the early 1960s, when the Castro regime banned professional sports and broke up century-old classic teams like Almendares and Habana, played baseball better than any other group of Cubans ever had in the Major Leagues.

They were at their peak in the mid- to late 1960s. First to make a splash was the Minnesota Twins' Tony Oliva, who in 1964 and 1965 became the first to win the batting crown in his first two years in the major leagues. He helped his team win the pennant in 1965, a season when his Cuban teammate Zoilo Versalles was named Most Valuable Player for his glove at shortstop and his timely hits. Another shortstop, Dagoberto "Bert" Campaneris, was a perennial All-Star and one of the majors' best base stealers; in 1965, he accomplished the feat of playing all nine positions in a single game.

Another great Cuban hitter of the era was Atanasio (Tony) Pérez. He never won a batting title, homerun crown, or led the league in RBIs. Yet he displayed such excellence and consistency over a 23-year career that in 2000 he was elected to the Baseball Hall of Fame at Cooperstown. He was the second Cuban so enshrined—and since the first, Martín Dihigo, never played in the

Tony Pérez, the Hall of Fame slugger, trotting home after hitting a home run for the Cincinnati Reds in the 1970s.
(Courtesy Cincinnati Reds)

majors because of the color barrier, Pérez became the first Cuban Major Leaguer in the Hall.

The top Cuban pitchers of the era were also among the best in the sport. Luis Tiant of the Cleveland Indians struck out 19 in one game in 1968, a year when he also led the American League in ERA. He would go on to fool hitters with his tricky delivery well into the 1970s with the Red Sox and Yankees. Another American Leaguer, Mike Cuellar (who actually began his Major League career in 1959), spent his best years with the Baltimore Orioles and won the Cy Young award in 1969. That year, too, the expansion San Diego Padres named Preston Gómez manager. He was the first Cuban appointed to a permanent position as a Major League manager (Mike González was temporary manager of the Cardinals in the 1940s).

There were also others who shone less brightly but still had lengthy careers in the majors: José Cardenal, Leo Cárdenas, Tony González, Tito Fuente, Cookie Rojas, Diego Seguí, José Tartabull. In all, 32 Cuban ball players made their Major League debut in the 1960s.

By the late 1970s most had retired. The stream of ball players from Cuba to the majors shut down. It was not until the 1990s that a generation of Cubans brought up in the United States and of defectors from the Cuban "amateurs" would equal their feats.

A DIFFERENT *EXILIO*

Whatever the exact number, all authorities who studied the exodus agree that these new Cubans were substantially different from the first wave of the early 1960s. They were much more likely to be working class.

SUPER MARKET

EL TIGRE DE ORO

La Casa de los Especiales
VIVERES FINOS EN GENERAL
Carnes Vegetales, Cafe al Minuto

Productos Espanoles
JESUS DOMINGUEZ Prop.
235 - 48th STREET- Union City, N. J.
FREE DELIVERY   TEL. UN 5-9880

An advertisement for "El Tigre de Oro," one of the first Cuban bodegas to open in Union City after Cubans began to settle there following the revolution.
(Courtesy Emilio del Valle)

While 34 percent of Cubans in Miami by 1963 were professionals or managers, just 12 percent of those who arrived in the Freedom Flights were so classified, and in one study, 57 percent of the newcomers were classed as "blue collar, service or agricultural workers."

One reason for the difference is logical: professional men and women could not leave, as ordered by the Cuban regime. Another reason was political. By the mid-1960s the government had nationalized small private businesses, shattering the lives of tens of thousands of working class Cubans who managed to open corner *bodegas*, neighborhood restaurants or other small shops after years of toiling in sugar mills or chopping down cane in the fields. Also, the regime had tightened its grip on the populace, organizing "Committees for the Defense of the Revolution" in every neighborhood to spy on and harass the disaffected.

No one was more openly disaffected, of course, than those who applied to leave. They were considered "enemies of the state." Most were fired from their jobs, and so found themselves unemployed for months or years while waiting for a seat on a Florida-bound flight. Many were forced to work in the fields at collective farms cutting cane, pulling potatoes, hoeing weeds—"volunteer work," it was officially termed. Upon their departure, household property was confiscated. "Two government officials entered my home unannounced," remembers Raúl García, a small business owner in Cuba. "They screamed obscenities and took away all of our possessions. We managed to leave with a small suitcase with some personal belongings and with the clothes on our backs."

Upon their arrival in Miami, many Cubans lived temporarily in barracks nicknamed *Casas de la Libertad*, the "Houses of Liberty," set up at Miami International Airport. Thousands were resettled away from South Florida; others chose to stay in the community and found jobs.

Many Cubans in the United States continued to believe they were here temporarily, until the Castro regime could be overthrown. And they were here temporarily as far as the law was concerned, too. The legal term for their immigration status was "parolees," suggesting they were to stay only for a limited period of time. This ended in 1966, when President Johnson signed into law the Cuban Adjustment Act. Cubans who had lived in the United States for one year could now apply for permanent residency, which enabled Cuban professionals to qualify to take tests to meet state licensing requirements in various occupations and the elderly to receive benefits available only to permanent residents or American citizens.

It was a sign that the United States would welcome and even grant special preferences to Cubans fleeing communism. It was also a beginning of the exiles' realization that their stay in the United States was going to be much longer than they once had believed.

And so the population of America's Cuban neighborhoods began to grow again after the respite between the Missile Crisis and the opening of Camarioca. By 1970 the census found that 439,048 people born in Cuba lived in the United States; another 121,580 were U.S.-born of Cuban origin.

In Miami, the number of Cuban students in public schools shot up from a little over 10 percent in 1965 to more than a quarter in 1973. In Union City and West New York the population was smaller in raw numbers but even more concentrated. Nearly half of the students in public schools were of Cuban origin by the 1969–1970 school year.

Watergate's Cubans

Three Cubans who gained unwanted notoriety in the 1970s were Bernard Barker, Virgilio González, and Eugenio Martínez, among the "Watergate burglars" caught while breaking into Democratic Party headquarters to photograph documents for the reelection campaign of Richard M. Nixon. A year later, their actions brought down a presidency.

Why Cubans in the middle of a great American scandal? Most Americans thought of Watergate as proof of the manipulative and unlawful extremes to which Nixon and his aides would go to win reelection, a matter of domestic politics. To the Cuban burglars, the break-in was a continuation of the struggle against Castro. *El exilio*, distrustful of Democrats to begin with, was deeply worried that an ultraliberal administration under George McGovern would embrace the Cuban regime. Barker, González, and Martínez believed the Democratic files at the Watergate would help Nixon win a second term and prevent a McGovern presidency, which they saw as disastrous for the cause of Cuba.

SETTLING IN

As the number of exiles climbed, the community at large greeted them with mixed reactions. "Some resented us because we spoke Spanish, we would talk too loud, and took jobs away from them," remembers Luis Botifoll. "In fact, there were signs that stated: No Pets, No Children and No Cubans." A columnist at the *Miami Herald* complained that Miami was "up to (its) armpits with Cuban refugees." Letters to the editor expressed outrage at the growing number of Cubans and how they "were sacrificing our welfare and security."

But others welcomed the newcomers and offered a helping hand. Many Americans from all walks of life sent checks and money orders to the relief efforts to help the new refugees. For their part, Cuban exiles were grateful and humbled by the positive reaction they received from American citizens. One wrote to the *Miami Herald*, "(We) never will forget (the American) people and (their) president. Each Cuban refugee feels very deeply indebted to you from the bottom of his heart and has with the United States of America an eternal debt of gratitude." Determined to succeed, the Cuban exiles went about their daily life, working hard and deeply motivated to prove their worth.

The exiles continued to settle mostly in Little Havana, the four-square-mile area in Miami's southwest district where Cubans had gone since the early 1960s. Hundreds of Cuban-owned businesses that began to open up along Southwest Eighth Street. There they catered to the growing exile community by providing what Cubans needed to feel somewhat at home: supermarkets, cafeterias, clubs, gas stations, bakeries, laundromats, lawyers, accountants, dentists, and a host of other services. The city of Hialeah, neighbor to Miami, also attracted thousands of exiles. They opened garment and textile factories that provided employment to many hardworking individuals.

Exiles in South Florida found their own ways to capitalize at least middle-sized businesses. With established banks unwilling to risk lending money to unknown Cubans, Cuban bankers stepped in. Carlos Arboleya, who had become president of Fidelity National Bank in the mid-1960s, and Luis Botifoll, who became president of the small Republic National Bank in 1970 after it had been bought by a group of fellow Cubans headed by Alberto Díaz Masvidal, were among the first to establish what were called "character loans." Often with no collateral and no more assurances than a gentleman's handshake, Arboleya and Botifoll made loans to entrepreneurs with whom they had done business back in Cuba. They knew that the businessmen they were lending to had the business know-how to make their firms succeed.

"They were small loans, because the bank was small and the businesses that asked for financing were small too," Botifoll recalled. "They wanted to buy a gasoline station, build a duplex, open a supermarket." Looking back three decades later, Arboleya believes that these small character loans formed the base upon which the multibillion economy of Cuban Miami was built.

Exiles who arrived on the Freedom Flights helped establish Cuban communities in other American cities beside Miami—Los Angeles, Chicago, New Orleans, Tampa, New York. The largest and most important outside of South Florida, however, was right across the Hudson River from Manhattan, in the Hudson County towns of Union City and West New York.

As late as 1966, Bergenline Avenue, the commercial thoroughfare that ran through those two neighboring cities, was practically abandoned by second-generation Italian Americans who were moving to suburbia and leaving behind their immigrant parents' urban neighborhood. Store after store was shuttered, the windows whitewashed, the street empty of shoppers.

Cubans would utterly transform the area. By the early 1970s Cuban retailers selling just about everything exiles desired were open for business on Bergenline.

Professionals, too, were now beginning to settle in. Cuban physicians, dentists, and accountants established themselves around Bergenline Avenue. But there were no Cuban lawyers until the middle of the 1970s. Those who could prove they had been attorneys in Cuba could practice if they passed the New Jersey Bar exam, but many of those who knew English well enough to take the exam found it too difficult to bridge the differences between common law as practiced in the United States and the codified civil-law system, prevalent in most of Europe and Latin America, for which they had been trained in Cuba. As to the younger generation, it was still too young—few had been in the United States long enough to graduate from college and go on to a law school.

The economic success of Cubans in South Florida and Hudson County signaled something had changed in the Cuban community. The same people who in the early 1960s refused steady jobs that might interfere with the struggle to free Cuba had a decade later repeated the classic tale of the American immigrant. "Their overwhelming success, in the span of one generation, has been virtually unprecedented in American history," wrote Elaine Condon in "The New Jersey Ethnic Experience."

Heberto Padilla, considered by many the foremost Cuban poet. (Courtesy *Miami Herald*)

Poet in Prison

In 1971 the Castro regime instigated a sort of Cultural Revolution that banned the works of foreign literary figures including Eugene Ionesco, Samuel Beckett, and Jorge Luis Borges, as well as Cubans such as Virgilio Piñera, Antón Arrufat, and Guillermo Cabrera Infante.

Most famously, Heberto Padilla—considered one of the greatest Cuban poets—was imprisoned and only released when he agreed to publicly castigate himself for writing poems like "Fuera del juego, or "Out of the Game," which were critical of the regime. Padilla was forced to make a speech based on a self-flagellating text written for him by Communist bureaucrats. But the world learned of the farce when the poet read it out loud exactly as it was handed to him, including grammatical mistakes.

The Padilla case became a cause celebre when intellectuals the world over like Jean Paul Sartre and Mario Vargas Llosa, who had once supported the Revolution, likened the humiliation of Padilla to a tropical version of the Stalinist show-trials of the 1930s when Russian writers were forced to denounce themselves. It was the first break between the literati and the Revolution.

After the scandal subsided, Padilla was put under house arrest and prohibited from writing. He was not authorized to leave Cuba until 1980, when Senator Ted Kennedy interceded on his behalf. Padilla then moved to the United States, where he taught at several colleges and cofounded the literary magazine *Linden Lane* with his then-wife, the poet Belkis Cuza Malé, while they lived in Princeton. He also wrote a novel, *Heroes are Grazing in my Garden*, and a memoir, *Self Portrait of the Other*. It is his poems of the 1960s and 1970s, however, that earn him a permanent place in Cuba's literary canon. In 2000, Padilla died in a hotel room near the University of Alabama.

There was growing clout in domestic politics, too. In Union City, Bob Menéndez won a seat on the local board of education—the first step of a political career that would take him to the Congressional Democratic leadership. And in 1973 Miami's Dade County officially became bilingual. Legal documents, government services, and election ballots all became available in English and Spanish.

DIEHARD EXILES, STUDENT ACTIVISTS, AND PARAMILITARIES

While most Cuban exiles were rebuilding their lives in America, some continued to actively try to overthrow Castro. In the mid-sixties the head of the Bacardí empire, Pepín Bosch, backed a referendum in which some 75,000 émigrés selected representatives for an organization named Representación Cubana del Exilio (RECE), whose objective was to create a united front to raise funds for propaganda and paramilitary operations against Castro's Cuba. Other groups that were actively involved in mounting commando raids against Castro's regime included Comandos L, 30th of November Movement, MIRR (Insurrectional Movement of Revolutionary Recovery), and the best known—the only one that survives today—Alpha 66. They spent as much time avoiding federal authorities as they did fighting Fidel Castro, a historically familiar position for Cuban activists to find them-

selves in. These groups considered themselves the inheritors of a fighting tradition that stretched more than a century
for Cubans in America, from Narciso
López to the wars of independence to
the struggle against Machado and on to
Prío and Castro's own fight against
Batista from the United States.

*Emblem for the paramilitary anti-Castro
group Alpha 66.* (Courtesy Alpha 66)

At first, the paramilitary's principal
strategy was to conduct hit-and-run
raids on military installations and political targets in Cuba, and sabotage economic centers such as sugar mills and
cane plantations. By the end of the
1960s their strategy had changed. Now
the emphasis was on landing small
armed parties (after the fiasco at Bay of
Pigs there was little wish to repeat a
large-scale, U.S.-sponsored invasion) who hoped to spark guerrilla warfare, as
both José Martí and Fidel Castro had done in their day.

The best remembered of these landing parties was organized by Alpha 66 (it
was one of twenty-two such landings it organized) and commanded by a *guajiro*—
a peasant from the Cuban countryside—named Vicente Méndez.

A MYSTERIOUS PLAN, A MYSTERIOUS MURDER

One of the oddest episodes in the history of anti-Castro exiles in the United
States involved the so-called *Plan Torriente*.

In February 1970 José de la Torriente, a distinguished-looking 66-year-old
retired accountant for Coca-Cola in Chicago, held a unity rally in Miami attended by thousands of exiles to announce he had a secret plan to overthrow
Castro. The following year at a press conference in New York he took credit for
organizing a commando raid on a Coast Guard station at Boca de Samá,
Oriente, resulting in six Cuban government casualties. De la Torriente produced official documents taken during the attack and indicated that in the future, his group would not publicly acknowledge further actions.

Over the next two years he made the rounds of exile communities throughout the United States asking for financial backing, and raised perhaps $200,000 to $300,000. He refused to provide details of his plan, which brought him heavy criticism—particularly from some of the more militant exile groups.

On Good Friday 1974, de la Torriente was assassinated in his Miami home by a sniper firing through a rear window. The culprit was never arrested. In 1988, a highly placed Cuban defector stated that the murder was carried out by Cuban intelligence.

Méndez, who grew up on his father's tiny tobacco farm in Las Villas province, had fought in the Escambray mountains against Batista. After the triumph of the Revolution he was made a lieutenant in the Rebel Army. But when he learned that the Agricultural Reform law of 1959 would turn large farms over to the state rather than to the direct ownership of landless peasants, he took up arms again and returned to fight in the Escambray.

Over the next two years the Rebel Army cleared the Escambray of anti-Castro guerrillas. Méndez, wounded in the foot and hand, escaped to Miami on a boat. There he hooked up with Nazario Sargén, whom he knew from the anti-Batista struggle, and joined Alpha 66. For the next few years Méndez and Sargén traveled through Cuban communities in the United States, raising money to buy arms for a new landing. They visited Tampa, Houston, New Orleans, Chicago, New York, and New Jersey. Back in Miami, they trained at Alpha's secret military camps in the Everglades. By 1969 Méndez was one of the best known anti-Castro activists among Cuban exiles. As Alpha 66 made no secret of its intentions, everyone expected a landing any day and figured it would be the beginning of the end of Fidel Castro.

After a tropical storm forced back the first attempt, Méndez finally arrived on Cuban soil April 17, 1970, with thirteen men armed with M-16 rifles. They were detected immediately. Méndez was killed in action after two days of fighting. The rest of his party was quickly killed or captured.

Others within the exile community took a different approach in their anti-Castro struggle. In an effort to bring international attention to the plight of the Cuban people back on the island, a group of young émigrés formed the Federation of Cuban Students (FEC), with chapters in several U.S. cities, Puerto Rico, and Costa Rica. They published a monthly paper, *Antorcha*, and organized several protests aimed at raising public awareness about Cuba's human rights violations. Another group of students in New York founded Abdala, named after a

1970s advertisement for a Cuban-Chinese restaurant in West New York.
(Courtesy Emilio del Valle)

play written by José Martí. In 1971, sixteen Abdala members chained themselves to the United Nations building to protest repression in Cuba. Over time, most of the student groups vanished as its members returned to school, graduated and found jobs, got married, and began to raise families.

Coming to an end, too, were the Freedom Flights. As early as May 1969 the Castro government decided that the escape valve had been open long enough and stopped accepting new applications for exit visas. The regime also periodically interrupted already scheduled flights. Still the number of Cubans arriving in Miami held steady at an average of about 50,000 each year between 1966 and 1971. Then in 1972 less than 24,000 arrived. On April 6, 1973, the last of the Freedom Flights landed at Miami International Airport.

Other Cubans

By the end of the Freedom Flights the majority of Cuban Jews and Chinese-Cubans were gone from the island and into exile in the United States.

Cuba had been home to some 15,000 Jewish people, most of them immigrants who arrived in the period between the World Wars. After the Revolution, some 10,000 headed to Miami, where they found a home not only among other Cubans, but also among the large community of American Jews who had moved to South Florida from New York and other northeastern cities.

In Miami Beach, the exiled Cuban Sephardic community founded Congregación Sefaradí de la Florida, which included Templo Moises. The Ashkenazi founded Círculo Cubano Hebreo along with its temple, Beth Shmuel.

The Cuban Chinese population was roughly the same size as the Jewish. It had its origins in 1847 when Chinese laborers were first brought to Cuba as indentured servants. Many fought in the 1895 War of Independence, winning a reputation for bravery that survives in Cuban historical folklore.

The Chinese-Cubans lived in Havana's Chinatown, where they ran restaurants and other small businesses. Following that tradition in the United States, they opened restaurants such as "La Campana China" in West New York and "Chino-Latino" near Manhattan's Chinatown, serving Chinese fried rice as well as Cuban rice and beans.

Most of Cuba's blacks and mulattos, a population that makes up perhaps half the island, stayed in Cuba. *El exilio* was largely white and would remain so even after the Mariel boatlift brought to America a substantial number of non-white Cubans.

CHAPTER 8

Living in America

1973–1980

By the time the Freedom Flights ended, Cubans in Miami, Hialeah, Union City, and West New York could live nearly complete lives immersed in a Spanish-speaking Cuban environment, a subculture that they had wholly constructed inside the larger American society.

Cuban retailers filled Bergenline Avenue in Union City/West New York, Miami's Calle Ocho, and the strip malls that dotted Hialeah. Nostalgic exiles kept alive the music of old Cuba by buying everything from old danzones of the 1920s to the 1950s songs of Beny Moré and the cha-cha-chas of Orquesta Aragón. Mom and pop bodegas (and in Miami, large Cuban-owned supermarkets) kept Cuban stomachs filled with staples like black beans and yuca. There were Cuban-owned furniture stores, dry cleaners, auto repair shops. Restaurants where people sidled up to the counter to sip strong Cuban espresso. Bakeries where parents brought their children for a *pastelito*, a pastry filled with meat, cheese or guava. Clothing stores where older men bought *guayaberas*. In South Florida—although not in the New Jersey enclaves—there were even bilingual Cuban private schools where the children of exiles learned more about Cuban history and culture than they could possibly have learned in a public school. The schools were fully certified, but modeled on the schools of old Cuba.

It was an attempt to recreate what was lost in Cuba. Older exiles got health care from Cuban doctors, ate only Cuban food, had only Cuban neighbors, read

By the 1970s South Florida was so thoroughly Cubanized it was not unusual to see an entire block of shops with signs in Spanish. (Courtesy *Miami Herald*)

their favorite columnists from old Cuba now in Miami newspapers, listened to anti-Castro radio stations, worked for Cuban companies. As Gustavo Pérez Firmat put it in his memoir, *Next Year in Cuba,* those who lived in such neighborhoods "could be delivered by a Cuban obstretrician, buried by a Cuban undertaker, and in between birth and death lead a perfectly satisfactory life without needing extramural contacts." Satisfactory was the right word, nothing more than that. For Cuba still loomed—elusive, a long-ago memory, perhaps unattainable. These Little Havanas were "a golden cage, an artificial paradise, the neighborhood of dreams," in Pérez Firmat's words.

Only 12,579 Cubans arrived in 1973. That was about half the number that arrived in 1972, which in turn was half the number that arrived in an average year during the Freedom Flights. With fewer newcomers to keep the flame burning, older exiles resigned themselves to living in the United States.

Cuban arrivals registered at Refugee Center from the end of the Freedom Flights to before Mariel

1973 —	12,579
1974 —	13,670
1975 —	8,488
1976 —	4,515
1977 —	4,548
1978 —	4,108
1979 —	2,644

ONE-AND-A-HALFERS

After the Freedom Flights, enough time had elapsed since the first post-Castro arrivals for a generation to have grown to adolescence in America. Most grew up in Cubanized neighborhoods, yet they could not help being exposed to the sweeping power of American culture. They were Cuban like their parents, but also American, and they had to figure out what it meant to become that new thing, a Cuban-American. In the words of Pérez Firmat, they were the one-and-a-half generation, not "entirely American, but too young to be anything else." Life for the one-and-a-halfers like himself, he wrote, was "a delicate balancing act between two countries, two cultures, two languages."

The one-and-a-halfers learned English in the schools, listened to American music—disco was particularly popular among Cuban teenagers of the 1970s—and dressed in hip American fashions. When they began to adopt the mores of the sexual revolution and the post-hippie age, they clashed with their parents' traditional Spanish Catholic values.

A girl allegorically dressed as the Cuban nation in chains and a boy wearing the costume of "Liborio" (the Cuban equivalent of Uncle Sam) at an anti-Castro march in the 1970s. (Courtesy *Miami Herald*)

Although not all Cubans were economically successful, their achievements as a community seemed remarkable. By 1979, over 60 percent of Cuban families owned their own homes, more than one-third of Miami's businesses were owned or operated by Cubans, and 90 percent of the residential and commercial construction industry in Miami was controlled by Cubans. At that time, for every twenty-seven Cubans, there was one exile business. As the 1970s drew to a close, the small corner of metropolitan New York that Cubans occupied across the Hudson from the skyscrapers of Manhattan was thoroughly Cubanized. In Florida the changes Cubans wrought were more dramatic. They not only lived in

The Union City area was a hotbed of anti-Castro activity in the 1970s, as shown in this meeting of the politically active Cuban Lions Club in Exile. The father of one of the authors, Roger Hernández, is third from right. (Author's collection)

thoroughly Cuban neighborhoods—they had in fact become involved in every aspect of South Florida's economic, social, and political life.

This brought friction with the other ethnic groups of Greater Miami—Jews and blacks not of Cuban origin, and "Anglos," the term for non-Hispanic whites.

Las Cubanas

As Cuban families struggled to find their way in America after the Freedom Flights, women became the backbone of exile communities. They often found jobs faster than Cuban men, working in factories and as waitresses, manicurists, cashiers, and domestic help. They would work at minimum wage and hold two jobs to make ends meet—and at the same time they made sure the family stayed together, taking care of the children and tending to their often demanding Cuban husbands.

Cuban women carry a large Cuban flag during a 1970s demonstration in Miami.
(Courtesy *Miami Herald*)

These women were following an old tradition. Cuban women have played a much larger role in the exile communities through the years than is commonly known. Unfortunately, few scholars have given much attention to the contributions that since the nineteenth-century Cuban exile women have made to further the cause of Cuban freedom, or to their contributions in the economic, political, and cultural fields.

During the Ten Years War, Cuban women organized fund-raising events to help the rebel forces. Many opened their homes in exile to patriots fleeing Spanish persecution. A generation later that tradition lived on. When José Martí was preparing the War of Independence and became ill due to exhaustion during a stay at Ybor City, a Cuban woman of African descent named

Paulina Pedroso nursed him back to health and offered her residence free of charge. After hearing of Martí's death, she sold her house and donated all the proceeds from the sale to the Cuban cause. On the site where her home once stood, a plaque reads, "Paulina Pedroso was one of the great women patriots of Cuba."

Today, Cuban women run some of the top Hispanic-owned firms in the country. Tere Zubizarreta is head of Zubi Advertising, Ada Levitan is CEO of public relations agency Sánchez & Levitan, Remedios Diaz Oliver runs All American Containers, Maria Elena Toraño is chairman of her own consulting firm.

Cuban women also shine in writing. *Miami Herald* columnist Liz Balmaseda received the Pulitzer Prize for commentary in 1993, Mariel arrival Mirta Ojito became a respected journalist for the *New York Times*, and Cristina García wrote critically acclaimed novels *Dreaming in Cuban* and *The Agüero Sisters*. In 1992, Ileana Ros Lehtinen became the first Hispanic woman to serve in the U.S. Congress. And entertainers such as Maria Conchita Alonso, Gloria Estefan, Celia Cruz, and Albita made a name for themselves.

One scholar/writer who has studied the role of women in Cuban society, both on the island and exile, is Ileana Fuentes. She founded the organization Mujeres Cubanas, or Cuban Women, and has written works such as *De Patria a Matria, (From Fatherland to Motherland)* and *Cuba sin caudillo,* or *Cuba Without a Caudillo,* a critique of *machismo* in political leadership.

ETHNIC TENSIONS

Not since the European immigrations of the nineteenth century to New York had an American city experienced a transformation as profound and in as short a time as Miami did in the years following the Cuban Revolution. As late as 1960 the census estimated only 4 percent of Dade County's population was of Hispanic origin. By the late 1970s it had grown to nearly half.

Hostility toward the newcomers did not take long to show. Old-time residents of the Miami area saw Cubans as clannish, noisy, and unwilling to adapt to life in the United States. "Will the Last American Leaving Miami Please Bring the Flag," said a popular bumper sticker of the time.

The black and Cuban communities were, and remain, highly segregated. Few American blacks were seen in Little Havana. Few Cubans ventured to Liberty City. There was resentment that Cuban businesses would not hire American blacks. Blacks feared Cubans were taking over Miami and leaving them behind.

EL DIÁLOGO

By the end of the decade, the older exile activists began to disappear from the scene and the return to Cuba seemed further away than ever. Carlos Prío committed suicide in Miami in 1977. José Miró Cardona became a law professor at the University of Puerto Rico, and died on that island in 1974. Manuel Urrutia led a quiet life as a Spanish teacher in Queens, and died in 1981. Their contemporaries who survived wondered how many more exiles would die without ever again setting foot on the Cuban land they so deeply loved.

It seemed for a time that exiles' main focus was building new lives in America. But the flow of international events brought the struggle for Cuba to the forefront.

In 1977 the administration of Jimmy Carter established contact with the government of Fidel Castro. The reasoning was that political and economic agreements with Havana might moderate Castro's behavior, or at least provide instruments for U.S. leverage, something difficult in the absence of U.S.–Cuban diplomatic relations since 1961. For its part, Cuba was feeling Soviet pressures to open détente with the United States. Besides, normalization with Washington would offer Havana advanced technology, commercial trade, and a break in its hemispheric isolation.

By April, the two governments signed an agreement relative to each others' fishing grounds, the boundaries of which had been long in dispute. The following June, agreement was also reached for establishing an "Interest Section" in each capital starting in September 1977 (sort of unofficial embassies). These diplomatic steps were accompanied by an exchange of visits between United States and Cuban trade officials and businessmen. But President Jimmy Carter emphasized that the Cuban government would have to respect human rights and stop sending troops abroad in support of revolutionaries in order to establish full diplomatic relations.

Dissidents Stir

Repression was so heavy handed in Cuba that nonviolent dissident groups like those forming in Eastern Europe did not have a chance to organize. It took until 1976, after seventeen years of revolution, for the first internationally recognized human rights organization to come into existence. The Comité Cubano Pro Derechos Humanos, (Cuban Committee for Human Rights) was founded by Ricardo Bofill, a former professor of Marxist philosophy at the University of Havana.

Because of his activities, Bofill was jailed for more than eight years. After he was freed in 1989 he went to Miami, where he continued to monitor human rights conditions in Cuba. "Our objectives were clear," says Bofill, "We wanted to raise the level of consciousness in Cuba and international forums about what was truly happening on the island with respect to human rights. From personal experience, we had lived under the repressive apparatus of Castro's Cuba and we wanted the world to know it."

Bofill is regarded as the father of the dissident movement. Today there are hundreds of small dissident groups on the island, the members of which are systematically harassed—they suffer arbitrary detentions, loss of employment, attacks by government-sponsored mobs—or are put in prison whenever and for as long as the regime desires. The groups cover the political spectrum, from those who believe in lifting the embargo to those who oppose closer relations between Cuba and the United States. In spite of their own political differences and the repression they endure, they manage to send to the world testimony about human rights violations in Castro's Cuba.

The prospect of normalized relations with the United States never materialized because Castro's foreign policy got in the way. In late 1977, Castro dispatched a second Cuban expeditionary force to Angola and combat troops to defend Ethiopia against Somalia, the latter at the request of the Marxist regime of Lieutenant Colonel Mengistu Haile Mariam. Cuba also resumed excursions into Central America, sending military advisors and large-scale shipments of arms to Nicaragua at the end of 1978. For Castro, the time was not right to normalize relations with the United States as he was at the zenith of his power internally as well as being a third world leader.

Oppression Required by Law

In 1976 Cuba adopted a new constitution. Fidel Castro became president and first secretary of the Communist Party, the only one the constitution permitted. It also recognized freedom of speech, of the press, and of religion, but only "as long as it conforms to the ends of socialist society." In short, totalitarianism was institutionalized at the highest level of Cuban law, even as the Carter Administration made efforts to moderate the regime.

In this 1970s Miami street protest Cubans demand the U.S. government permit militant exile organizations to wage war against Castro. (Courtesy *Miami Herald*)

Meanwhile, restrictions were eased for exiles to travel to Cuba to visit loved ones. More than 100,000 exiles went back to their hometowns to visit with friends and family. Many of the visits were bittersweet. On the one hand, they had a chance to see their country of origin once again and to see family and friends. On the other hand, Cuba had deteriorated beyond what many expected. The harsh, repressive political apparatus was firmly in place and the dire economic situation was unbearable for many.

Investigators in 1977 inspect a cache of arms meant for anti-Castro raiders intercepted in South Florida. (Courtesy *Miami Herald*)

"I remember walking the streets of Havana thinking to myself how sad Cuba and its people had become," recalls one older exile. "People were afraid to talk about the political situations fearing reprisals from the government and no one dared to criticize the economic conditions." For many Cubans, the visits proved that the government propaganda against *el exilio* and the United States were groundless rhetoric. Many exiles brought medicine, food, clothing, and dollars to their loved ones and countless spoke of living under a democratic form of government, of the political freedom they enjoyed in the United States, and the opportunities that those freedoms provided. Such ideas would have a profound effect on the minds of hundreds of thousands of Cubans and would plant the seed for future departures.

But not all visits were family related. One group made the trip with a political agenda.

Most Cubans in America were outraged when a group of young exiles that called itself the Antonio Maceo Brigade, after the general of the wars of independence, traveled to Cuba. The trip was not regarded by most exiles as merely another well-meaning if misguided way to convince a tyranny to ease up; rather, it was seen as an open show of support for the Castro regime. And it was. The *maceítos*, as they were derisively called ("little Maceos"), were open admirers of Revolution, uncritical of its record on human rights. Yet being small in number—only fifty-five traveled to Cuba—they were seen as an insignificant group of "traitors" to the exile cause.

It was another development that proved explosive.

In the summer of 1977 the prominent Miami exile banker Bernardo Benes held secret talks in Panama with top officials of the Cuban regime. Benes's intention was to promote Cuba–United States relations, open exile travel to the island, and convince the Castro regime to free political prisoners. Castro's aim was to end the embargo and gain recognition from the U.S. government. The Carter Administration, against the advice of National Security Advisor Zbigniew Brzezinski (an exile from communist Poland himself), encouraged the contacts that followed in the next few months.

These talks laid the groundwork for the electrifying announcement Fidel Castro made at a Havana news conference in September 1978. In front of the largest group of Cuban-American journalists ever permitted to travel to Cuba (the group included such exile establishment figures as the city editor of *El Herald*, the Spanish-language edition of the *Miami Herald*, and a reporter and crew from Miami's Channel 23) Castro said he wanted to end nearly twenty years of antagonism and establish a dialogue with "the Cuban community abroad."

More talks followed. That November, Benes and a "Committee of 75" chosen in consultation with the Cuban regime was in Havana in face-to-face negotiations with Fidel Castro. Agreements were reached to free political prisoners and allow exiles to travel to the island.

The Plantados

Exile politics have always been so marked by rivalries between groups that few figures are universally admired by Cubans in America.

An exception: The two or three hundred *plantados* (roughly, "the Ones Who Stood Up"), political prisoners who survived twenty or more years in Castro's jails, subject to sadistic physical and psychological torture.

Their plight became internationally known in the mid-1980s with the publication of *Against All Hope*, the memoirs of Armando Valladares, who spent twenty-two years in Cuban prisons "solely for having espoused and expressed principles distinct from those of the regime of Fidel Castro," as he put it. In his harrowing book Valladares wrote of guards murdering in cold blood, of having protein-rich food withheld from prisoners in order to make them guinea pigs in medical experiments on nutrition, of being forced at bayonet point to dive into a sewerage ditch filled with "islands of excrement" and "clouds of green flies."

That was when they were punished. Roberto Martín Pérez, who spent twenty-eight years in prison, learned that regular, everyday treatment consisted of beating prisoners and then feeding them just enough so they could

Osvaldo Cabrera celebrates his newfound freedom with his family, after being released from the Cuban political prisons in which he spent sixteen years. (Courtesy *Miami Herald*)

stand the next beating. "We would get macaroni water and peas cooked in a vat where they'd throw dead rats," he recalled years after his release. "When we got meat, we got rotted meat."

Some of the *plantados* had been convicted of taking arms against the Castro government; others were charged with nothing more than philosophical opposition against the regime. But what made them stand apart from the rest of the political prisoner population (in *Cuba: Mito y Realidad* Juan Clark estimates it at 60,000 during the 1960s) was a struggle over a uniform.

Political prisoners had been allowed to wear a distinctive yellow uniform, while those jailed for common crimes wore blue. But in the mid-1960s prison authorities decreed everyone would wear blue. The *plantados*, nearly 1,200 of them at first, refused.

Because of their refusal, they were stripped and forced into the infamous *gavetas,* solitary confinement cells that prisoners likened to the drawers of a dresser, so small that there was only enough room inside for an average-sized person to kneel. Many stayed like that for months.

The punishment continued when they were let out. From 1968 until 1987 Martín Pérez lived in his underwear in a cell "the size of a phone booth, about one and a half meter wide, two meters long, and maybe seven meters high," he recalled. "The walls were iron plates, so it got very hot in the sun."

Nevertheless, the *plantados* held on and never wore the blue uniform.

By the late 1980s most of the veteran *plantados* who survived the ordeal had been released and were living in the United States and have become heroic figures in Cuban communities, such as Valladares and Martín Pérez. Or Pedro Luis Boitel, who died of dehydration in 1972 after a 53-day hunger strike to protest the inhuman conditions; or Huber Matos, the former *comandante* of the rebel army who spent twenty years in prison; or Mario Chanes de Armas, a member of the *26th of July Movement* who had taken part in the Moncada assault and the *Granma* expedition. He was at his release in 1991 after thirty years, the world's longest-held political prisoner.

An unidentified former political prisoner in Cuba shows his gratitude to America upon being freed. (Courtesy *Miami Herald*)

The exile community was shaken to its very core. *El Diálogo,* as the talks became known, was not simply between Castro and leftist fringe groups like the *maceítos.* Castro, of course, had insisted on their attendance as well as that of members of the group that published *Areíto,* a New York City–based magazine that was openly pro-Castro. Also involved in the talks were stalwarts of the exile community such as Benes himself and Orlando Padrón, owner of Padrón Cigars.

Their talks with Castro violated the principle held sacred by a large majority of Cubans in America: No communication with the dictator who had forced them to leave their homes.

Thus began the most painful era *el exilio* has witnessed. In South Florida and the Union City area, families and friends were bitterly divided; some wanted desperately to go see relatives in Cuba, others opposed the trips on grounds that the very expensive costs of travel subsidized the Castro regime with dollars. Also, a number of political prisoners, who stood to gain their freedom, smuggled a petition out of Cuba's jails calling for an end to any talks with the Cuban government.

The dominant view among exiles was that the Castro regime was completely unwilling to move toward democratization, negotiations or not. So negotiations were viewed as nothing more than a way for naïve American policymakers to strengthen a tyranny by granting it official recognition.

Critics of *el Diálogo* took action. There were marches in Washington, Miami, and Union City to protest against exile *dialogueros* as well as the Carter Administration, which seemed to back the talks. Businesses of exiles involved in the Castro talks were boycotted. Exile radio stations and the small exile newspapers known as *periodiquitos* charged that the *dialogueros* were communist (not an altogether false charge when applied to the *maceítos*). In a community where hundreds of thousands had lost everything to a Marxist regime, it was about the gravest accusation that could be made, similar to being called a racist in the African-American community.

People became violent. In the 1960s and early 1970s militant groups mostly targeted places in Cuba itself. A new group Omega 7 went after exiles in the United States suspected of collaborating with the Castro regime. The militants bombed Miami and Union City travel agencies that arranged trips to Cuba. They threatened the life of Bernardo Benes and bombed Miami's Continental Bank, of which he was president. In May of 1979, Carlos Muñíz, a member of the Committee of 75, was assassinated in Puerto Rico. In November, men wearing ski masks shot to death another member of the Committee, José Eulalio Negrín, as he stepped out of his car on Tenth Street in Union City. Investigations later revealed Muñiz and Negrín had ties to Cuban intelligence.

A caller to the Associated Press claimed responsibility on behalf of Omega 7. "We will continue with these executions until we have eliminated all of the traitors living in this country," the caller said.

Sporadic bombings continued over the next few years. Then the FBI came

Political rally in Miami to demand the release of Cuban militants in U.S. jails for anti-Castro activities. (Courtesy *Miami Herald*)

down hard on Omega 7. By the mid-1980s most of its members had been tried in federal courts and condemned to prison. Its alleged leader, Eduardo Arocena was convicted on weapons and explosives charges; he began to serve a life sentence in 1983. Other exiles spent months in jail when they refused to testify before federal grand juries during the Omega 7 investigations.

But *el diálogo* was losing momentum even by the time Negrín was killed. With Cuba sending tens of thousands of soldiers to fight on behalf of fellow Marxists in Angola, Ethiopia, and elsewhere in Africa, the Carter Administration reconsidered its policy of improving relations. The Cuban military presence in Nicaragua (there were advisors and large-scale shipments of arms sent to the Sandinistas) and the August 1979 discovery of a Soviet combat brigade of 3,000 troops in Cuba ended whatever good feelings remained.

Besides, by late 1979, most political prisoners had been freed, exiles had been allowed to visit their relatives. There was nothing left to discuss. The Cuban government was not about to dismantle its machinery of oppression—dissent remained strictly prohibited, *diálogo* or not. It said so right in the constitution. Benes and other leaders of the negotiations withdrew from politics, partly because there was nothing else to say to the Cuban regime, partly because of the threats on their lives.

Was *el diálogo* a failure? Certainly, it did nothing to improve the human rights situation in Cuba. As to the freeing of political prisoners, opinion remained divided. Its supporters say that if not for the talks, prisoners would not have been released. Critics claim that international pressure would have resulted in the release of prisoners anyway.

The violent reaction to *el diálogo* proved a failure, too. The killings and bombings discredited the anti-Castro cause in the eyes of the American public, as exiles were seen more as extremists. It wasn't until the 1980s that Cuban-American organizations turned to politics American-style. Then they would gain greater influence at the highest political circles in Washington.

Perhaps the most important impact of *el diálogo* came through the exile visits that the talks authorized. Tired of the dire conditions suffered under the regime throughout the years, Cubans in Cuba saw the sharp difference between their own ordeal and the exiles' freedom and economic success.

Such internal turmoil within the island rekindled Cubans' desire to join exiles in the United States. Many risked their lives in small boats and rafts, as they tried to cross the Florida Straits to get to America. Others found a way out of the island by crashing the gates of the heavily guarded Latin-American embassies in Havana, where they knew diplomatic tradition granted asylum to those who made it in. Still others, some 20,000 over the decade, continued to come through Spain or Mexico, as they had during the period between the missile crisis and the Camarioca exodus.

But getting out was difficult, as reflected in the number of Cubans who arrived on American shores in 1979. That number, 2,644, was the smallest since the triumph of the Revolution.

The 1980 Census recorded 803,226 people of Cuban birth living in the United States. By the end of that year, the figure was badly outdated. Census takers had finished their enumeration just days before 125,000 Cubans flooded South Florida in the space of a few weeks.

Terrorist or Freedom Fighter

The most controversial figure that *el exilio* has produced is a former pediatrician named Orlando Bosch. To some, he is a hero who gave up everything to dedicate himself to the violent overthrow of Fidel Castro. To others, he is a terrorist.

Bosch fought with Castro's *26th of July Movement* against Batista, but quickly turned against him and joined rebels fighting the new revolutionary government in the Escambray Mountains. In 1960 he left for Miami.

During his first months in the United States, Bosch trained with the CIA, which was recruiting exiles for military operations against Castro. After the Missile Crisis, the Kennedy Administration decided to stop sponsoring armed raids. But the CIA-trained Cubans would not stop. And American law enforcement went after them.

The irony did not escape these Cubans. The same government that had trained them to fight Castro was now persecuting them for fighting Castro.

Between January 1961 and May 1968 "more than 30 violent acts were either claimed by or attributed to Bosch. These included bombings, armed incursions, and aerial attacks against targets in Cuba, Panama, and the United States," according to a Justice Department report. He was arrested by federal authorities at least five times, but was always acquitted until November of 1968, when he was found guilty of firing a bazooka at a Cuba-bound Polish freighter in the port of Miami. He served four years of a ten-year sentence at federal penitentiaries before being released on parole.

In 1974 he fled the United States, in violation of the terms of his parole, to travel in Latin America, finding ways to fight the Castro regime from there. In the Dominican Republic in 1976 he founded CORU, United Coordination of Revolutionary Organizations, which federal authorities maintain acted as an umbrella group for the most militant exile groups.

The same year he headed to Venezuela, where he was arrested and charged with masterminding the bombing of a Cuban airliner in which 73 people died. Bosch was twice tried and acquitted. He spent eleven years in Venezuelan prisons.

The year after his release, Bosch arrived in Miami and was immediately arrested by U.S. Marshals for his 1974 parole violation. He served three months in prison. Eventually, he was admitted to the United States. Since then, the Cuban government has accused him of being behind several bombings on the island, charges he has consistently denied.

Cuban Miami welcomed Orlando Bosch. The 24th of March 1983 was officially proclaimed "Orlando Bosch Day" in the Dade County cities of Miami,

Hialeah, Sweetwater, and West Miami. A radio marathon raised $137,000 to pay legal costs of his court battle to stay in the United States. Prominent politicians such as Florida Governor Bob Martínez and Congresswoman Ileana Ros Lehtinen pressured Ronald Reagan and the Justice Department to allow him to stay in the United States, as did major exile groups including the Cuban American National Foundation.

CHAPTER 9

Mariel and the Rise of Cuban-Americans

1980–1989

The Mariel boatlift began with a dramatic but relatively small-scale incident in Havana. On April 1, 1980, six Cubans stole a bus and crashed the gates of the Peruvian embassy, making it alive through a fusillade of machine gun fire opened by Cuban state security forces stationed outside the compound. Once inside, they asked for and were granted political asylum.

The six were following an old Latin-American diplomatic tradition: People who fear arrest for their political activities have the right to seek asylum in foreign embassies. The Castro government had tried to prevent these kinds of defections by posting guards outside embassy entrances throughout Havana—which did not prevent a handful of Cubans over the years from finding a way inside. But after these six came through in such spectacular fashion, word of their exploit spread through the city. Thousands of people headed to the Peruvian embassy to see what was going on.

On the street outside the embassy citizens began to shout anti-Castro slogans. Forces from the Interior Ministry and pro-Castro civilian goons responded by beating up demonstrators. The crowds continued to grow. With events spinning out of anyone's control, the Castro government tried to convert its crisis into a crisis for Peru: It removed its security detail, bulldozed the fences around the compound, and announced that the Peruvian embassy was wide open. Within forty-eight hours, 10,800 men, women, and children had taken refuge inside. All

Tired and uncertain, a couple who arrived during the Mariel boatlift wonders about life in America. (Courtesy *Miami Herald*)

were granted asylum by the Peruvians. The Castro government, embarrassed at the spectacle of Cubans desperate to flee, quickly reversed itself and sealed off the entire neighborhood. No one else would get in. Then it mobilized huge pro-government marches.

"People turned on each other . . . and those of us who did not want to participate in the rallies had to hide inside our homes," remembers Mirta Ojito, who eventually escaped and became a reporter in the United States. "It was one of Cuba's darkest periods."

It was also dark for those in the Peruvian embassy. Officials there suddenly found themselves having to provide for a population the size of a small town while the Cuban government blocked humanitarian assistance from the Red Cross and exiles who had donated food and medical supplies. Needless to say, the embassy did not own 11,000 beds; neither could it feed that many people or provide adequate sanitary facilities. People slept on the lawn, on trees or on the roof; when food ran out, they resorted to killing and eating cats and small birds.

Mariel refugees eating at one of the temporary camps in which they lived.
(Courtesy *Miami Herald*)

Portable toilets were set up outside the embassy, but everybody was afraid to leave the diplomatic sanctity of the compound, so they went largely unused. The grounds became a putrid swamp of mud littered with excrement and garbage. Parents feared for the health of their children.

At first the refugees' stay under such horrific conditions seemed indefinite—the Castro government had insisted through its official newspaper *Granma* that "no person who enters a foreign embassy by force will be granted safe conduct to leave the country." But eventually it agreed to let Peru evacuate the asylum-seekers, most to be settled in Peru itself while others would go to the United States (the

Carter Administration announced it would accept 3,500) and several countries in Latin America and Europe.

The airlift began April 16, with Costa Rica volunteering to be the staging area before refugees departed for their destinations. However, after two days the Cuban regime suspended the flights, claiming they were being used for propaganda purposes by the governments of Peru and Costa Rica. Meanwhile, thousands of Cubans continued to gather in the vicinity of the embassy.

It was all too much for the Castro government. It came to the realization that, as in the time of Camarioca fifteen years earlier, it was facing enormous internal pressure, and that the way to relieve that pressure was to open an escape valve. And so it did. On April 20 the government announced that Cubans who wished to leave the island could do so through the northern port city known as Mariel. Those who wanted to leave were branded by Castro as *escoria*, scum. It was a new addition to the official lexicon that described the politically disaffected, heretofore referred to as *gusanos*, worms.

El exilio reacted with euphoria despite the *comandante's* insults. On Calle Ocho, people honked their car horns and waved Cuban flags when they learned that Mariel was open. In Union City and West New York, exiles hurried down to Miami to see what they could do about going to Cuba to bring back family members they had not seen in years. Those who were not well off sold their possessions or took out second mortgages—if reunification meant they had to spend their life savings to buy a boat or pay a boat owner to sail with them to Mariel, so be it.

In less than a week, up to 500 exile vessels had docked at Mariel. What followed was pandemonium. In Mariel, Cuban officials abused refugees waiting to be picked up and their exiled relatives—physically roughing them up, stealing personal possessions, gouging them on the cost of food and gas for the return trip. At sea, overcrowded boats sank or broke down and had to be rescued by an overburdened Coast Guard.

It seemed like a replay of Camarioca. But this time there were many more boats, many more refugees, and the boatlift went on for a much longer period of time.

René Rodríguez was one of the Cubans who rushed to Mariel hoping to find a boat willing to take him to the United States. "Seeing thousands of people boarding all those boats docked in Mariel is a memory I will never forget. People frantically trying to find loved ones to come aboard, men, women, and children all frightened and at the same time excited to be reunited with their loved ones," Rodríguez said. "But after you find yourself stranded in the middle of the ocean in the dead of the night, an overwhelming sense of fear engulfs you." When the

A family just arrived through Mariel drafting a letter to family in Cuba to tell them they arrived safely in America. (Courtesy *Miami Herald*)

boat ran out of food and water, passengers prayed while waiting for dawn to arrive. "When we finally saw the coast of Key West we cried, hugged and kissed each other, grateful to be alive and thrilled to have finally made it to America."

There were other, unexpected difficulties. Exiles who went to Mariel to pick up relatives were forced by Cuban government officials to take onboard persons they did not know. As it turned out, many of those strangers were mental patients or criminals released by the regime for the express purpose of being sent to the United States.

Mariel and Crime

Even though the vast majority of the men and women of Mariel had no criminal past, among them were some 2,000 hard-core felons who had been purposely let out of prison by Fidel Castro.

The American news media, naturally, had to report the crime wave they caused in Miami, but it did so without the context needed to explain that the relatively high percentage of criminals in the Mariel population was due to the fact that they came straight from prison. It created the stereotype of the crazed, homicidal Mariel Cuban.

Many of the most violent offenders never made it to American streets. As early as June the Carter Administration realized that Castro had put criminals aboard the exile vessels, and ordered the expulsion of refugees who had committed serious crimes in Cuba. But the Castro government would not take them back, and the United States would not release them. They were incarcerated indefinitely.

As years went by, they were joined in prisons by other Mariel refugees, some 3,800 of them who had committed crimes on American soil after their arrival. After they served their sentences, these men were also deemed deportable and detained indefinitely.

A few hundred were repatriated to Cuba under various short-lived immigration agreements. In 1987, after one such deal between American and Cuban officials, more than 2,000 Mariel inmates who feared returning to Cuba rioted at federal prisons in Atlanta and Oakdale, Louisiana. They had control of both facilities for eleven days. Through the mediation of Miami's Bishop Agustín San Roman, the men surrendered on condition that each detainee's repatriation would be reviewed. In effect, they said they preferred life in an American prison to life in Cuba.

The felons of the Mariel exodus remained locked up in U.S. jails until 2000, when federal courts ordered most should be released.

By mid-May 3,000 Cubans were arriving every day. During that month alone, more Cubans arrived than in any one year previously. On June 3, the peak day, more than 6,000 landed on Floridian shores including 731 on the Panamanian freighter *Red Diamond*. The Coast Guard was so overwhelmed—by early June it had conducted some 1,000 search-and-rescue operations—that it had to call up reservists and ask the Navy for warships to help control the tide of Cuban immigrants. Together, Navy ships and Coast Guard cutters began to turn back exile boats on their way to Mariel.

By July the flow of refugees had slowed to about 1,000 a week, enough for the Navy to pull out and let the Coast Guard handle the crisis by itself. Some 10,000 arrived through the rest of the summer. Then on September 25, the Cuban government shut down the port of Mariel, ordering all boats docked at the time to leave even if they had not picked up anyone.

In total, 2,011 vessels took part in the Mariel boatlift. They brought to the United States 125,266 Cubans seeking the liberty denied them in their homeland.

The Artists of Mariel

To the American public at large, the Mariel exodus still summons forth a disturbing image of ragged refugees on overcrowded boats and cold-blooded murderers like the character played by Al Pacino in *Scarface*.

But on those overcrowded boats, wearing the same ragged clothes of other refugees, was the cream of Cuba's art and cultural world. There were writers Reinaldo Arenas and Andres Reynaldo, painters like Juan Abréu.

Freed from the artistic censorship of the Castro regime, they ignited a burst of creativity in Cuban Miami. They revived the cultural life of a community too long consumed with business and politics. Those who were writers founded a literary magazine, *Revista Mariel*. Painters and sculptors exhibited in the galleries of Coral Gables.

Arenas, the best known of the Mariel generation, had been sent to labor camps by the Castro regime in the 1970s for "ideological deviation," which in his case meant homosexuality. Novels such as *Adios al mar*, pub-

The late novelist Reinaldo Arenas, the most celebrated of the Mariel artists.

lished in English as *Farewell to the Sea*, won critical praise for unsparing critique of life in Castro's Cuba that never lost the power and lyricism of literary fiction.

Arenas found Miami too intolerant for a gay man and moved to New York. There sick with AIDS, he committed suicide in 1990, alone in his apartment surrounded by books and manuscripts, raging against the injustices that had plagued him and his native land. His memoir, *Antes Que Anochezca,* of his life and persecutions in Cuba was made into the internationally acclaimed film *Before Night Falls.*

A VERY DIFFERENT *EXILIO*

The new arrivals had one thing in common with the older exiles: *Necesidad de Libertad,* as the writer Reinaldo Arenas, a member of the Mariel generation, put it in the title of one of his books, *A Need for Freedom.* But they were very different in other ways.

The most readily visible difference was that the Mariel exodus included a lot of Cubans who were not white. Because of the Latin-American tradition of seeing "race" as a continuum rather than in the stark black-white terms understood in the United States, it can be difficult to classify Hispanic individuals by race. Nevertheless, the percentage of non-whites who came through Mariel has been estimated at anywhere from 15 percent to 40. In contrast, the pre-Mariel non-white exile population—or at least the black exile population—was certainly under 5 percent. After Mariel, the racial demographics of *el exilio* began to resemble that of Cuba itself.

Another difference was gender—nearly 70 percent of Mariel entrants were male. It was also disproportionately young—nearly half were between the ages of 15 and 45. At the time, Cuba prohibited young men of draft age from leaving.

Then there was occupation and social class. Although the Mariel exodus included a large number of writers, musicians, painters, and other artists, most of the refugees were blue collar workers. In this they were unlike the professionals in the first wave of exiles, but similar to their fellow working-class Cubans of the Freedom Flights. However, there was an important distinction: The Freedom Flights Cubans had come of age before the revolution and arrived in the United States with entrepreneurial skills they quickly put to use in a free-market economy; in contrast, the Mariel Cubans fifteen years later were largely young men who had grown up in Cuba's communist economy and arrived in the United States with little business or professional experience.

Precisely because of these social, economic, and racial characteristics, the Mariel exodus proved to be an international embarrassment for Castro. The newcomers who were young, poor, black, or of mixed race "were supposed to be the very same people that benefited most from the Revolution," pointed out historian

The Mariel exodus was more racially mixed than earlier waves of Cubans, with black individuals, white individuals, and people of every shade in between.
(Courtesy *Miami Herald*)

Mark Falcoff. "But they wanted to leave. It was indeed a terrible blow to Castro's prestige."

SOUTH FLORIDA IN SHOCK

The more than 125,000 Cubans who arrived in the United States within the space of five months were a shock to South Florida in every conceivable way. Nobody was ready for them.

The Carter Administration realized that the large number of refugees had

Bishop Agustín San Roman in front of the Hermita de la Caridad, *Catholic Miami's shrine to Cuba's patron saint, the Virgin of Charity. The prelate played the leading role in quelling the riots by Mariel refugees who were imprisoned in the United States and faced deportation to Cuba.* (Cuban Heritage Collection, University of Miami)

turned Mariel from a diplomatic to a domestic crisis. It declared a state of emergency for Florida, authorizing $10 million to help with the refugees. But the brunt of the work fell, at least initially, to local officials and volunteers in South Florida.

First, the newcomers had to be administratively "processed." In Key West, Tamiami Park, Opa-Locka, and the Krome Detention Center near the Everglades the first Cubans to arrive through Mariel were photographed, fingerprinted, given medical tests, and questioned about their jobs and political affiliations back on the island. But registering every single person took time, so authorities had to scramble to find places for tens of thousands of people to live and eat while they waited.

And so many were waiting that volunteer housing centers in churches, gymnasiums, and armories quickly filled. Miami officials had to open up the Orange Bowl as an emergency shelter. Later that summer they also established the infamous "Tent City" under the I-95 overpass between Little Havana and downtown. It was an open-air disaster. When it finally closed at the end of September, four thousand refugees had passed through, living in crowded tents among exposed wires, broken plumbing, and garbage.

Those refugees with the good fortune to find a "sponsor" in South Florida—such as family members or a charitable institution willing to guarantee to the government that they would not let the newcomers become a public charge—left the camps fairly quickly, but found it difficult outside. The economy was in recession and jobs were hard to come by. One report published by Dade County officials in

1981 said that of 3,046 people on an employment waiting list at the Little Havana Manpower Agency, 95 percent had arrived during Mariel.

More than 60,000 refugees who did not find sponsors were transferred to four military bases, Eglin Air Force Base, on the Florida panhandle; Fort Chaffee, Arkansas; Fort Indiantown Gap, Indiana; and Fort McCoy, Wisconsin. There they remained virtual prisoners until they found a sponsor.

The hardened criminals that the Castro government had dumped made life hell for the majority of law-abiding refugees in those resettlement camps. There was prostitution, beatings, rapes, stabbings. Because of the Mariel refugees' violent reputation, sponsors were hard to find. Some of the refugees waited as long as a year to get out. Frustration built up and exploded in riots at Forts Chaffee and Indiantown Gap that summer. Some one thousand Cubans in each camp went on a rampage, looting and setting fires. State troopers and federal marshals tear-gassed the mobs to restore order. The

The children of Mariel had problems adjusting to schools and to life in America at first. Eventually, most caught up to their classmates—today the Mariel generation is similar to other Cubans in most measures of socioeconomic well-being. (Courtesy *Miami Herald*)

national publicity that followed worsened the already bad reputation of the Mariel refugees.

The Mariel children—and their teachers—also found that first year a nightmare. Dade County schools had two decades of experience in dealing with newly arrived Cuban students. But earlier waves of exiles were spread out over a relatively long period of time. When classes started after the Mariel exodus, Dade County schools suddenly had more than 12,000 new Cuban students to cope with. Almost none of them spoke English or had any familiarity with American culture, or even with the Cubanized American culture of Miami. A disproportionate number of them were violent or emotionally unstable. "They had no concept of self-discipline. Their concept was one of terror," a Cuban-American teacher was reported as saying in a monograph published by the Cuban American National Foundation. "They embodied in their vocabulary, their manners and their actions, the communist system of Cuba."

"*Marielitos*" was the pejorative term longer-established exiles used to refer to the newcomers. Miami Cubans at first welcomed the Mariel Cubans, giving time and money to help the latest wave of fellow exiles settle in. But after the initial euphoria died down, many longtime exiles who got to know their newly arrived compatriots came to believe that two decades of communist dictatorship had changed Cubans, and not for the better. *Marielitos* had no work ethic, it was believed. They were wont to use communist-inspired words like *compañero*, comrade. They were violent. They stole. They had no respect for authority. Old-time exiles needed only to point to the frightening rise in crime. According to the *Miami Herald*, robbery shot up 775 percent in Little Havana the year following the exodus, auto theft 284.2 percent, burglary 190.8 percent, and assault 109.5 percent.

If fellow Cubans thought badly of *Marielitos*, non-Cubans thought worse. A poll taken by the *Miami Herald* showed 68 percent of non-Hispanic whites and 57 percent of non-Hispanic blacks in Dade County thought the exodus had damaged South Florida. These Americans had put up with the arrival of half a million Cubans over the past twenty years, and they wanted no more—particularly not Cubans with a reputation for crime. Many moved out. The Mariel exodus was followed by "white flight" to Broward and Palm Beach counties, where fewer Cubans lived. Two years after the exodus, resentments lingered, and not just in Miami. In a national Roper Poll conducted in May of 1982, Americans were asked to rank fifteen immigrant groups according to their positive influence on the United States. Cubans were dead last.

MARIELITO *SUCCESS*

By the end of the decade the old fears and resentments had largely dissipated, because the exiles of Mariel and other Cubans had become virtually indistinguishable. The children of older exiles and of *Marielitos* were graduating from high school and going on to college at approximately the same rate, and families who came from Mariel were already almost as likely to own businesses or own their homes as Cubans who came earlier. In fact, the major remaining differences were perhaps to the advantage of the Mariel group—a disproportionate number of the artists, cultural figures, and intellectuals of Cuban Miami arrived during the exodus of 1980.

The Mariel Cubans have been absorbed so successfully (if not into mainstream America, at least into mainstream Cuban America) that even the word *Marielito* lost its sting. For some, being a *Marielito* has become a source of pride.

"The biggest irony of Mariel is that it was the migration most stereotyped, yet it has been the most diverse of all waves from Cuba" Lisandro Perez, director of the Cuban Research Institute at Florida International University, told the *Miami Herald* during the newspaper's coverage of the twentieth anniversary of the exodus. "Who's to say who is a Mariel refugee anymore? You can't tell."

Cuban America after Mariel

By the late 1980s Miami and Cuban America in general were both on the rebound from the shock of Mariel. Not only had *marielitos* begun to catch up to other exiles in terms of education and economic success, but Cubans overall could boast of a remarkable adaptation to life in America.

The 100,000 Cubans of Hudson

Paquito D'Rivera, from a publicity poster for one of his albums. The world renowned saxophonist defected in Madrid while on tour with the jazz band Irakere at the same time Cubans were boarding the boats at Mariel. To punish him, the Castro government denied his son Franco an exit visa for eight years.
(Courtesy Paquito D'Rivera)

County, New Jersey, made up as much as three-quarters of the population of Union City and West New York. One had to strain to hear English spoken on the street, unless it came from the mouth of a Cuban youngster whose dominant language had become English. Just about every store on Bergenline was owned by

Domino tournament at the Domino Park on Miami's Calle Ocho.
(Courtesy *Miami Herald)*

Cubans, whether a restaurant that sold *arroz con frijoles* or a culturally "neutral" dry cleaner.

Cubans had also spread out to other sectors of the local economy. Many of the lace factories that had been the lifeblood of Hudson since the nineteenth century were now owned by Cuban exiles who had started off as workers there when they first arrived in the 1960s. In this decade, too, the region's first Cuban-American lawyers began to practice. They and prominent local businessmen met every Wednesday at the Federación Mercantil Hispana, a chamber of commerce. Exiles would spend the afternoon drinking, eating a Cuban meal, reminiscing about pre-Castro days, discussing the latest plans to liberate Cuba, and talking local politics.

That was a new development. Cubans were now among the leading political figures in the region—a major change from the days in the 1960s when exiles took little interest in domestic American politics because they thought their return to Cuba was imminent. Now Cuban-Americans were beginning to supplant the Italian-Americans who had in their day displaced the Irish-Americans who once dominated town halls in these eminently immigrant cities. In 1986 Union City elected its first Cuban mayor, Bob Menéndez, the New York–born son of immigrants from the 1950s. There were Cubans elected to the city commissions of West New York and Union City, to the boards of education, to the state legislature in Trenton. No candidate for office in the region could afford to ignore the Cuban vote.

The Cuban enclave in Union City and West New York, successful as it was, began to break up by the end of the decade. The two towns had always been rough-edged cities, waystops for immigrants where the first generation got its feet on the ground of America long enough to allow the second generation to move to more affluent neighborhoods. Cubans followed this traditional pattern in the wake of Italians, Irish, and Germans. The children of exiles went off to college, became professionals and never returned except to visit, choosing instead to live middle class lives in the leafy suburbs of nearby Essex and Bergen counties, or to move to Miami, where their "Cubanness" opened doors that might have been closed elsewhere. By the late 1980s their parents, the generation that had come in the 1960s or in the Freedom Flights, began to retire and leave Hudson County, too. Inevitably, they headed for Miami.

In essence, the Union City-West New York region had never been more than a Cuban-influenced speck across the river from mighty New York. Miami was different. It was like North Hudson, but more so. In Miami, Cubans exerted enormous influence on the life of an entire major American city.

The pervasiveness of Cuban culture in Miami happened because Cubans were not limited to owning small mom-and-pop shops on Calle Ocho. They were also connected to the city's leading centers of power. In politics, Miami and Hialeah elected their first Cuban mayors, Xavier Suárez and Raúl Martínez in the early 1980s. During the period, Dade County sent seven representatives to the

Robert Menéndez began his political career with his election to the Union City Board of Education in 1974 when he was a 20-year-old college student. He later became the first Cuban mayor of Union City and the first Hispanic State Senator in New Jersey. He was elected to Congress in 1992 and in 1999 named Vice Chair of the Democratic Caucus, which made him the fourth-ranking Democrat in the House of Representatives. (Courtesy *Miami Herald*)

Florida legislature and three to the Senate, and in 1989 voters made Cuban-born Ileana Ros Lehtinen the first Hispanic woman elected to Congress. She would later be joined by Lincoln Díaz-Balart, a member of a prominent political family in Cuba with ties to both Batista and Castro. Union City's Bob Menéndez got elected to Congress, too, and eventually became the fourth-ranking Democrat. There was even an echo of an earlier Cuban presence, that of the nineteenth-century exile community in Tampa, when third-generation Cuban-American Bob Martínez was elected governor of Florida.

High-level business affairs also came under Cuban influence. By the mid-1980s more than a dozen bank presidents and more than a hundred vice presi-

Chef Pepín, a popular Miami television cook-show figure, preparing a dish to start off the Calle Ocho festival. (Courtesy *Miami Herald*)

dents were of Cuban descent. They and the lawyers of Cuban origin at Miami's top law firms were instrumental in the city's rise as Latin America's financial and banking capital. In the import/export sector, too, hundreds of Cuban entrepreneurs established business that helped make the Port of Miami a point of departure for much of the trade between the United States and Latin America. And locally, Cubans were influential in industry, through the Latin Builders Association and executives like Armando Codina, a business partner of future Florida governor Jeb Bush.

Also telling was the Cuban influence on Miami's mass media. There were at least ten radio stations that broadcast in Spanish, featuring either Cuban music or the extremely popular news and talk shows about Cuban politics. Two television stations broadcast in Spanish, part of the Telemundo and Univision networks; their ratings rivaled and sometimes topped those of the English-language stations, a phenomenon new to American broadcasting. Miami was also the only American city with two daily Spanish-language newspapers. *Diario La Américas* was still strong after four decades of publication. *El Nuevo Herald* started as *El Herald* in 1976, an insert with little more than translated articles from the English-language edition of the *Miami Herald*. But as Cubans' predominance continued to grow, the Knight-Ridder Corporation, owner of the *Herald*, decided in 1987 to publish a stand-alone Spanish-language newspaper with its own staff of editors and reporters under publisher Roberto Suárez, who had arrived from Cuba in the 1960s and worked his way up the Knight-Ridder hierarchy. It now has a circulation of more than 100,000.

Nuevo Latino Cuisine

There was a culinary revolution in the America of the 1980s, as chefs began to experiment with new and intriguing flavor combinations, based on fresh ingredients and techniques inspired by cuisines from around the world. Cubans were part of the movement, too.

A Cuban-American chef named Douglas Rodríguez caused a sensation at Yuca Restaurant in South Florida with his innovative "Nuevo Latino" cuisine. Rodríguez refined the traditional cooking of Cuba and other Hispanic countries, giving it a modern sensibility. The result was dishes like plantain fettuccini, shredded pork in black bean broth, and a puree of *boniato*, a traditional Cuban tuber.

Rodríguez eventually brought his style to the demanding palates of "foodies" in Manhattan. He opened the Nuevo Latino dining establishment Patria and later a restaurant/tapas bar named Pipa.

Particularly of note during the 1980s was the rise of younger Cuban-Americans who grew up and were educated in the United States. They were not only bilingual, but also bicultural, able to navigate the sometimes treacherous currents of Miami's "American" and "Cuban" cultures. Their social circles were more likely than their parents' to include non-Hispanic friends, which to some extent alleviated ethnic tensions. In business, they understood modern American savvy in marketing and finance, yet retained the traditionally Cuban, highly personalized way of doing business that they learned from their parents.

All in all, the Cuban economic success story can hardly be overstated. The median Cuban-American family had income rates in line with the national average, one in sixteen Cubans owned his own business and over 20 percent had incomes above $50,000, according to sociologist Alejandro Portes and Alex Stepick's *City on the Edge*.

As Cubans became better off financially, they began to move out of urban neighborhoods like Calle Ocho and into the suburbs of Southwest Dade in Florida. But there was an important difference between them and the Cubans of Hudson County who had moved to suburbs outside Cuban enclaves there. Those Cubans who left Union City and West New York went on to live among middle-class "Anglos" and created no distinctively Hispanic suburban community—they had to travel back to Bergenline for their fix of Cubanness. In contrast, those who moved to suburban Dade County took their Cubanness with them, introducing a Latin flavor to suburban life.

Over the years following Mariel, the Cuban-origin population of the United States reached one million persons. They scored higher than other groups deemed "minorities," and close to the national average, in socioeconomic measures such as home ownership, income, health, and education. In many ways, Cuban-Americans as a group were indistinguishable from the national non-Hispanic white population. Except, of course, that many preferred to speak Spanish, clung tenaciously to Cuban culture, and continued to feel passionate about their troubled ancestral nation.

ETHNIC TENSIONS

American-style success and cultural identity strained relations between Cubans and non-Hispanics, whether white or black.

Language remains the major issue. Cubans were seen as either unwilling to learn English or unwilling to speak it. "What happens is that in an open store there will be two or three women talking in an incomprehensible language, and people, I think, sometimes just get tired of being surrounded by Spanish," a "native white business executive" told Alejandro Portes and Alex Stepick, scholars who studied tensions between Cubans and Miami's other ethnic groups in the 1980s. Spanish- and English-speaking communities clashed the November following the Mariel exodus in a bitter fight over a referendum to overturn Dade's 1973 bilingual ordinance, which required that many county documents be printed in the two languages. Voters repealed the law, and Dade adopted English as its sole official language. Cubans and other Hispanics saw it as an attack on their heritage, a heritage in which the Spanish language was indispensable.

There was also a more general question of assimilation. Unlike nearly every other ethnic group to arrive in America, the Cubans of Miami climbed the local socioeconomic ladder inside one generation—enough time to become successful, but not enough time for the community's successful elders to fully assimilate. As a result, there was a well entrenched Cuban upper class that preferred to speak Spanish and considered itself fully the equal of the upper class Anglo establishment. A "parallel social structure," sociologists have called it. Upper class Cubans ran major businesses, ate in the best restaurants, lived in the best neighborhoods and (particularly those who had arrived in the United States as adults) moved in their own Hispanic circles. Exclusive old social clubs of Havana like the Vedado Tennis Club and the Miramar Yacht Club were recreated in South Florida. This rapid ascendancy, accomplished without the degree of acculturation expected of immigrants, irritated many non-Hispanic Miamians.

Tensions were particularly high between Cuban and non-Cuban blacks, particularly after Mariel, when even in the midst of an economic recession *Marielitos* found it easier than American-born blacks to find work. A major part of the problem was the difference between the ways African-Americans and Cuban exiles saw their place in American society. A black lawyer and community activist told Portes and Stepick, "I said to Cubans in a speech that there was going to be a time when white folks were going to treat you all like niggers . . . but unlike black Americans, Cubans had no history of being kept in their place, and as a result, they responded differently. We black folks were saying to white folks, 'Let us in.' Cubans were saying to white folks, 'Let us in so we can take over.'"

Most of those Cubans who wanted to "take over" were of course themselves white; they had once already reached success, as businessmen or professionals in Cuba, which helps explain how they saw their "place" in the new Miami.

Part of that place was to be successful newcomers. And part of it was to continue to battle the dictatorship of Fidel Castro.

THE REAGAN YEARS

With the election of Ronald Reagan in 1980, a new era of United States–Cuba relations began, one characterized by increased hostility and aggressiveness on both sides. However, early on in his administration President Reagan, unbeknownst to most of his staff and the public at large, attempted to establish common ground with Havana. He sent his advisor, Ambassador-at-Large Vernon A. Walters, to Cuba to meet with Fidel Castro in April 1982.

"We met for almost six hours, we spoke in Spanish, and discussed our profound differences," Walters recalled. "At the beginning, Castro was amiable and appeared willing to negotiate our pressing issues, but as the hours passed his demeanor changed drastically. He went on a rampage about U.S. ills and his vision to be the sole vanguard of the oppressed masses due to U.S. imperialism."

Days later, during a meeting at the White House with Reagan, Walters informed the president that Castro was not serious about negotiations and that a new approach was needed to deal with him. Given Walters's report, as well as the experiences of the Carter years and Cuba's financial and military dependence on the U.S.S.R., Reagan's foreign policy advisors became convinced that Castro was not willing to negotiate legitimately with the United States.

It was not to Castro's advantage to negotiate. His relationship with the Kremlin had yielded substantial advantages for the Cuban government over the past decades, in the form of generous subsidies and increased military aid. Such backing served to strengthen Castro's standing among Third World nations and increased his stature in the international arena.

In response to Castro's dependence on the U.S.S.R. and his newly acquired ascendance in the Third World, the Reagan Administration began an even tighter economic boycott of the island. All U.S. tourist and business travel to Cuba was banned. Moreover, in an effort to thwart Cuban support of the Sandinista Front for National Liberation in Nicaragua, the Reagan Administration funneled financial assistance, military advisors, and weaponry to the Nicaraguan Contras.

The Reagan Administration also aimed its arrows at Castro's Achilles' heel, human rights violations. American officials concluded that documentation of the Cuban regime's systematic violation of the thirty articles of the United Nations Universal Declaration of Human Rights (to which Cuba was a signatory) could be used to discredit Castro both in Cuba and abroad. As the then U.S. Ambassador to the United Nations Jeanne Kirkpatrick, put it, "condemnation by the United Nations Human Rights Commission would be a heavy blow to the prestige of Fidel Castro's government." Furthermore, it would interfere with Castro's ambition to be seen as a leader of, and as a spokesman for, Third World nations. Such condemnation would impede Cuba's efforts to improve its ties to Western Europe, Latin America, and Canada.

Cuba's Human Rights Record Condemned

A six-member U.N. delegation, headed by the United Nations Human Rights Commission (UNHRC) Chairman Alioune Sene of Senegal, visited Cuba September 16–25, 1988. For the dissident movement there, headed by Ricardo Bofill, the day to show the world the truth about Cuba's dismal human rights record had finally arrived. The dissidents handed the UNHRC representatives a 110-page report outlining serious violations encompassing the thirty articles of the United Nations Universal Declarations of Human Rights.

Over 1,600 people went to meet with the delegation personally to denounce the state of human rights in Cuba, including Cubans who had been tortured, beaten, denied jobs due to political causes, or denied the right to leave the island. Months later, the delegation published a critical report raising serious questions about the state of human rights in Cuba.

For the next couple of years, Cuba faced mounting pressure at the UNHRC's annual meetings. Finally, in March 1992, with votes from the former Soviet bloc abstaining or switching sides, the UNHRC voted to condemn Cuba. Their findings showed in great detail that liberties of speech, movement, and assembly, among others, where routinely denied to the Cuban people by their government. "It was something unprecedented," recalls Bofill later in exile. "It made us feel optimistic. It gave us hope that our people could have liberty someday."

THE RISE OF THE CUBAN-AMERICAN LOBBY

Emboldened and energized by the new administration's tough stance toward Cuba, a group of Cuban-American businessmen in 1981 organized a lobbying group aimed at influencing U.S. foreign policy toward the island, the Cuban American National Foundation (CANF). Modeling themselves after Jewish lobbying groups, CANF gained access and acceptance in the corridors of power in Washington. Its leader was Jorge Mas Canosa.

Mas Canosa was not only the most influential of Cubans in Washington, but also by far the most popular in Miami. In a poll taken in October of 1996 by Miami Spanish-language television station WSCV, 66 percent of Cubans in South Florida chose him as the exile leader who "best represents the ideals of a free Cuba." In addition, 93 percent had a "very favorable" or "favorable" view of him.

Mas Canosa's exile in the United States began in 1960. He joined Brigade 2506 and was set to take part in the Bay of Pigs invasion, but his ship never re-

Exile leader Jorge Mas Canosa, left, with the late South Florida Congressman Dante Fascell. Mas Canosa, who died in 1997, was known for his access to people of power in Washington. (Courtesy *Miami Herald*)

Mas Canosa at a rally for the election of George Bush. (Courtesy *Miami Herald*)

ceived orders to land. He then worked at various blue collar jobs for some years, as a milkman, dock worker, and shoe salesman. In 1971, with a $50,000 loan, he bought a small telecommunications company in Puerto Rico named Iglesias y Torres. He anglicized the name to Church & Tower and began to do business in South Florida. The firm won contracts to lay down telephone cables in South Florida. It is the foundation of the present-day MasTec, Inc., which by the late 1990s had annual revenue of more than one billion dollars.

Yet his prominence in the history of Cuban America rests not on his business acumen, but on his political prowess. Mas Canosa had extraordinary personal access to decision makers in Washington, the kind that few leaders of any other cause could match. Every American president since the creation of the Cuban American Foundation in 1981 sought his advice, and few decisions regarding Cuban policy were made against his wishes.

"The objectives were clear," Mas Canosa recalled years later. "To keep the pressure on Castro and to inform the American public and the international community about his atrocities." Mas Canosa, along with his powerful friends, proved to exercise considerable influence over Cuban policy during the 1980s and into the following decade.

One impressive initiative by Mas Canosa and CANF was the establishment of Radio Martí. Created with the objective to "disarm Castro's monopoly of information on the island," Radio Martí provided news and entertainment programs to Cuba. Despite opposition from congressmen who believed it inappropriate for the United States to fund a station with such a mission, the Radio Martí bill passed Congress and was signed into law by President Reagan. On May 20, 1985, the first broadcast was heard over shortwave radio inside Cuba. Henceforth, the

Cuban people had a window to the outside world to view events in a more objective manner than previously possible.

There were other triumphs. In an effort to tighten the U.S. embargo on Cuba, CANF was instrumental in the passage of the 1992 Cuban Democracy Act and the 1996 Cuban Liberty and Democratic Solidarity Act. No other Cuban-American organization has had more influence and effectiveness in forming U.S. policy to Cuba than the Cuban American National Foundation. And it became involved in humanitarian causes, too. CANF created the Cuban Exodus Relief Fund, aimed at bringing Cuban exiles in other countries to the United States. By 1987, the program had brought to America more than 10,000 Cubans without costing the U.S. taxpayers a penny. The foundation found the new arrivals jobs and provided rent payment, scholarships, and medical care.

Most of the Cuban exile community supported Mas Canosa's actions—CANF was beyond argument the most popular organization in the four-decade-old history of *El Exilio*. But there were difficulties. One of the most public fights was with the *Miami Herald* and *El Nuevo Herald* in the late 1980s, when CANF accused the newspapers of being too easy on Fidel Castro. The editors fought back, saying no other newspapers in the United States—the rival *Diario Las Américas* excepted—denounced human rights violations and uncovered economic shortcomings in Cuba anywhere near as regularly. CANF called for a boycott of both dailies, but the dispute eventually wound down, ending up as a sort of draw. Cubans didn't stop buying the paper, and CANF lost none of its influence in Washington or Miami.

CANF was also unpopular with those within the exile community who argued for a softening of the U.S. embargo and a dialogue with the Castro regime. "Soft liners" such as Eloy Gutiérrez Menoyo were critical of CANF's policies and lamented the influence the organization had achieved. They would grow in power during the 1990s.

CANF succeeded because it had the backing of many exiles eager to see their cause represented at the highest levels of power. In turn, CANF's influence depended to a large extent on the Cuban-American vote. So many exiles became American citizens in the 1980s that the percentage of Dade County voters of Cuban origin tripled from what it was at the beginning of the previous decade. They registered for the most part as Republicans, unlike voters from other Hispanic groups, who largely vote Democrat. Cuban voters gave GOP candidates large margins in national elections—upward of 85 percent of the Cuban vote went to the hugely popular Ronald Reagan.

However, Cubans voted for Democrats, too, as long as they had a "hard line" policy regarding the Castro regime. Menéndez, the influential congressman from New Jersey, is a Democrat and so is Florida Senator Bob Graham, who won Cuban votes by margins similar to those that usually go to Republicans. Still, the legacy of the perceived betrayal by Kennedy during the Bay of Pigs lived on—there weren't many Democrats Cuban voters trusted when it came to U.S. policy toward the Castro regime.

CULTURAL RENAISSANCE

As Cubans were growing in economic and political power, they also asserted themselves in the arts. After Mariel—probably in large part because of the artistic figures who arrived in the exodus—a period of creative talent and artistic training generated a cultural awakening in the exile community throughout the United States. Exile publishers in Miami printed hundreds of new titles, nearly all in Spanish. Other Cuban authors had their works published by major English-language houses.

Modern-day writers of the first rank such as Guillermo Cabrera Infante, Heberto Padilla, Severo Sarduy, and Lydia Cabrera made their international reputations while still in Cuba and enhanced their prestige while in exile. Cuban exiles in the United States had a long literary tradition, too, exemplified by José María Heredia in the middle of the nineteenth century and José Martí some decades later. They both are part of the canon of Cuban literature.

In the first narratives by Cubans in America following Castro's takeover, the omnipresent theme was the revolution. There were memoirs, novels, short stories, poems—all of them trying to come to grips with what the authors lost when they had to leave Cuba. Much of it was the work of men and women who were not professional writers, who wrote simplistic sketches of the very real pain the revolution had caused them. Most of the time, they found no publisher so they paid out of their own pockets to have their work printed and distributed.

Still others during this period, most notably Carlos Alberto Montaner, analyzed the revolution with great depth and insight. His work, and the works of many others, were published by Ediciones Universal, a Miami publishing house founded by Juan Manuel Salvat in 1965. Over thirty-five years, Universal has kept Cuban memories alive by publishing everything from the memoirs of ordinary exiles to the sophisticated works of academics. Salvat's bookstore on Calle Ocho has long been a place where Cuban writers and intellectuals sip *cafecito* and talk about literature, history and, inevitably, politics.

The authors of the first two decades of *El exilio* wrote mostly in Spanish, for fellow Cubans. They were almost exclusively interested in exploring their relationship to Cuba and to the Castro regime. They showed little interest in writing about the United States, even about Cuban Miami. The writers of the Mariel generation also focused on similar themes, albeit with the experience of having lived under Castro much fresher in their minds.

This began to change in the 1980s with the emergence of Cuban writers who grew up in the United States. They made the choice to write in English, for a wider audience through mainstream American publishing houses, and to focus on what it meant to be a Cuban in America.

The best known of them is Oscar Hijuelos, winner of the Pulitzer Prize for fiction in 1990 for *The Mambo Kings Play Songs of Love*. Hijuelos, born in New

A tour bus taking part in the New York City Cuban parade of 1989, flying (left to right) *Cuban, American, and Puerto Rican flags.* (Courtesy Emilio del Valle)

York in 1951 of Cuban immigrant parents, explored the Cuban-American condition by setting most of his fiction in the decades before *El exilio* had even begun. Another approach is that of Gustavo Pérez Firmat, a professor of literature with a flair for the popular essay, who is the author of *Next Year in Cuba* and *Life on the Hyphen*, meditations on Cuban-Americanness. Other writers who achieved popularity writing in English include novelists Cristina García, who established her reputation with *Dreaming in Cuban*, and Virgil Suárez, who wrote *Latin Jazz* and *Havana Thursday*.

Cubans also shined in academia. They founded and developed notable Cuban collections at Florida International University and at the University of Miami. The latter had existed for decades, but it expanded greatly during the 1980s. Cuban-born scholars including Jaime Suchlicki at the University of Miami, Jorge Domínguez at Harvard, Luis Aguilar León at Georgetown, Roberto González Echevarría at Yale, and Lisandro Pérez at Florida International University were among the national leaders in their investigations of Cuban history, Castro's rev-

An old Cuban tradition that thrives in the United States is the celebration of formal "Quince" party, given when girls turn fifteen years old. (Courtesy *Miami Herald*)

olution, Cuban literature, and what it meant to be Cuban in the United States. Two other Cuban-born academics, Modesto Maidique and Eduardo Padrón, became presidents of Florida International University and Dade County Community College, respectively.

Over the 1980s, hundreds of events maintained the cultural traditions of the exiles alive, such as the Miami Book Fair International, the Miami Film Festival, the International Hispanic Theater Festival, the Calle Ocho Street Festival, the Miami Carnival, and innumerable concerts of Cuban music and popular plays in the small theaters of Little Havana. Thousands of exiles also kept memories alive in hometown-based social clubs that organized dinners, dances and lectures. These groups came together politically under the umbrella of *Municipios de Cuba en el Exilio*.

By the late 1980s, *El exilio* could look back upon thirty years as Cubans in America. It was in many ways a story of success. Yet the longing for a free Cuba remained unabated, at least for the older generation. They continued to see themselves as a part of Cuban history, the heirs of earlier *exilios* dating back to Félix Varela and José Martí.

However, there was something else now. Over three decades exiles had established themselves culturally and economically in a way earlier Cuban émigrés never had. They brought up a generation that was not only Cuban, but Cuban-American—a five-year-old girl who arrived with her parents in the first waves of 1959 or 1960 was by the end of the 1980s a grown woman in her mid-30s with little if any memory of Cuba, a career "Made in the USA" and American-born children who struggled to speak Spanish even in the cauldron of Cubanness that Miami had become. *El exilio* and its progeny remained part of Cuban history, but almost without realizing it had also become part of the history of the United States.

CHAPTER 10

Rafters and Bittersweet Dreams

1990–Present

During the early 1990s *el exilio* became convinced that the long awaited return to a Cuba free of Castro was imminent. The topic became the obsessive preoccupation on the airwaves of exile radio stations, in homes, and at the outdoor espresso stands. People talked of their own plans to go back, of kneeling down to kiss the Cuban soil, about what kind of future awaited a post-Castro Cuba. Everybody seemed to know somebody who had already packed their bags.

A sense of anticipation pervaded the community. The small theaters of Little Havana put on popular plays about the great day, and a short novel by the popular comedian Guillermo Alvarez Guedes, *El día que cayó Fidel Castro*, or *The Day Fidel Castro Fell*, became a local best-seller. Alvarez Guedes imagined Cubans from all over the United States heading to Miami to celebrate the fall of the dictator in a giant street party.

What had happened to lift expectations so high? One decade earlier, Cuban America was deeply troubled. On the island, Castro was at the height of his international prestige, with troops winning battles in African wars, a new ally in power in Nicaragua, and communist guerrillas in El Salvador fighting to get power. In Miami, the Mariel boatlift had filled neighborhoods with struggling newcomers.

Ten years later the picture had changed completely. The *Marielitos* had joined the broader community, the Sandinistas had been voted out of power, the

Salvadoran guerrillas had become just one more political party, most of the soldiers in Africa had been withdrawn. Even more significant to Cuba's fortunes, the world watched in amazement as communism in Europe collapsed. The Castro regime was isolated. *El exilio* fully expected that without the backing of the now-disappeared Soviet Union—$4 billion a year in subsidies plus the political and military support of what had been a superpower—the regime of Fidel Castro would surely be next to go.

Restoring the Old San Carlos

One sign that Cuban-Americans had come into their own by the early 1990s was that they began to look back—not just to Cuba, which they always had, but to Cuban history in the United States.

Key West's San Carlos Institute, built in 1924 as a successor to the establishment where José Martí did so much for Cuban independence in the nineteenth century, fell into disrepair with the coming of the Castro revolution. In 1973 the bilingual school that had functioned there for almost fifty years closed. Vagrants moved in; books, paintings, and other historically valuable material was lost or damaged. After its façade collapsed in 1981 some locals called for the building's demolition.

Then Rafael Peñalver, a Miami attorney, made saving the San Carlos his personal crusade. He raised $4 million from historic preservation grants from the State of Florida and thousands of private donations. Finally on January 3, 1992, exactly 100 years to the day that José Martí first visited the Institute, the San Carlos reopened.

Today it houses an art gallery, a theater, and a library of books and historical documents relating to the history of Cuba and the Keys. In 1999 it became an affiliate of the Smithsonian Institution, with which it sponsored an exhibit of Cuban postal stamps. The San Carlos has once again become a shrine of Cuban-American culture.

Authorities took the excitement seriously. Local police in Dade County made plans to control the huge crowds expected in the wild celebrations the day Castro fell from power; the state government busied itself with the long-range—Governor Bob Martínez formed the Free Cuba Commission to study how the collapse of the Castro regime would impact Florida.

Anti-Castro political groups looked to the future, too. CANF and other exile organizations began to draft plans for a new Cuban constitution. One umbrella

Ileana Ros Lehtinen celebrating after winning her South Florida Congressional seat in 1992. She was the first Hispanic woman elected to the United States House of Representatives. (Courtesy *Miami Herald)*

group called Unidad Cubana, organized by former *plantado* Andrés Vargas Gómez and radio commentator Armando Pérez-Roura, sought to reopen the armed struggle against Castro. In 1992 it turned over to President George Bush a 300,000-signature petition asking for the annulment of the Kennedy– Khrushchev accord reached during the 1962 Missile Crisis, under which the United States pledged it would not permit U.S.–based exiles to undertake military operations against the Cuban regime in return for the Soviets withdrawing their missiles from the island. Bush, unsurprisingly, turned down the request.

To more effect, Cuban-American organizations worked in Washington to ratchet up economic and political pressure on the Cuban regime. As a result, in 1992 Bush traveled to a public ceremony in Miami to sign into law the Cuban Democracy Act, originally introduced by New Jersey Democratic Congressman Robert Torricelli with the strong backing of CANF. It tightened the embargo by prohibiting foreign-based subsidiaries of U.S. companies to trade with Cuba.

Passage of the law was a reminder that the Cuban-American lobby, with CANF in the lead, wielded enormous influence in official Washington. What is more, everyone expected it to be the final shove that pushed Fidel Castro out of power. Even in domestic politics Cubans in the United States were triumphant, particularly after the 1993 reinstatement of the Dade County bilingual ordinance that had been rescinded at the time of Mariel. *El exilio* felt itself powerful, and on the march.

Nevertheless, Castro did not fall. But he faced serious difficulties. With the economy in a freefall, the regime announced the establishment of an official

Two Bay of Pigs veterans meet in an embrace at the headquarters of Brigade 2506 during ceremonies for the 33rd anniversary of the battle. (Courtesy *Miami Herald*)

"Special Period." It cracked down on the dissident movement with renewed vigor and rationed just about everything, including cooking oil, electricity, and water. This created additional discontent among a populace weary of having to use the infamous rationing cards even when store shelves were practically empty of anything to buy. There seemed no way out, other than leaving the country.

Cubans knew full well that leaving the island without an official exit permit was illegal. But they also knew that acquiring the necessary permit exposed them to the wrath of the regime. As Amnesty International put it, "The desire to emigrate is in itself seen by the Cuban authorities as tantamount to a rejection of the

Cuban political system . . . and those who seek to do so are often labeled as 'counter-revolutionaries' or 'traitors.'"

But the pull of Florida proved powerful. There, just 90 miles from the communist island, was a place where Cubans lived free and had reached a standard of living impossible for Cubans in Cuba to attain. People once again began to take to the sea in leaky boats or flimsy homemade rafts.

MASSACRE AT SEA

One group of 72 Cubans departed the island at three in the morning on July 13, 1994, aboard an old tugboat named *13 de Marzo*. They were immediately spotted by two vessels from the Cuban Ministry of Transport, which gave chase. They followed the refugees for about 45 minutes and caught up to them about seven miles off Havana.

What happened next has made the date a day of mourning in Cuban America. The government vessels rammed the *13 de Marzo* to make it capsize. They fired high pressure water hoses at the refugees on deck that tore off their clothes and ripped babies from the arms of their mothers.

According to the account of a survivor, made public by Amnesty International, "The mothers screamed and implored the attackers to stop directing the water hoses at them because they might cause the young ones to drown. The perpetrators continued using the hoses against the citizens, including the children, trying to drown them by suffocation . . . a third tugboat appeared and attacked forcefully from behind, splitting the boat in two."

The men, women, and children were thrown into the water; then, the account continues, "After nearly an hour of battling in the open sea, the other boats circled round the survivors, creating a whirlpool so that they would drown."

At least 41 people perished, including at least 12 children. The survivors were arrested by Cuban state security.

The Castro regime called the sinking an accident. Two years later the Inter-American Commission on Human Rights concluded that the Cuban government was responsible for the deaths of the 41 people, and that it refused to recover the bodies or allow others to recover them. The regime has never acceded to international calls for an investigation.

It did respond, in its own way, to calls for justice from the people of Cuba. Citizens began wearing black armbands as a sign of mourning, and planned a special mass for the victims of the *13 de Marzo* tragedy. The government detained and questioned those wearing the armbands, and forced cancellation of the church service.

On August 5, in a show of defiance to continued government violence against citizens trying to leave, the people of Havana—according to press reports almost 30,000 of them—took to the streets to demonstrate against the government's actions. It was the largest antigovernment disturbance to have taken place in revolutionary Cuba. The regime quickly stopped it by beating up demonstrators and taking into custody scores of protesters.

But with the dire shortages of goods that the country faced, the intensified crackdown on basic liberties, and now the widespread anger about the victims of the *13 de Marzo*, the Cuban kettle was boiling. Fidel Castro turned once again to his old strategy of opening an escape valve: In the late summer of 1994 he ordered his security forces to stop intercepting those trying to flee.

THE RAFTER EXODUS

What had been a trickle of a few thousand rafters over the first years of the decade became a flood. By mid-September some 32,000 Cubans had arrived in the United States or been picked up by the U.S. Coast Guard It was the largest mass departure of Cubans since Mariel.

But there was one big difference. During Mariel, and also during the Camarioca boatlift, many refugees had been picked up by relatives on boats procured in the United States. Even though many of these vessels were unseaworthy, there was no large-scale loss of life either in 1965 or in 1980.

In the summer of 1994 refugees took to the sea on their own. People were so desperate to leave they used pieces of Styrofoam or plywood, inner tubes or empty oil drums tied together. They would throw in provisions for a few days and hope to somehow get across the stormy, shark-infested Gulf Stream.

"When dreams don't move forward, they fall behind forever," one young man whispered in Cuba to a visiting European camera crew as he sat by his bedside with the lights off shortly before he left the island on a raft. Wishing to remain anonymous and fearing government retribution, explained why he took the enormous risk of leaving clandestinely. "You can risk your life, but if you arrive you have the opportunity to break with everything. . . . It's madness, but sometimes madness is a way out. . . . And such madness may be the only thing that saves you."

The U.S. Coast Guard gets ready to tow a boat jammed with Cuban refugees during the "rafter" crisis of 1994. (Courtesy *Miami Herald*)

Many of the rafters arrived traumatized after seeing loved ones drown. Many of those survivors additionally suffered exposure, sunburn, dehydration. The disasters were engraved in the collective consciousness of Cuban America, particularly those that involved children. There was 8-year-old Daniel Bussot, who helplessly watched as his mother, Julia, and his father, Juan Carlos, disappeared under the waves. He survived the horrifying ordeal with his skin burned by a gasoline spill on the boat. There was Raisa Teresa Santana, a 28-year-old mother who drank sea water after giving her young son Frank the last of the fresh water remaining on her raft. She went into a coma and died two weeks later at a Miami hospital after doctors disconnected life-support. She was declared brain-dead from brain swelling induced by the sea water.

Determination in the face of rafters leaving Cuba. (Courtesy *Miami Herald*)

These deaths, well publicized by Miami's Spanish-language media, became symbols of Cuba's tragedy. They foreshadowed the emotions five years later that surrounded another child survivor of a catastrophic rafter voyage, a boy named Elián González.

Nobody really knows how many other rafts disappeared with no survivors. Some experts have estimated that only half of the rafts that set out from Cuba made it across. Even if that figure is speculative, few people doubt that thousands of Cuban men, women, and children lie dead at the bottom of the sea in the Straits of Florida.

With immigration from Latin America at a high point, the United States was in the midst of one of its periodic outbursts of xenophobia. In this political atmosphere President Bill Clinton—who had faced a Cuban refugee crisis of his own when *Marielitos* rioted in Fort Chafee while he was governor of Arkansas—was not about to tolerate a second Mariel.

His administration ruled that the rafters would not be admitted to the United States. It was a stunning change in American policy, which had traditionally offered almost automatic asylum to Cubans fleeing the island. Instead, the rafters were taken to detention centers in the U.S.–run Panama Canal Zone, or to the

Fear—and relief—in the faces of rafters being rescued. (Courtesy *Miami Herald*)

The risk worked. Young Cuban men and women on a homemade raft made the journey across the Straits and are about to be rescued. (Courtesy *Miami Herald*)

These rafters being held at the Guantánamo Naval Base cut out a model of the Statue of Liberty to remind America of its immigrant traditions. (Courtesy *Miami Herald*)

American naval base at Guantánamo. There rafters were to be warehoused for an indefinite period. Like the felons who arrived during Mariel, they could not go back to Cuba, and were not permitted to enter the United States. They, too, were prisoners in limbo. Except they had been charged with no crime.

That September, the Clinton Administration and Cuba reached an agreement on immigration. The United States reaffirmed its decision to no longer grant automatic asylum to Cuban refugees and agreed to issue 20,000 visas to Cubans each year. The Castro regime, for its part, pledged to return to its former policy of preventing Cuban citizens from leaving without permission.

The pact was criticized by human rights organizations, and by many Cubans in the United States. There was concern that the U.S. government would ignore the needs of Cubans who had a legitimate fear of persecution. There were also denunciations that the United States was, in effect, collaborating with a foreign nation in denying its citizens an internationally recognized right—the right to leave their country of birth without the permission of the government.

Meanwhile the rafters languished in Panama and Guantánamo. That February, the 7,500 held in Panama were airlifted to Guantánamo, where they joined

One of the rafters who evaded the Coast Guard and made it to the shoreline.
(Courtesy *Miami Herald*)

some 20,500 others. Over the first few months, some 10,000 were granted entry on a case-by-case, humanitarian basis. Then in May of 1995 the American government decided it could not keep the refugees in the camps forever. They were finally permitted to enter the United States.

There were, of course, problems in adjusting to life in a new society. But the rafters did not prove a shock to the system, like the Mariel refugees fifteen years earlier. There were fewer newcomers. And the Cuban community of South Florida was much stronger, better able to provide jobs, housing, and training. CANF guaranteed employment and temporary health insurance benefits for a number of the newly arrived refugees; another group, the Cuban American National Council, set up the Hialeah Institute and the Little Havana Institute, alternative educational centers for kids who had trouble adjusting to public schools. The Dade County school system, too, was more prepared; it established the Félix Varela Centers, named for the nineteenth-century exiled educator-priest, easing the transition into the public schools for children who had not only gone through harrowing experiences at sea, but had also lost a year of schooling while held in Guantánamo.

Rafters continued to come regularly, albeit in smaller numbers, for the next few years. There was an increase in the number who arrived on high-speed boats owned by smugglers who charged their U.S.–based relatives thousands of dollars for the ride north. Whether they were smuggled in or came on rickety rafts like their predecessors, they faced one odd provision of the immigration agreements between Cuba and the United States: the so-called wet-dry policy. Those rafters caught in the water were immediately returned to the island; those found on land were permitted to plea their case for asylum.

The difference was not always clear-cut. In one famous case, televised throughout South Florida, dozens of beachgoers watched as a group of six rafters pulled up in the water just yards off the sand at Surfside and jumped and ran and twisted and dove to avoid Coast Guard personnel trying to catch them. The refugees and the Coast Guard both knew that if they made it to the dry sand they could apply for asylum and almost be sure to get it, but if they were caught with their feet still in the water they would be sent back to Cuba. They made it.

Baseball Renaissance

After the retirement of the last generation of players who learned their trade in Cuba before the revolution—Tony Oliva, Luis Tiant, Tony Pérez—Cubans almost disappeared from the major leagues. While 38 Cubans debuted during

Orlando "El Duque" Hernández, who defected after a brilliant career with the Cuban national team and became one of the best post-season pitchers in the storied history of the New York Yankees. (Courtesy *Miami Herald*)

the 1960s, only seven made it between 1970 and 1983.

The following year Danilo Tartabull, son of former outfielder José Tartabull, was called up from the minors by the Seattle Mariners. Then José Canseco made his debut in 1985 with the Oakland A's, and in 1986 Rafael Palmeiro made his initial appearance with the Chicago Cubs. It was the beginning of a wave of Cuban Major Leaguers brought up in the United States, who would go on to shine in the 1990s.

Canseco and Palmeiro, in particular, became true superstars. In 1988 Canseco became the first player to hit 40 home runs and steal 40 bases in one season. Although he was notoriously injury-prone (there were four different years in which he appeared in fewer than 100 games) he had hit 462 career home runs by the end of the 2001 season, the most ever by a player of Hispanic origin. Palmeiro, too, became one of the best sluggers in baseball. Playing for the Cubs, Baltimore Orioles, and Texas Rangers, he had more than 100 RBIs and no fewer than 37 home runs in every season except one between 1993 and 2000.

The Cuban-Americans were joined in the Majors by defectors from the Cuban national team beginning in 1994, when pitcher René Arocha signed with the St. Louis Cardinals. Another defector, Liván Hernández, became the idol of all Miami when he pitched the Marlins to victory in the 1997 World Series. His half-brother, pitcher Orlando "El Duque" Hernández, became one of the most celebrated players in the star-studded New York Yankees, winning a remarkable eight post-season games with no defeats between 1998 and 2000 as his team won three straight World Series.

El Duque's half-brother, Liván, also deserted the Cuban national team. Here he lifts the
MVP trophy he won when he led the Florida Marlins to the 1997 World Series.
(Courtesy *Miami Herald*)

BROTHERS TO THE RESCUE

One of the most visible of exile groups during this time in South Florida was
Hermanos al Rescate, or "Brothers to the Rescue," founded in 1991 by Bay of
Pigs veteran José Basulto in response to the growing number of rafters heading
across the Straits. The Brothers flew small planes between Miami and Havana, ra-
dioing the Coast Guard when they found rafters in trouble. By 1996 they had
flown 1,800 search-and-rescue missions that had helped save the lives of some
4,200 rafters.

That year everything would change for them.

Hermanos al Rescate was more than a strictly humanitarian organization. It

A Brothers to the Rescue plane. (Courtesy *Miami Herald*)

was also a human rights group. Basulto believed that its mission, apart from saving rafter lives, should also be to help nonviolent dissidents in Cuba. In particular, the Brothers became involved with Concilio Cubano, a network of 160 peaceful—and illegal—opposition groups in Cuba that had been formed in late 1995. The Concilio formally asked the Cuban government for authorization to hold its first national meeting on February 24, 1996.

It was an unprecedented development in the history of Castro's Cuba. Never had dissidents united in a single front, and never had any opposition group publicly announced its intention to hold a national assembly.

To spread the word about Concilio Cubano that January, planes flown by the Brothers dropped leaflets over Havana (although the Brothers have acknowledged flying in Cuban airspace, Basulto says this time the leaflets were dropped outside the 12-mile territorial limit and carried to shore by the wind) printed with the thirty articles of the United Nations Declaration of Human Rights. One month later, the Castro government arrested some 180 Concilio members and declared that the group would not be permitted to hold its planned national meeting.

An international scandal began to brew. Here was an unquestionably nonviolent group of individuals in disagreement with the Castro regime, who sought to do no more than get together to discuss that opposition. Yet its leaders were in prison for merely asking for permission to have the meeting. The move against

José Basulto, president of Brothers to the Rescue. (Courtesy *Miami Herald*)

Concilio secured Castro's domestic hold over his people, but at a high price—international human rights organizations as well as American, European, and Latin-American leaders demanded the Concilio leaders be released and permitted to have their meeting.

With pressure mounting against him, many exiles speculate, Castro decided to divert the attention of the world.

The day that Concilio had hoped to have its meeting, February 24, Basulto was piloting his Cessna over the Florida Straits. Alongside him were two other Cessnas carrying four other members of the group. Mario de la Peña was flying one with Armando Alejandre Jr; on the other was Pablo Morales and Carlos Costa, the pilot. Of the four, only Morales was not a U.S. citizen—he was a rafter who had himself been rescued by the Brothers in 1992.

At 3:20 P.M. Basulto was exchanging greetings with Cuban air traffic controllers, informing them in Spanish that he was flying "12 miles to the north of Havana, proceeding on course for a search-and-rescue mission to the east," according to a cockpit recording. He added, "It is a gorgeous day and Havana looks beautiful from where we are. A cordial greeting to you and all the people of Cuba from Hermanos al Rescate."

Suddenly Basulto spotted two aircraft he immediately recognized as Cuban airforce fighter jets, a MiG 29 and a MiG 23. "They are throwing MiGs at us!" he said to three passengers flying with him. "They are going to shoot! They are going to shoot us!"

At about that same moment, according to transcripts obtained by the International Civil Aviation Organization during the subsequent investigation, Cuban ground control radioed to its MiG pilots, "Authorized to destroy."

Basulto saw what he thought was a flair, followed by a plume of smoke rising from the sea. He and de la Peña, on the other plane, tried to radio Costa. There was no answer.

It was no flair. The MiG 29 had fired an R-73 missile that blew up the plane with Costa and Morales. The MiG 29 radioed back to base, "We hit him! ¡Cojones! We hit him! We retired him!" Added the MiG 23, "This one won't fuck around anymore."

Back in Basulto's plane, passenger Sylvia Orondo pulled out a rosary from her purse and started to pray. The Cessna continued to head east, still outside of Cuban waters. De la Peña's plane headed north.

The MiGs radioed their intention to return home, but were ordered to follow the two remaining aircraft. Seven minutes after the first shootdown, the MiGs found the Cessna with de la Peña and Alejandre in international waters, at least eighteen miles outside Cuban airspace.

"We have it, we have it, we're working, let us work!" radioed the MiG 29. It fired another R-73 rocket.

On a fishing vessel below, Tim Reilly looked up to see a streak through the sky, and then something burst in flames. Large pieces of metal fell to the water all around him.

"The other is destroyed, the other is destroyed," radioed the MiG 29 in a frenzy of excitement. "Fatherland or death! ¡Coño! The other one is also down!"

Basulto had seen the streak of the second rocket followed by a ball of smoke suspended in midair. A radio message to de la Peña got no response. Desperate, he tried again several times. Still no answer. Incredulous, Basulto realized that the Cuban jet fighters had shot down two unarmed civilian planes over international waters. He turned off all communication and turned north to try to get back to the safety of American waters. A second set of MiGs went after him, making visual contact with the fleeing Cessna somewhere south of Key West. Then at 3:53

P.M. the jets fighters were ordered to return to base. Basulto made it back to the airport at Opa-Locka.

The shootdown caused an uproar not just in Miami, as had been the case with the sinking of the *13 de Marzo,* but throughout the world. Governments condemned the action as murder. Exiles called for immediate retaliation. President Clinton's advisers even presented him with options for a military strike.

It did not matter to Castro. The day after the shooting, Juan Pablo Roque, a member of Brothers to the Rescue, turned up in Havana to denounce the rest of the group. He along with thirteen others were later indicted for spying for the Castro regime on charges that included conspiracy to shoot down the planes. Five pleaded guilty. Five were found guilty in June 2001 after a six-month trial that caused a sensation in Miami. The remaining four, including Roque, are believed to be living in Cuba. Attention had been diverted to people who were now dead, and away from the dangerous demands of the dissidents of Concilio Cubano.

Two Flights to Freedom

One of the most spectacular defections from the Castro regime was that of Orestes Lorenzo, veteran jetfighter of the war in Angola and a major in Castro's airforce who in 1991 flew his MiG 23 into Boca Chica Naval Air Station in the Florida Keys and asked for asylum.

But his most spectacular deed was yet to come.

Lorenzo's escape had come at the price of leaving behind his wife Victoria, and their two sons, Reyniel, 11, and Alejandro, 6. After his defection, Vicky was harassed by authorities who demanded she call her husband a traitor. When she refused to condemn him, the regime denied the family an exit visa to join Lorenzo in the United States.

He feared his family might never be together again. "If Lorenzo had the balls to take one of our MiGs, maybe he'll also have the balls to come get his family," said Raúl Castro, Fidel's brother and Cuba's Minister of Defense.

Just before Christmas of 1992, after months of secret messages to his wife and preparations based on his intimate knowledge of Cuba's air defense system, the former major took off from Marathon Key flying a 30-year old Cessna and landed on a two-lane highway near the city of Matanzas. There his wife and his children waited. They ran to the old airplane and climbed in, crying and kissing each other for a few seconds that "seemed in slow motion," Lorenzo recalls in his memoirs *Vuelo al Amanecer.* Then he shouted, "Let's go."

The plane took off and headed back to the United States where their new life together awaited.

Former Cuban Air Force Major Orestes Lorenzo, who deserted on a MiG and later flew back to Cuba clandestinely to pick up his wife and children. (Courtesy Zoe Blanco-Roca)

A TOUGHENED EMBARGO

What Clinton actually did, three weeks later, was toughen the embargo by signing the Helms-Burton Act, which he had been reluctant to approve before the shootdown. Helms-Burton, officially known as the Cuban Liberty and Democratic Solidarity Act, was sponsored by Republican Senator Jesse Helms of North Carolina and Republican Congressman Dan Burton of Indiana. It sought to internationalize the embargo by imposing trade sanctions on foreign firms that utilized confiscated American properties in Cuba and by allowing federal authorities to deny visas to executives of such companies. The new law allowed former owners of confiscated properties the right to sue in American courts.

CANF and most other exile groups supported the legislation strongly. So did most Cubans in America. Signing Helms-Burton made Bill Clinton seem tough on Fidel Castro. That perception, along with a concern that Republican candidate Bob Dole had not distanced himself from the anti-immigrant, anti-Hispanic rhetoric that characterized the Republican campaign of 1996, brought Clinton to levels of popularity among Cuban voters unmatched by any Democratic presidential candidate since the disaster at the Bay of Pigs.

In that year's presidential election, just 46 percent of Florida's Hispanic vote—which was largely Cuban—went to Bob Dole, with Clinton winning 42 percent. It was a huge contrast to the days when Republican presidential candidates won 80 percent of the Cuban vote. "Even in the most lopsided Republican stronghold precincts of Hialeah and Little Havana, which Bush and Reagan were sometimes able to carry by margins as high as nine to one, Dole barely received 60 percent of the vote," wrote Darío Moreno, a political scientist at Florida International University.

One of the strongest anti-Castro voices in Congress belongs to Lincoln Díaz Balart. The representative from Miami drafted much of the language of the Helms-Burton Law that strengthened the embargo. (Courtesy *Miami Herald*)

Cuban-American Entertainers Shine

By the 1990s a number of Cuban-American performers had burst into the American pop culture mainstream. Andy García was recognized as one of the greatest actors of his generation, winning an Oscar nomination for his work in "The Godfather Part III." He also produced "Cachao . . . cómo su ritmo no hay dos," a feature-length documentary about the legendary Cuban bass player

Three Cuban divas: talk show host Cristina Saralegui, salsa star Celia Cruz, and Gloria Estefan. (Courtesy *Miami Herald*)

and composer Israel "Cachao" López, co-creator of the mambo. He continued bringing Cuban themes to American audiences in 2000 when he starred in "For Love or Country," in which he portrayed Arturo Sandoval, the jazz virtuoso who defected from Cuba in 1990.

One of Sandoval's partners in founding the celebrated jazz group Irakere in Cuba during the 1970s was another jazz virtuoso, saxophonist/clarinetist Paquito D'Rivera. He defected in 1980 and went on to win three Grammys in the United States. Aside from being one of the world's best instrumentalists, D'Rivera is a composer, known for his work blending rhythms from throughout Latin America, jazz, and elements of classical chamber music.

Another artist who made a splash was the legendary Cuban salsa singer Celia Cruz. Playing to sold-out concerts everywhere, and with nearly seventy-

Miami's favorite star Gloria Estefan waves to her fans during a concert at the American Airlines Arena. (Courtesy *Miami Herald*)

five recorded albums, "The Queen of Salsa," has won a Grammy and the National Medal of Arts, presented by President Bill Clinton in 1994. Other Cuban artists that left their mark include Jon Secada and Albita.

Beginning with her group Miami Sound Machine in the 1980s, Gloria Estefan became perhaps the most recognizable Cuban-American in the United States and certainly the best-selling Cuban-American musician of all time. She sang in both English and Spanish, combining traditional Cuban rhythms with an American pop sensibility in a dozen best-selling albums. The bicultural music she made with her husband, producer Emilio Estefan, was emblematic of the Cuban experience in the United States.

Emilio Estefan founded Miami's Crescent Moon recording studios, where he has been on the leading edge of bringing "Latin pop" into the American mainstream. He has produced songs by Ricky Martin, Jennifer López, Jon Secada, Marc Anthony, Colombian superstar Shakira, and of course his wife Gloria. (Courtesy *Miami Herald*)

RISE OF THE "SOFTLINERS"

Helms-Burton was not universally well received outside of Miami. Internationally, the law angered Canada, Japan, and U.S. allies in Europe and Latin America, who saw it as American interference in their internal affairs. As a result of the pressure, Washington never permitted the provision that allowed lawsuits to go in effect.

In addition, not all Cubans in the United States supported a toughened embargo, or even supported an embargo at all, for that matter.

There still remained far left factions that openly supported the Castro dictatorship, such as the *Maceítos* and their leader Andrés Gómez. They had little credibility and remained inconsequential. One left-wing voice that did become louder in the 1990s was that of radio commentator Francisco Aruca, whose program "Radio Progreso" presented a view that was sympathetic to the Castro regime. Aruca, a Maceíto and participant in *el Diálogo* in 1978, also owned Marazul Tours and Charters, a travel agency with specialization in arranging travel to Cuba that was firebombed a few times.

Aruca became the target of a steady barrage of vehement criticism from anti-Castro exile groups, who campaigned unsuccessfully to get his program off the air. To many people outside of Miami, the crusade against Aruca was evidence of *el exilio's* intolerance for dissenting views about the Castro regime. But to anti-Castro exiles, Radio Progreso was the equivalent of what a Ku Klux Klan radio program would be to African-Americans. They wondered how tolerant blacks would be of a blatantly racist, regularly scheduled broadcast.

The "softliners" also tried to revive the failed *Diálogo* of the 1970s. In May of 1994 a group of Cuban-Americans selected by Fidel Castro traveled to Havana to open talks with the regime. The "negotiations," however, were restricted to issues having to do with U.S. foreign policy toward Cuba. Any discussion of political prisoners or the treatment of dissidents was off limits.

Not that the group had much interest in discussing human rights in Cuba. The regime had, naturally, not invited "hard-line" groups such as CANF or Unidad Cubana. But neither did it invite more "moderate" groups such as CID, which was led by Huber Matos (the former *comandante* in the struggle against Batista who turned against Castro and spent twenty years as a political prisoner) or the Madrid-based Cuban Liberal Union, led by the writer Carlos Alberto Montaner. As a result, the meeting between the Cuban government and its supposed exile adversaries turned out to be a meeting between the Cuban government and its Cuban-American supporters.

Little was accomplished beyond calling for improved relations between Havana and Washington, precisely what Castro had intended. The group exploded in a chant of "Fi-del, Fi-del" when he appeared at a reception. Magda Montiel-Davis, a Miami Democrat who had lost a Congressional election to Ileana Ros Lehtinen two years earlier, stood before Castro visibly awestruck and told him, "Fidel, thank you for all you have done for my people. You have always been my teacher." The scene was broadcast on the news stations in Miami, putting an end to whatever political aspirations Montiel-Davis had left—and to any claim that the *dialoguistas* of 1994 had about holding a middle ground, against the embargo yet concerned about human rights in Cuba.

Despite the blunders of those who traveled to Havana that year, two other groups that opposed the embargo, both founded in 1993, began to be taken seriously. One was the Cuban Committee for Democracy (CCD), noted for its ties to academia; the other was Cambio Cubano, or Cuban Change, led by Eloy Gutiér-rez Menoyo. Both groups stopped short of endorsing the Castro regime; instead, they positioned themselves as middle-of-the roaders in the labyrinth of exile politics—they held themselves out as advocates of a peaceful transition toward democracy in Cuba, a transition they believed the embargo impeded.

The Warrior Turned Dove

Eloy Gutiérrrez Menoyo arrived in Cuba as an exile when his parents left Spain after Franco's triumph in the Spanish Civil War. In the 1950s he fought in the mountains against Fulgencio Batista as a member of the Second Escambray Front, a guerrilla group that was independent of Castro's *26th of July Movement* but allied with it. After falling out with Castro, he went to the

Eloy Gutiérrez Menoyo, the best known of the exile "softliners" who sought negotiations with the Cuban government. (AP/wide world)

United States in 1961 and became a cofounder of Alpha 66, one of the most active of exile paramilitary groups. After being captured in 1965 while in Cuba on a military mission, he spent twenty-two years in Castro's prisons. Upon his release in 1987, exiles hailed him as a hero.

But he abandoned his former militancy and began to advocate negotiations with Castro regime. Those on the other side of the exile political spectrum accuse Gutiérrez Menoyo of naivete for believing Castro can be talked into changing the totalitarian nature of his regime. He has also been accused of not being vocal enough in his criticism of human rights violations on the island.

Gutiérrrez Menoyo remains the most recognizable exile advocate of dialoguing with the Castro government.

CCD focused its efforts in Washington, hoping to become a player equal in stature and influence to its pro-embargo rival, CANF. It attracted eloquent spokespersons such as Alejandro Portes, a sociologist at Princeton University; Marcelino Miyares, who ran a successful television production company in New York City; Alfredo Durán, chair of the Florida Democratic Party from 1976 to 1980; and its executive director Elena Freyre. "Since the end of the Cold War, many Cuban analysts have agreed that U.S. policy toward Cuba is not driven by international concerns but rather by domestic ones [that] reflect the success of conservative Cuban-Americans in mobilizing political support for an agenda that favors the isolation and punishment of the Cuban people because of their government," CCD explains in its official statement of policy. "Our position is that the goal of promoting a democratic Cuba would be better served by constructive engagement rather than by fruitless isolation."

Cambio Cubano, for its part, focused less on Washington than in actively seeking contacts with Havana. Gutiérrez Menoyo met with the then-foreign minister of Cuba, Roberto Robaina, in 1994 in Madrid and again in New York four years later. He also traveled to Cuba in June of 1995, where he met with Fidel Castro. "If the Cuban government is now prepared to show tolerance and respect for the views of those like myself," he wrote in the *Washington Post* op-ed page after his return from Havana, "then indeed a new beginning can be made and we can face the future with renewed hope."

But the Cuban government was not prepared. It refused to negotiate any increase in tolerance or respect for opposing views, regardless of whether Gutiérrez Menoyo, the CCD, or even the U.S. government itself held out improved relations as a carrot. "Our position is that we do not accept any types of conditioning that may affect the country's sovereignty and independence

Alfredo Durán, veteran of the Bay of Pigs and a leading figure in the Cuban Committee for Democracy, which espouses an end to the embargo and negotiations with the Castro government.
(Courtesy *Miami Herald*)

(in order) to solve economic problems or political problems between the United States and Cuba," Castro told CNN when he visited the United Nations in 1995. The theme was repeated in speech after speech, which typically ended with the slogan "Socialism or Death."

And the inflexible position was more than rhetoric. In 1998 a new law established twenty-year prison terms for Cuban citizens who possess or disseminate "subversive literature" or "collaborate" with foreign-based media in an effort to support the U.S. embargo. It was a reaction to a growing movement of "independent journalists" who smuggled to the outside world articles denouncing human rights conditions on the island. Even before the law was passed, in July of 1997, Cuban state security arrested four dissidents who had written a critical document entitled "La Patria es de todos," or "The Homeland is For All." Vladimiro Roca, Felix Bonne, René Gómez Manzano, and Marta Beatriz Roque were imprisoned without trial until March 1999, when they were sentenced to terms of up to five years in prison. They became the most celebrated of imprisoned Cuban dissidents.

The pro-embargo forces in Miami did not keep still as anti-embargo groups grew in importance. Most spectacularly, Jorge Mas Canosa did the unthinkable: He spoke, publicly, to a top official of the Castro regime. The exchange came in a debate broadcast in 1996 by television network CBS Telenoticias between Mas Canosa, the leader of CANF, and Ricardo Alarcón, president of Cuba's National Assembly. "What we want for the Cubans on the island is precisely a system that guarantees them the opportunity to be what we are today—independent people," Mas Canosa said. To the shock of many viewers, he added that if Alarcón were elected president of Cuba in a free election, "we would support him." On the other side, Alarcón denied the charge that basic liberties were suppressed on the island, and declared he would never support a Mas Canosa presidency "because he's not a Cuban."

Many in the press declared Mas Canosa the winner of the debate for presentation of the exile viewpoint with clarity, factual information, and persuasive arguments against the less prepared and seemingly dogmatic Alarcón.

Mas Canosa died a year later. But *el exilio* as a whole continued to make its opinion known. A coalition of several anti-Castro groups organized a pro-embargo march on Calle Ocho in 1998. The 8,000–10,000 demonstrators waved Cuban and American flags, demanding an end to any attempt at improving relations with Cuba while Castro remained in power.

They had reason to worry. The late 1990s were a time when the policy of maintaining the embargo was coming under increased assault, and not just because of the rise of Cambio Cubano and the CCD.

With the death of Jorge Mas Canosa in 1997, many believed—and his enemies hoped—that the influence of CANF, and of pro-embargo groups in general, would be diminished. No doubt, exiles lost their most effective and best known spokesman. Around the time of his death, the move toward improved relations and trade with Cuba, once supported almost exclusively by liberal Democrats, became a favored cause of conservative Republicans from farm states who wanted to sell their produce to Cuba. Three years later, the Congress approved legislation permitting just that—the first significant easing of the embargo since it was imposed.

There was also the pope's milestone visit to Cuba in January 1998. The pontiff's most widely quoted declaration, his hope that "the world open to Cuba, and Cuba to the world," was unmistakably a reproach to the Castro regime as well as a criticism of the U.S. embargo. It lent the moral prestige of the Catholic Church to the anti-embargo cause, but had no effect on the behavior of the Castro government toward political opponents. By the end of the year Cuba Verdad (Cuba Truth), a group of independent journalists, delivered a letter to the Papal Nuncio in Havana that said, "After the Holy Father's visit to our homeland, the world opened to Cuba, but Cuba does not open to the world because this is prevented by the exclusive, intolerant and aggressive nature of the political order imposed by the Communists."

The embargo continued to come under assault in the cultural sphere, too. "The Buena Vista Social Club," an album of traditional Cuban music recorded in Havana with the blessing of the Castro regime, became a top seller in the United States. The group itself, composed of older musicians who had not recorded for years until producer Ry Cooder brought them together, embarked on several highly successful tours

Aerial view of the 1997 Calle Ocho Festival. The annual event has become one of the largest outdoor celebrations in the United States. (Courtesy *Miami Herald*)

of the United States. Their success brought other musical groups from Cuba to America. Los Van Van, a popular dance band, even played in the Miami Arena, inciting the anger of anti-Castro demonstrators who yelled obscenities and threw eggs at concert goers.

Outside of Cuban circles, the controversy was incomprehensible; the exile objections against the musicians from Cuba seemed reactionary. Why protest against such great music?

Most Americans did not understand the political connotations that *el exilio* attached to these concerts. Many Cuban-Americans feared that popularizing what was in essence a product of the Castro regime would open a back door to those hoping to normalize relations regardless of whether the right to dissent was respected on the island. They drew a parallel to the days of apartheid in South Africa when Steve Van Zandt, a member of Bruce Springsteen's E Street Band, brought together an all-star group of international musicians to record "Sun City," an album in which the artists pledged to support the economic and cultural boycott against the apartheid regime. If music was a legitimate weapon to denounce a dictatorship in Africa, Cuban-Americans asked, why were they perceived as intolerant for protesting music that at least indirectly supported a dictatorship in Cuba? Cuban-Americans also wondered why the same people who criticized them for picketing Cuba-based performers did not also criticize the Castro government for not permitting U.S.–based Cuban musicians—like Gloria Estefan, Celia Cruz, or the popular Miami singer Willie Chirino—to perform on the island.

These controversies remained unsettled. What was not in question was that as the century drew to a close Cuban-Americans continued to increase their already profound influence in America.

ELIÁN ARRIVES

At about 8:30 on the morning of Thanksgiving Day 1998, Donato Dalrymple and his cousin Sam Ciancio, out fishing off the coast of Fort Lauderdale, saw something dark and round bobbing in the choppy three- to five-foot seas. When they came closer they saw a hand and a small head of wet hair. To their astonishment, they had found a young boy. They pulled him out of the water. "¿Hablas español?" Dalrymple asked in his rudimentary Spanish. The child, weak and sunburned, answered, "Sí."

His name was Elián González, and he was five years old. Elián spent Thanksgiving at Joe DiMaggio's Children Hospital, in nearby Hollywood. To the surprise of doctors, the next day he was well enough to be discharged. He was picked up by Miami relatives that included his great uncle Lázaro González and Lázaro's daughter Marisleysis. They took him to their home in a working class section of Little Havana.

As it turned out, Elián was one of three survivors among the fourteen people who had left the Cuban coast near the city of Cárdenas the previous Monday aboard a 17-foot boat.

Although the exact details of the disastrous trip remain clouded, authorities believe that the motor stopped running one day into the trip. Sometime later, it is unclear when, a storm made the boat capsize. The passengers desperately clung on in the darkness to two inner tubes, tossed by the waves. Hanging on to one of the big truck tires were Nivaldo Fernández and Ariane Horta, the only two others who lived through the ordeal. Hanging on to the other tube was a group that included Elián and his mother, Elisabet Brotons. As time passed people began letting go, and drowning. The inner tubes continued to drift, coming closer to shore. In the dead of night that Wednesday but in sight of the lights of South Florida, an exhausted Elisabet gave Elián the last of the fresh water and tied him to the inner tube. Then she implored Fernández and Horta, they have said, to "help me, help me make sure the boy makes it to freedom." Later that night waves separated the two groups.

Elián González salutes the media while playing with other children in his Miami relatives' home. (Courtesy *Miami Herald*)

Before the sun rose on Thanksgiving morning, Elián watched his mother disappear below the waves. He was alone on that inner tube, floating semiconsciously and traumatized when the fishermen found him.

It might have been one more of the thousands of "rafter" tragedies, surely heart-rending and laden with symbolism about the plight of Cuba but ultimately forgotten except by the people who lived through it. But that was not to be.

The night Elián left the hospital he spoke by telephone to his father Juan Miguel, who was divorced from Elisabet. The same night, standing outside his small Little Havana house, Lázaro said to reporters that the boy should not be sent back to Cuba. "His mother lost his life for him to be here," he said according to the *Miami Herald*. "God wanted him here for freedom, and he's here and he will get it."

That Sunday the government of Cuba demanded the immediate return of the boy. The same day in Miami Congresswoman Ileana Ros Lehtinen visited the González home to offer support, as did well-known exile leaders such as Brothers to the Rescue leader José Basulto. CANF printed posters with a photo of Elián. Prominent lawyers volunteered their services.

The battle lines were drawn.

MORE THAN A FIGHT FOR CUSTODY

To many Americans the Elián González case could not have been simpler or more clear-cut: The boy belongs with his father. To Cubans, it was not at all simple. Escaping Castro and living in freedom in the United States was the core of the Cuban-American identity; losing loved ones in the treacherous flight from Cuba made the experience even more powerful. It was inconceivable to most of Cuban Miami that the very country which had given them freedom would send a boy back to the country his mother had given her life to flee.

Almost immediately, the case became an obsession. Large crowds of exiles demanding that Elián be allowed to stay gathered in front of the González home. The fascination spread well beyond Miami. Throughout the United States and even much of the world the name "Elián" became a household word, the face of the boy with the short dark hair and impish smile recognizable to millions of people. They asked, Should Elián go or stay? Of course, what ultimately would decide the question was the law.

Attorneys for the Miami relatives took the position that Elián had as much right to petition for political asylum as any adult refugee. The Immigration and Naturalization Service (INS) would have none of that. In a nationally televised news conference in early January, INS Commissioner Doris Meissner, with President Clinton by her side, announced the official ruling that because Elián was a minor, he had no right to seek asylum without the consent of his father. The boy had to be returned to Cuba within one week, she said.

Cubans in Miami took to the street to protest, interrupting traffic at several key intersections. The family filed an appeal. Elián stayed put for a time.

Late that month, the Castro government surprised exiles by allowing the boy's grandmothers to go to the United States. They arrived in New York City, their trip arranged by the National Council of Churches, an organization that had long been active in opposing the embargo. At first the grandmothers lobbied in Washington and New York for the boy's return. Then, three days after their arrival, they flew into Miami to see their grandchild.

Demonstrators in front of Elián's home. (Courtesy *Miami Herald*)

Outside the González home, exiles made a carpet of flowers to welcome the grandmothers. But after landing at Tamiami Airport the women refused to go to Little Havana, citing fear of violence from the anti-Castro crowds. They turned around and flew to Washington that evening, the plane taking off at the same time that Lázaro and Marisleysis pulled up at the airport—without the boy—to meet with them.

Then the INS ordered Lázaro to bring Elián to his grandmothers on neutral ground. All parties agreed on the home of Sister Jeanne O'Laughlin, a nun who was president of Miami's Barry University.

The Miami relatives stayed in one room while nuns brought Elián to his grandmothers in another. The child, O'Laughlin later said, appeared nervous at first but eventually became playful. The adults remained distrustful, the atmosphere tense. The Miami group worried that the child would be snatched. The grandmothers refused to greet or even see Lázaro and Marisleysis.

Inside the González home, (from left) *Gloria Estefan, Andy García, Emilio Estefan, and Miami-Dade Mayor Alex Penelas plan what they are going to say outside the house at a news conference the day that the boy's Miami relatives defied a federal government deadline.* (Courtesy *Miami Herald*)

The meeting's end brought yet another twist to the Elián saga: O'Laughlin, who had initially supported the boy's return to Cuba, changed her mind.

"Somewhat naively I felt that this was a straightforward custody case, and that Elián should be returned to his surviving parent. My position changed after witnessing the fear which existed in the eyes of Elián's grandmothers, and absorbing the events which unfolded in my home," she testified in an affidavit before a Miami federal court. "I am convinced that the grandmothers were not free to respond or act as they would toward their family, and that the situation was controlled by Cuban officials."

The women flew back to Cuba without their grandchild.

As the saga continued, crowds in front of Elián's Miami home grew larger and more fervent. They saw something mystical, even religious, in the story of the

A young woman's reaction to a judge's ruling in favor of the INS. (Courtesy *Miami Herald*)

boy. People left flowers in front of a bank in Little Havana, insisting they had seen an image of the Virgin Mary on its glass door—a heavenly message for Elián, they believed. There was a story that he was saved by dolphins who kept him afloat on that inner tube. "The son of dolphins," wrote Zoe Valdés, an award-winning Cuban novelist living in Paris.

On a more practical note, a radio marathon raised $240,000 for the boy's legal defense. And to the shock of most non-Cuban—or at least non-Hispanic—South Floridians, Miami-Dade County Mayor Alex Penelas and Joe Carollo, mayor of the city of Miami, pledged that their police departments would not cooperate with the INS if it decided to actually go in and remove Elián from his Little Havana home.

Much speculation centered on the insistence of Elián's father Juan Miguel, still in Cuba, that he wanted the boy returned and had no wish to live in the United States or even go there to get his son. Exiles wondered whether he was speaking freely or being coerced by the Castro government. In a way, it did not seem to matter. Guillermo Cabrere Infante, Cuba's foremost novelist and an exile in London, summed up what so many Cuban-Americans felt when he wrote, "They ask me if I agree that the boy Elián should be returned to Cuba. My answer is always a question. How can an exile agree, an exile who fled Castro and took with him his two daughters because he did not want them to live in misery and fear?"

In Cuba the regime organized marches to claim the boy. It also accepted the designation of Greg Craig, one of Bill Clinton's lawyers during the impeachment proceedings over the Monica Lewinsky scandal, as Juan Miguel's attorney in Washington.

The father won a legal victory in late March when a federal judge upheld the INS ruling of January. The Miami family appealed. Tens of thousands of people holding candles and flashlights took part in a prayer vigil for Elián on the streets of Miami.

Less than a week later, the Castro government surprised everyone again: Juan Miguel González was allowed to travel to Washington with his new wife and six-month-old child. He met with Attorney General Janet Reno, alone in her office. Sitting in front of the top law enforcement officer in the United States, it was the perfect opportunity for Juan Miguel to defect. That he did not choose to do so was the first indication that he indeed had no wish to ask for political asylum.

Over the next days Juan Miguel met with anti-embargo activists and congressmen sympathetic to Castro such as José Serrano and Charles Rangel, Democrats from New York. But everybody knew he was in America for his son. And public opinion, at least among people who were not Cuban, was firmly on his side. In a *Miami Herald* poll, 71 percent of non-Cuban whites and 84 percent of non-Cuban blacks said that Elián should be returned to his father "immediately"; 55 percent of non-Cuban Hispanics and 80 percent of Cubans said he should stay.

The presence of Elián's father in the United States upped the pressure, as well as the stakes for everybody. To those who wanted Elián to stay, taking the boy back to Cuba would be not just a misfortune for one child, but also a very public defeat in their struggle against Fidel Castro. Senator Bob Torricelli tried to use his good relationships with the Justice Department, Craig, and CANF to broker a compromise under which the Miami relatives, Elián, and his father would all

Arturo Sandoval played the Cuban and American national anthems before thousands of people outside the house in Miami. (Courtesy *Miami Herald*)

meet at the Vatican Embassy to talk things out. But the deal fell through. The Miami relatives wanted no preconditions, just a family discussion about Elián's future; Juan Miguel and his lawyer insisted there had to be a transfer of custody.

Late that night Lázaro stood outside his door speaking to a large group of reporters. He said he would obey any INS order to give up the boy, but insisted they would have to come get him. It was, in essence, a dare. A meeting the next day at the home of Sister Jeanne O'Laughlin between Janet Reno and the Miami family with its lawyers changed nothing.

But on April 13, the next day, a judge from the 11th Circuit U.S. Court of

Protest leader Ramón Saul Sánchez addresses the crowd outside Elián's home.
(Courtesy *Miami Herald*)

Appeals ordered that Elián González could not be taken out of the country until the full court reviewed the motion for asylum. Although the ruling did not actually prohibit the INS from taking the boy and turning him over to his father, the simple knowledge that the boy was going to remain in the United States at least until the case could be heard was enough for Cuban Miami to celebrate a victory.

That day the crowd near the González Little Havana home grew larger than ever, "energized by people who had not previously participated in the protest—well-dressed bankers clutching cell phones, uniformed dental hygienists, suburban mothers pushing baby strollers," reported the *Miami Herald*. Tens of thousands of people crowded the neighborhood's streets praying, singing, crying, cheering, hugging one another, all for a little boy. A national television audience watched the extraordinary outpouring of emotion.

Well known Cuban-Americans also came to lend Elián their support, from exile activists to politicians to prominent businessmen to celebrities like Andy García and Gloria Estefan. Outside the house before the huge crowd, Arturo Sandoval, the great trumpet player who had escaped Castro's Cuba nearly ten years earlier, played a moving rendition of the "Star Spangled Banner" and the Cuban National Anthem. People listened spellbound, in complete silence, tears running down many cheeks.

Nothing like it had happened in forty years of exile. The modest little stucco house on NW Second Street and 23rd Avenue had become the epicenter of *el exilio*, the very soul of a people who had lost nearly everything to Castro's regime but managed to rebuild their lives in a new nation. It was a defining moment. Thousands of Cuban-Americans were united by a profound emotional certainty that little Elián González embodied their own stories and that he, like them, deserved to live in freedom. A buzz of pride ran through the crowd like electricity. It was a fine day to be Cuban in America.

Elián González, calm in the midst of the storm, shortly before the INS raid that forcibly removed him from his relatives' home. (Courtesy *Miami Herald*)

The huge crowd remained outside the house over the next few days, waiting for a ruling from the full court. They bedecked the outside of the modest González home with homemade signs and flags, not only of the United States and Cuba, but also the flags of Israel and just about every Spanish-speaking nation.

One group was making other preparations. Knowing that the INS was still not barred from getting Elián, Ramón Saul Sanchez, of the exile group Movimiento Democracia, borrowed from Martin Luther King's techniques of civil disobedience and began to train people to form a human chain to block the door of the González house. Their practice sessions were watched by throngs of reporters and beamed to the world by the dozens of television satellite trucks parked around the neighborhood. Whatever happened, the world was sure to see it.

The ruling from the full court, or at least a temporary one, was handed down April 20. It changed nothing, actually, since it simply affirmed the single judge's order of the previous week that Elián was to stay in the United States until the court heard the appeal. But once again thousands of people made their way to join the thousands of others celebrating outside the González home. People cheered, cried, hugged each other. "Let's thank God. Let's thank America," said Sánchez to the joyful crowd. "This is not a final victory, but a step in the right direction, that Elián is beginning to be heard by the court system."

There was still, of course, the matter of the INS. Although Elián was required by law to stay in the United States for now, there was no legal bar to prevent federal agents from taking Elián to his father, as long as Juan Miguel promised to wait out the appeals process.

BROKEN HEARTS

And so it happened. Two days after the court ruling, at about 5 A.M., some thirty federal agents drove up in four white vans to the González home. The throngs had thinned out after the festivities of the last few days, leaving only a few dozen protestors outside the house. The agents jumped out of their cars, firing tear gas to hold the crowd back. They used pepper spray to subdue the few who tried to stop them, and held some of them down with shotguns aimed at their heads.

The agents broke down the doors to the González house and burst in, guns drawn. They ransacked Marisleysis's bedroom, where Elián slept, and found him in a closet in the arms of Donato Dalrymple, the man who rescued him at sea five months earlier. "¿Qué está pasando, qué está pasando?" the boy screamed. "What is happening, what is happening?" One agent leveled a semiautomatic weapon at Elián and Dalrymple, as shown in the now famous photograph taken by AP photographer Alan Díaz. A female agent took the boy and wrapped him in a blanket. She ran outside surrounded by other agents, carrying the crying, panic-stricken child into a van. They sped off.

Inside the house people were in shock. Among them was the prominent Miami lawyer Aaron Podhurst and Carlos Saladrigas and Carlos Manuel de la Cruz two of the most influential business and community leaders in South Florida. As the agents rushed in, they were on the telephone with Janet Reno herself, trying to work out a last-minute compromise. "We were in the house negotiating in good faith when we heard a noise and everyone started saying they are here,"

Angry demonstrators after the raid. (Courtesy *Miami Herald*)

Saladrigas told the *Miami Herald*. "They pointed guns to our heads and released pepper spray. I've never felt so betrayed in my whole life."

Elián was taken to Homestead Air Reserve Base, and from there he flew to Andrews Air Force Base, where he reunited with his father.

By the time people woke from bed that morning news of the raid was all over television. Marisleysis seemed to be on every channel, weeping, taking cameras on a tour of the wrecked home to show what had happened. Lázaro, too, cried. Outraged people took to the streets in anger. The demonstrations lasted almost the entire day. In some places, young men turned over garbage containers and bus benches and threw rocks at passing police cars. They set more than 100 fires. Police in riot gear quelled the disturbances, firing tear gas and making some 270 arrests.

It was not a good image of Cubans for the country to see. The cream of Cuban Miami organized a peaceful protest one week later, to show America that Cubans knew how to show their pain without violence. Some 100,000 people filled Calle Ocho to mourn for Elián.

The massive demonstration and prayer vigil in Little Havana one week after the INS raid. (Courtesy *Miami Herald*)

Members of Mothers Against Repression marching in Washington, D.C., in front of the White House. They are protesting the INS's forced removal of Elián from his Miami relatives' home. (Courtesy *Miami Herald*)

Elián spent the next two months with his father at the Wye Plantation in rural Maryland and later at a home in Washington, both sponsored by the federal government. It was almost anti-climactic when the 11th Circuit Court of Appeals rejected the last legal pleas from Elián's Miami relatives on June 23. Lawyers filed an appeal with the Supreme Court. Five days later it issued a terse one-sentence statement, "The application for stay presented to Justice [Anthony] Kennedy and by him referred to the court is denied." It was the final word in Elián González' American odyssey.

That evening Elián flew back to Cuba with his dad, seven months after his miraculous rescue at sea.

The saga of Elián González shook *el exilio* like nothing had since the fiasco at the Bay of Pigs. For all of its success in business affairs, for all of its influence on life in Miami, for all of its considerable political clout in Washington, it helplessly watched its cherished dream of keeping the little boy in the United States come to an end in the federal agents' storming a small home in Little Havana.

What's more, the deep anguish that afflicted so many Cubans after the raid was not shared by other Miamians, widening the already wide gulf that split the local ethnic groups. At workplaces, Cubans and non-Hispanics who worked together spent days studiously avoiding each other. Some places it got worse—at one anti-Cuban demonstration, blacks marched next to whites waving Confederate flags to protest Cuban influence in South Florida.

Top journalists at the newsweeklies and leading newspapers in the country felt free to write things about Cuban-Americans that would never be written about any other ethnic group. *Philadelphia Inquirer* columnist Elmer Smith said Cubans were "shameless zealots." To Pete Waldmeir of the *Detroit News*, Cubans were "a bunch of wackos." Syndicated columnist Molly Ivins wrote of "revanchist nutters." Even in milder allusions, there was a decided lack of sympathy for the anti-Castro cause. *Time* referred to "Miami's rabidly anti-Castro lobby," while *Newsweek* said the controversy over Elián is a reminder of "the Cuban exile community's endless feud with Fidel Castro."

Cuban-Americans saw a double standard: Would the NAACP ever be characterized as a "rabidly anti-racist lobby"? Were anti-apartheid activists ever depicted in a mainstream publication as stuck in an "endless feud with P. W. Botha"?

Opponents of the embargo, too, saw an opening. That April, former Democratic Senator Gary Hart wrote an op-ed piece in *The New York Times* suggesting that with Cuban-American's political power weakened by the Elián controversy, the time was ripe to move toward lifting the embargo. Neither did the National Council of Churches nor an anti-embargo congressman hesitate to tie a change in America's Cuban policy to the fortunes of little Elián.

The Cuban-American Economic Miracle

Cuban-Americans have an outstanding record of success in business affairs. According to *Hispanic Business* magazine, Cuban-Americans own almost 30 percent of the largest 500 Hispanic-owned businesses in the United States, even though they make up less than 5 percent of the 13.7 million Hispanics age 15 or older. They own 40 percent of the top 25 firms, including number one MasTech, Inc., a publicly traded billion dollar engineering firm.

One outstanding story is that of Carlos Saladrigas and José Sánchez, founders of Vincam Group, an employee leasing company. Both arrived penniless but eager to succeed in their adopted homeland. Their success was largely based on achieving higher education, having a tremendous work ethic, and possessing plenty of perseverance and drive. In 1999, their company was sold to Automatic Data Processing for almost $300 million.

Cubans also distinguished themselves at the highest levels of corporate America. Carlos Gutiérrez was CEO of Kellogg; Tony White was CEO of Fortune-1000 company Perkin-Elmer; Emilio Alvarez-Recio was vice president of global advertising for Colgate-Palmolive; Nestor Carbonell was vice president of international public affairs for PepsiCo; Angel Martínez was chief marketing officer at Reebok.

The best known and most widely admired Cuban-America executive was Roberto Goizueta. When he was named CEO of Coca-Cola in 1981, stock had plummeted by half and the company was barely making money. Goizueta took Coca-Cola, which then had a market value of $4.3 billion, and turned it into a $180 billion global enterprise— a whopping 3,500 percent turnaround during his tenure.

The late chairman of Coca-Cola, Roberto Goizueta.
(Courtesy *Miami Herald*)

The Elián effect made itself felt in the presidential election of 2000. It was one of the closest races in American history, but to Cubans it was no contest. Still embittered by the dawn raid that took the boy from his relatives' Miami home, some 80 percent of them voted for George W. Bush. They saw in Al Gore a continuation of the Clinton Administration under whose orders the raid had taken place.

Realizing the depth of the problem South Florida's most prominent Cuban leaders began to organize a national publicity campaign to rehabilitate the image of the community. Some even wondered whether *el exilio* had been too strident in its battle to keep Elián in America. The protests that snarled traffic, the street disturbances the day of the raid—perhaps it was not surprising that members of other communities would be angry. For his part, Mayor Penelas, under fire from non-Cubans for his announcement that local police would not help the INS in its raid, tried to reach out to non-Hispanic constituents. He met with community activists of all of South Florida's ethnic groups to put in place "Mosaic 2000," an initiative meant to promote interracial dialogue.

Changing times brought conflict among anti-Castro forces, too. In the summer of 2001 there was a rift in the Cuban American National Foundation, now under the leadership of Jorge Mas Santos, who had succeeded his late father Jorge Mas Canosa.

Earlier that year CANF helped the White House put together a plan that called for the United States to send financial support to dissidents and independent businesses in Cuba. This angered the more traditional activists, who worried that the money would support groups that worked against Castro but tacitly accepted Cuba's socialist constitution instead of challenging it altogether.

More controversially, CANF supported bringing the 2001 Latin Emmy Awards to Miami even though among the nominees were musicians from Castro's Cuba. It was a decision that broke with the long-standing opposition to contacts with musicians from the island, who were seen by many as envoys of the Castro dictatorship. Mas Santos said he took the decision to show that exiles understood tolerance and the right of free speech. But that summer Ninoska Pérez Castellón and her husband Roberto Martín Pérez, two of the best known members of the CANF leadership, resigned in protest. It was the most controversial development in Cuban America since Elián.

By then the preoccupation with Castro had taken on a new dimension, what some Cubans were calling "biological inevitability." The issue was not so much how to overthrow Castro the next day, but whether Castro, in his late 70s, would wake up alive the next day. To elderly exiles, it became a race against time. They wanted to outlive the dictator and see their decades-old dream of a Cuba without Castro come true.

Many questions remained after "biological inevitability" had reached its due course. What would happen in a post-Castro Cuba? Who would be its leaders? How could the nation recreate a democratic civic life after its people had endured four decades of repression? These questions haunted older Cubans. Yet it was the younger, U.S.–bred generation that was destined to deal with them. Although the future of their ancestral nation lay in the hands of the Cubans in Cuba, Cuban-

Miami schoolchildren march down Calle Ocho in the annual José Martí parade.
(Courtesy *Miami Herald*)

Americans will surely play a major role with their business know-how and their understanding of the workings of democracy.

They will also play a major role in shaping the future of South Florida. The younger generation of local Cuban-American leaders, it seemed, had come to terms with the realization that their community occupied a position unique in America. In other heavily Hispanic cities throughout America, Hispanics were demanding a fair share of power. In Miami, the question was how Hispanics should share with others the power they had already accumulated.

And so Cuban life goes on in the United States. Cubans in America at the beginning of a new century kept alive their dream of seeing democracy flourish in the island of their birth, just like Cubans in America had during the Spanish colonial days of Félix Varela and José Martí, during the *machadato*, and during the Batista dictatorship. They had inherited a legacy of tragedy.

But they had also turned it into a story of triumph over adversity. America's Cubans had created for themselves a narrative of success in a nation that was not always sympathetic to them, yet received them with generosity and provided the freedom and opportunity that they had been seeking.

Although there remain newcomers to assimilate, ethnic tensions to be eased, and Cuba policy to be fought over, Cuban-Americans have constructed their own identity. It has to do with the pain of an old homeland that is suffering, and the pride of having contributed so much to a new homeland.

The terrorist attacks of September 11, 2001, shook the United States to its core. The heinous crime left Americans filled with sadness, anger, and resolve to support our nation and the world in combating terrorism on all fronts.

The same emotions were palpable among Cuban-Americans. The day of the attacks, Cuban-Americans in Miami took to the streets to protest once again. But this time their protests were not aimed against Castro's Cuba—the protests were against those who had inflicted so much pain and suffering on their adopted homeland. They rallied around a flag, as they had so often done during so many exile crises, but this time it was the American flag they held, while singing "God Bless America." The flags stayed up, and not just in Miami. Cuban-Americans throughout the United States raised American flags in their homes, tied them to car antennas, pinned them to lapels. In Miami, they mobilized by the thousands in a show of support, standing in long lines to donate blood for victims, contributing large and small amounts of money to relief agencies, and taking part in the many spontaneous vigils that took place in the days following the attack. They realized they were more American than they thought before September 11.

Bibliography

Printed Books and Articles

Enciclopedia de Cuba, Playor, Madrid, 1974.

Aguilar, Luis: *Cuba 1933*. Cornell University Press, Ithaca, New York, 1972.

Alvarez Borland, Isabel: *Cuban American Literature of Exile*. University of Virginia Press, 1998.

Andrés Hernández (editor): *The Cuban Minority in the United States, Final Report*. Florida Atlantic University, Boca Raton, Florida, 1974.

Antonio, Jorge; Suchlicki, Jaime & Leyva de Varona, Adolfo: *Cuban Exiles in Florida: Their Presence and Contribution*. University of Miami, North/South Center Miami, 1991.

Arana, Luis Rafael & Manucy, Albert: *La construcción del Castillo de San Marcos*. Eastern National Park and Monument Association, 1992.

Arenas, Reinaldo: *Necesidad de Libertad*. Kosmos Editorial, Mexico City, 1986.

Batista, Fulgencio: *Respuesta*. Sánchez, Mexico City.

Bonsal, Philip W.: *Cuba, Castro, and the United States*. University of Pittsburgh Press, Pittsburgh, 1971.

Bonsal, Stephen: *When the French Were Here*. Kenikat Press, Port Washington, NY, 1968.

Bosch, Adriana: *Orlando Bosch, el hombre que yo conozco*. Editorial Sibi, Miami, 1988.

Boswell, Thomas & Curtis, James: *The Cuban-American Experience*. Rowmand and Allanheld, Totowa, NJ, 1983.

Bourne, Peter: *Fidel, A Biography of Fidel Castro*. Dodd, Mead and Co., New York, 1986.

Bretos, Miguel: *Cuba and Florida*. Historical Association of Southern Florida, 1991.

Carbonell, Nestor T.: *And the Russians Stayed: The Sovietization of Cuba*. William Morrow and Co., New York, 1989.

Casal, Lourdes & Prohías, Rafael: *The Cuban Minority in the United States, Preliminary Report*. Florida Atlantic University, Boca Ratón, Florida, 1974.

Clark, Juan, Jose I. Lasaga, & Rose S. Reque: *The 1980 Mariel Exodus: An Assessment and Prospect*. Council for Inter-American Security, Washington D.C. 1981.

Clark, Juan: *Cuba, mito y realidad*. Saeta Ediciones, Miami, 1990.

Clark, Juan: *The Cuban Exodus: Background, Evolution, Impact*. Union of Cubans in Exile, Miami, 1977.

Conde, Yvonne: *Operation Pedro Pan*. Routledge, New York, 1999.

Cortes, Carlos (editor): *Cuban Exiles in the United States*. Arno Press, New York, 1980.

Cortina, Rodolfo & Moncada, Alberto (editors): *Hispanos en los Estados Unidos*. Ediciones de Cultura Hispánica, Madrid, 1988.

Cunningham, Barbara: *The New Jersey Immigrant Experience*. Wm. H. Wise & Co., Union City, NJ, 1977.

Davis, Burke: *The Campaign That Won America: The Story of Yorktown*. Eastern Acorn Press, New York, 1970.

De Zéndegui, Guillermo: *Ambito de Martí*. Escuela Gráfica Salesiana, Madrid, 1954.

Dickinson, Jonathan: *Jonathan Dickinson's Journal*.

Dominguez, Jorge I.: *Cuba: Order and Revolution*. Harvard University Press, Cambridge, MA, 1978.

Encinosa, Enrique: *Escambray, la guerra olvidada*. Editorial Sibi, Miami, 1988.

Fermoselle, Rafael: *The Evolution of the Cuban Military*. Ediciones Universal, Miami, 1987.

Galván, Raúl: *Cuban Americans*, Marshall Cavendish, New York, 1995.

Garcia, Maria Cristina: *Havana/USA: Cuban Exiles and Cuban Americans in South Florida, 1959–1994*. University of California Press, Berkeley, 1996.

González Echevarría, Roberto: *The Pride of Havana, A History of Cuban Baseball*. Oxford University Press, New York, 1999.

González Pando, Miguel: *The Cuban Americans*. Greenwood Press, Westport, CT, 1998.

Griffin, William B.: *Here They Once Stood: The Tragic End of the Apalache Missions*. University of Florida Press, 1951.

Grillo, Evelio: *Black Cuban, Black American: A Memoir*. Arte Público Press, Houston, Texas, 2000.

Haslip-Vieira, Gabriel: *The Evolution of the Latino Community in New York City*. University of Notre Dame Press, South Bend, IN, 1996.

Henderson, Ann L. & Mormino, Gary R. (editors): *Spanish Pathways in Florida*. Pineapple Press, Sarasota, Florida, 1992.

Isern, José: *Pioneros Cubanos en USA*. Cenit Printing, Miami, FL, 1971.

Jiménez, Onilda: *La mujer en Martí*. Ediciones Universal, Miami, 1999.

LaFarelle, Lorenzo: *Bernardo de Galvez, Hero of the American Revolution*. Eakin Press, Austin, Texas, 1992.

Larzelle, Alex: *The 1980 Cuban Boatlift*. National Defense University Press, Washington D.C., 1988.

Llerena, Rafael & Phillipson, Lorrin: *Freedom Flights*. Random House, New York, 1980.

Lorenzo, Orestes: *Vuelo al amanecer*. St. Martin's Press, New York, 1994.

Mañach, Jorge: *Martí el Apóstol*. Espasa Calpe, Madrid, 1942.

Manucy, Albert: *Sixteenth Century St. Augustine*. University Press of Florida, Gainesville, 1997.

Marquez Sterling, Carlos & Marquez Sterling, Manuel. *Historia de la Isla de Cuba*, Regents Publishing, New York, 1975.

Marquez Sterling, Carlos: *José Martí, sintesis de una vida extraordinaria*. Editorial Porrúa, Mexico City, 1998.

Martí, José: *Obras Completas*. La Habana, 1953.

Moreno Fraginals, Manuel: *Cuba/España/Espãna/Cuba*. Grijalbo Mondadori, Barcelona, 1995.

Mormino, Gary R. & Pozetta, George E.: *The Immigrant World of Ybor City*. University of Illinois Press, Urbana, 1987.

Oppenheimer, Andrés: *Castro's Final Hour*. Simon and Schuster, New York, 1992.

Oviedo, José Miguel: *La niña de New York*. Fondo de Cultura Económica, Mexico City, 1989.

Pedraza, Silvia & Ruben G. Rumbaut (editors): *Origins and Destinies: Immigration, Race and Ethnicity in America*. Wadsworth, Belmont, 1996.

Perez Firmat, Gustavo: *Life on the Hyphen: The Cuban-American Way*. University of Texas, Austin, 1994.

Perez Firmat, Gustavo: *Next Year in Cuba*. Anchor Books, New York, 1995.

Pérez Jr., Louis A.: *On Becoming Cuban*. University of North Carolina Press, Chapel Hill, 1999.

Portes, Alejandro & Alex Stepick: *City on the Edge: The Transformation of Miami*. University of California Press, Berkeley, 1993.

Quirk, Robert: *Fidel Castro*. W. W. Norton and Co., New York, 1993.

Reiff, David: *The Exile: Cuba in the Heart of Miami*. Simon and Schuster, New York, 1993.

Santovenia, Emeterio & Shelton, Raúl: *Cuba y su historia*. Cuba Corporation, Miami, 1966.

Silva, Helga: *The Children of Mariel*. Cuban American National Foundation, Miami, 1985.

Silverio Sainz, Nicasio: *Tres vidas parelelas*. Ediciones Universal, Miami, 1973.

Suchlicki, Jaime: *Cuba: From Columbus to Castro*. Charles Scribner and Sons, New York, 1992.

Szulc, Tad: *Fidel, A Critical Portrait*. Avon, New York, 1987.

Tejera, Eduardo: *The Cuban Contribution to American Independence*. Ediciones Universal, Miami, FL, 1972.

Thomas, Hugh: *Cuba or the Pursuit of Freedom*. Harper and Row, 1988.

Thomas, Hugh: *The Cuban Revolution*. Harper and Row, New York, 1977.

Torres, Angel: *La leyenda del baseball cubano*. Review Printers, Miami, 1996.

Valladares, Armando: *Against All Hope*. Alfred Knopf, New York, 1986.

Vega, Bernardo: *Memoirs of Bernardo Vega*. Monthly Review Press, 1984.

Vilá, Herminio: *Historia de Cuba en sus relaciones con los Estados Unidos*. La Habana, 1949, reprinted by Mnemosyne Publishing, Miami, 1969.

Whitaker, Arthur Preston: *The Spanish-American Frontier 1783–95*. University of Nebraska Press, Lincoln, 1970.

Zayas Bazan y Perdomo, Hector: *Cubans' Contribution to the Independence of the United States*. Junta Patriótica Cubana, Santa Ana, California, 1987.

INTERNET

Articles from used from websites not otherwise specifically related to Cuba

Amnesty International 2000 Report on Cuba
http://www.web.amnesty.org/web/ar2000web.nsf/countries/d9e7ad0023a0bef18
02568f200552918?OpenDocument
Amnesty International Report on the sinking of the 13 de Marzo
http://web.amnesty.org/ai.nsf/Index/AMR250131997?OpenDocument&of=
COUNTRIES\CUBA
Cramer, Ralph: *Washington's Second Front: The Battle of Pensacola.*
http://www.flssar.org/cramer.html
Estefania, Carlos Manuel: *José Antonio Saco.*
http://home.swipnet.se/~w-91445/CubaNuestra/ghu1.htm
Greenbaum, Susan: *Afro Cubans in Exile: Tampa, Florida 1886–1984.*
http://scfn.thpl.lib.fl.us/bbs/tbhcessays1.txt
Howard, Frank: *Revolutionary War, Pensacola, Florida.*
http://polaris.net/~rblacks/fdh/pensacla-war.htm
Human Rights Watch 2000 Report on Cuba
http://www.hrw.org/wr2k/americas-04.htm
Moreno, Dario: *Cubans in the 1996 Presidential Election.*
http://www.fiu.edu/~morenod/scholar/1996.htm
Sánchez del Valle, Carmina: *Historical Background to the Story of St. Augustine.*
http://web.nwe.ufl.edu/pic/pres_intro/StGeorgeSt/history.html
Sheppard, Donald E.: *DeSoto Trails Through Florida.*
http://www.floridahistory.com/inset5.html
Westfall, Glenn. *Birth of Ybor City.*
http://www.datadepo.com/ohp/tbhcessays3.txt

Cuba-related websites used

Alpha 66 Homepage
http://www.alpha66.org/
Antonio de La Cova Home Page: Latin American Studies at Rose-Hulman University
http://www.rose-hulman.edu/~delacova/home.html
Cambio Cubano Homepage
http://cambiocubano.com/
Castro Speech Database at University of Texas

http://www.lanic.utexas.edu/la/cb/cuba/castro.html
Cuban American National Foundation
http://www.canfnet.org/
Cuban Committee for Democracy
http://www.us.net/cuban/
Cuba Freepress Project
http://www.cubafreepress.org/
"Cuba Megalinks" Page
http://www.lanuevacuba.com/megalinks.htm
Cuban Exile Documents
http://cuban-exile.com/
Felix Varela Foundation (New York) Home Page
http://www.pfvarela.org/index.htm
Felix Varela Foundation (Miami) Home Page
http://members.es.tripod.de/ppcruz/index-Varela.html
Florida Cuban Heritage Trail
http://www.flheritage.com/magazine/cht/index.html
Granma Digital
http://www.granma.cu/
Guaracabuya Electronic Magazine
http://www.amigospais-guaracabuya.org
Hermanos al Rescate
http://www.hermanos.org/
Miami Herald On-line Archive: Mariel
http://www.herald.com/content/archive/news/mariel/index.htm
Miami Herald On-line Archive: Brothers to the Rescue
http://www.elherald.com/content/today/archivos/cuba/hermanos/index.htm
Miami Herald On-line Archive: Elián Gónzalez
http://www.herald.com/thispage.htm?content/archive/news/rafters99/elian.htm
Miami Herald On-line Archive: Rafter Exodus
Ybor City and José Martí
http://www.contrib.andrew.cmu.edu/~dpeters/Ybor/Marti/#Visits
Cubans and Cuban Americans on the Internet, University of Miami
http://www.library.miami.edu/netguides/cubanet.html

Index

ABC organization, 115
Abdala, 180–181
academia, Cuban, 226–227
Adams, John Quincy, 28
airlift, Peruvian embassy, 204
Aldama, Miguel, 50–53
Alejandre, Armando Jr., 243–244
Almendares, 117–118, 121, 171
Alpha 66, 164, 178–180, 252
American Civil War, 46–47
American Revolution, 18–25
Amoros, Sandy, 138
anexionismo, 28, 31, 37–44
annexation movement, 37–44
Antonio Macao Brigade, 192
Arboleya, Carlos, 158, 160, 176
Arenas, Reinaldo, 207–208
Argamonte, Ignacio, 57, 59, 147
Armas, Ramón de, 74
Arnaz, Desi, 132–133
Artime, Manuel, 155–157
artists, of Mariel, 207–208
artists/performers, 123–125, 129–130, 132–133,
       149, 247–249, 255–256
Aruca, Francisco, 250
assimilation, into American society, 52, 100–112,
       148–151, 158–162, 172–178, 183–200,
       208–209, 213–219
asylum, political, 201–204, 235–239

autonomismo, 46–49, 83–84
Azpiazu, Don, 123

Bacardi Massó, Facundo, 153–154
Ball, Lucille, 132–133
Barquín, Colonel Ramón, 134
baseball, 117–122, 138, 170–172, 239–241
Basulto, José, 241–245, 258
Batista, Fulgencio, 115–117, 125–142, 146
Bauzá, Mario, 123–125
Bay of Pigs, 154–158, 221, 224, 231
Béisbol see baseball
Benes, Bernardo, 193–198
Berroa, Admiral Esteban, 14–15
Betancourt Cisneros, Gaspar, 31–32, 38–39,
       43–44, 47, 59
Betancourt, Ernesto, 137
bilingual, Dade County, 178, 218, 230
Black Cubans, in Florida, 109–111, 182, 188, 219
Bofill, Ricardo, 189–190, 220
Boitel, Pedro Luis, 195
Bolívar, Simón, 27, 33
Bosch, Orlando, 199–200
Botifoll, Luis, 150–151, 175–176
boycott, economic *see* embargo
Braga, Bernardo, 102
Brigade 2506, 154–158, 221, 231
"Brothers to the Rescue," 241–245
Brotons, Elisabet, 257

Buena Vista Social Club, 255–256
Buford, Lieutenant Harry, 46–48
Burriel, Juan, 61
Bush, President George, 230
businesses, Cuban in U.S., 127–128, 148–151,
    183, 185, 188, 212–213, 215–216, 270–271
Bussot, Daniel, 234

Cabrera Infante, Guillermo, 262
Cagigal, Field Marshall Juan Manuel de, 20–21,
    24
Camarioca boatlift, 165–169, 233
Cambio Cubano, 251, 253–254
Campaneris, Dagoberto "Bert," 171
Canseco, José, 240
Capablanca, José Raúl, 111–112
Carbonell, Nestor, 149
Cardona, President Miró, 147, 155–156,
    162–164, 189
Cartas a Elpidio, 33
Carter, President Jimmy, 189–200, 204, 206, 209
Castillo San Marcos, 9–15
Castro, Fidel
    and "Brothers to the Rescue," 241–245
    and Elián González, 262–272
    attempts to overthrow, 178–182, 189–190,
        192–200, 228–232, 241–245, 250–256
    el Diágolo, 189–200
    embargo, 246–247
    exiles under, 3–4, 148–151, 158–169, 172–178
    Freedom Flights, 166–182
    future after, 272–274
    Mariel boatlift, 201–227
    rafters, 232–240
    Reagan, 219–221
    revolution, 3–4, 128, 130–132, 134–142,
        145–165
    "softliners," 250–256
Cecilia Valdés, 30, 42
census, Cuban-Americans, 51, 99, 100, 109, 111,
    117, 126, 148–149, 174, 188, 198
Céspedes, Carlos Manuel de, 49, 52–57, 59, 79
Chanes de Armas, Mario, 195
"character loans," 176
children, of Mariel, 211–212
Chinese-Cubans, 182
cholera epidemic, New York, 34–37
cigar factories, Ybor City, 80–84, 103–106, 109,
    111
Círculo Cubano, 107–108
Civil War (American), 46–47
Clark, Juan, 154, 157, 194
Clemente Zenea, Juan, 57
Clinton, President Bill, 235–239, 245–247
Commitee of 75196, 193
communism, and Castro's regime, 147–148, 190

Concilio Cubano, 242–245
confiscation, of Cuban businesses/property,
    153–154, 173–174
Conquistadores, 4
conspiracies
    against Castro, 154–158, 161, 178–182,
        199–200
    against Prío, 129–130
    independence from Spain, 27, 38–43
Costa, Carlos, 243–244
Cova, Antonio de la, 43
criminals, in Mariel boatlift, 205–206, 210
Cruz, Celia, 248–249, 256
"Cry of Yara," 51–52, 74
Cuban Adjustment Act, 174
Cuban-American National Foundation (CANF),
    221–224, 230, 239, 246, 251–254, 258,
    272
Cuban artists/performers, 123–125, 129–130,
    132–133, 149, 247–249, 255–256
Cuban Cane Sugar Co., 102
Cuban Committee for Democracy (CCD),
    251–254
Cuban Constitutional Convention, 93, 117
Cuban cuisine, 216–217
Cuban culture in U.S. *see* artists/performers; as-
    similation
Cuban Democracy Act, 223, 230
Cuban flag, 39–41
Cuban Jews, 182
Cuban Liberty and Democratic Solidarity Act,
    223, 246–247, 250
Cuban Missile Crisis, 162–164, 199, 230
Cuban Refugee Program, 150, 158, 160–161
Cuban Revolutionary Council, 155, 157, 162–164
Cuban Revolutionary Party, 85–87
Cuellar, Mike, 172
Cugat, Xavier, 123
cuisine, Cuban, 216–217
culture, Cuban in U.S. *see* artists/performers; as-
    similation

Dade County
    bilingual, 178, 218, 230
    see also assimilation; Florida; Miami
Daíz Balart, Lincoln, 247
Dalrymple, Donato, 256, 266
dance, 129–130
    see also artists/performers
Dance of the Millions, 99
Daza, Ignacio, 9–12
De Grasse, Admiral, 24–25
defectors, 245–246
Delgado, Manuel Patricio, 79
detention centers, 235–239
Dihigo, Martín, 118, 121, 171–172

dissidents, 189–190, 192–200, 229–232
  "Brothers to the Rescue," 241–245
  "softliners," 250–256
Dole, Bob, 247
Dolores Poyo, José, 80
D'Rivera, Paquito, 248

Ediciones Universal, 224
Eisenhower, President Dwight, 154–155
El Baseball en Cuba, 118
el Diálogo, 189–200, 250–256
el Exilio, 148–151, 158–169, 172–178
El Grito de Yara, 51–52, 74
El Habanero, 32–33
el lechero, 127–128
El Mensajero Semanal, 33
El Porvinir, 78
El Pueblo, 45
El Yara, 80
embargo, U.S., 220, 223, 230, 246–249, 250–256,
  270
emigration, 231–233
  see also Camarioca; Mariel; rafters
English
  attack on Castillo San Marcos, 12–15
  conquest of Havana, 15–17, 21–22
entertainers, Cuban-American, 123–125,
  129–130, 132–133, 149, 247–249, 255–256
Estalella, Roberto, 118–120
Estefan, Gloria, 249, 256, 265
Estrada Palma, Tomás, 87–88, 91, 93–95, 99
Estrampes, Francisco, 44
ethnic tension, Florida, 107–111, 186, 188,
  208–209, 218–219
exiles
  under Castro, 3–4, 148–151, 158–169,
    172–178
  see also refugees
Exilios, 26–49

Federation of Cuban Students (FEC), 180
Fernández Cavada, Adolfo and Federico, 46, 47
Figueredo, Fernando, 79, 81
Finlay, Carlos, 94–95
Fish, Hamilton, 54, 61
Five Points Slum, 34–35
flag, Cuban, 39–41
Florida
  after independence, 102–112
  America's acquisition of, 22–23
  Black Cubans in, 109–111, 182, 188, 219
  José Martí in, 77–87
  racial tension, 107–111, 186, 188, 208–209,
    218–219
  Spanish, 4–12
  see also Miami

Fomenteros, 128
foreign policy
  el Diágolo, 189–200
  see also U.S.
fortress, St. Augustine, 8, 9–15
Freedom Flights, 163, 168–171, 181–182, 184,
  208
Freedom Tower, 150
Frente Revolucionario Democrático (FRD), 151,
  155
Fuentes, Ileana, 188

Gálvez, General Barnardo de, 18–23
Gálvez, Wenceslao, 118
García, Andy, 247–248, 265
García, General Calixto, 62, 68, 92–93
García Menocal, President Mario, 99, 114–115
García, Raúl, 174
Garesché, Lieutenant Colonel Julius P, 46
gavetas, 195
Gener, Tomás, 29–30
Gillespie, Dizzy, 124–125
Goizueta, Roberto, 271
Gomez, General Máximo, 60, 69–71, 74, 86,
  91–95
Gómez, Juan Gualberto, 86–87
Gómez, President José Miguel, 99
Gómez, Preston, 172
Gonzáles, Ambrosio José, 38, 40–43, 46, 52
González, Elián, xiii–xv, 235, 256–272
González, Juan Miguel, 257–272
González, Lázaro, 256–257, 259, 263, 267
González, Marisleysis, 256, 259, 266–267
"Good Neighbor Policy," 115–117
Grant, President Ulysses S., 53, 55
Grau Alsina, Ramón and Polita, 163
Grau, President Ramón, 117
Griffin, William B., 6
Grillo, Evelio, 110
Grillo, Frank, 123–125
Grito de Baire, 87
Guantanamo Naval Base, 237–239
Guerra Chiquita, 69
Gutiérrez Menoyo, Eloy, 251–253

Havana
  Chinatown, 182
  English conquest of, 15–17
Helms-Burton Act, 223, 246–247, 250
Henry, Patrick, 19–20
Heredia y Campyzano, José María, 30–31
Hermanos al Rescate, 241–245
Hernández, Orlando (El Duque); Liv/'an, 240–241
Herrera, Martin, 80
Hevia, President Carlos, 130, 135
Hijulelos, Oscar, 225–226

Hinestrosa, Juan de, 8
History of Cuba in its Relations with the United States, 54
Hone, Philip, 34
Hudson County, 127–128, 176–177, 213–214, 217
human rights, 180–181, 189–200, 220–221, 232–233, 238, 242–243, 251

Ilse Volmaner, 114–115
immigration, 99–125
Independence, War of, 87–90
independence from Spain
    1789–1868, 26–49
    1868–1902, 50–95
independentistas, 28, 31, 48–49
INS, and Elián González, 258–272
Isern, José, 8
Ismaelillo, 73

Johnson, President Lyndon, 168–169, 174
Jorge Mas Freedom Foundation, 150
Junta Central Republicana de Cuba y Puerto Rico, 53
Junta Promovedora de los Intereres Políticos de Cuba, 40

Kennedy, President John F., 155–158, 162, 199, 224
Key West, 79–81
"Kid Chocolate," 100–102

La Edad de Oro, 66
La Libertad, 58
La Liga de Instrucción, 75
La Patria Libre, 63
la Torre de la Libertad, 150
La Voz de América, 48
Labada, Gilberto, 128
Lamadriz, José Francisco, 85
language, bilingual Dade County, 178, 218, 230
Laurent, Emilio, 115
Lecciones de Filosofía, 29, 33
Lecuona, Ernesto, 149
Lemus, José Francisco, 27, 52–57, 91
Lersundi, Captain-General Francisco, 48–49, 53
Little Havana, 159, 175–176, 183–188
López, Israel "Cacho," 248
López, Narciso, 38–43
Lorenzo, Orestes, 245–246
Luque, Adolfo, 120–121

maceítos, 192, 195–196, 250
Maceo, Antonio, 59, 61–62, 69–71, 74, 86, 89
Machado, Gerardo (The Machadato), 112–117
"Machito," 123–125

Macías, Juan Manuel, 40, 48–49
Mackenna, Benjamin Vicuña, 48–49
Madan, Cristóbal, 30
Maine, 91–92
Mambises, 87–90, 92
mambo, 129–130
Mañach, Jorge, 70
Mantilla, Carmita (Carmen), 71–74
Mantilla, María, 72, 74
Mariel boatlift, 182, 201–227, 233
Marielitos, 211–213, 219, 228, 235
Martí Bazan, José, 72
Marti City, 81
Martí, José, 62–70, 187–188
Martí-Maceo Union Club, 109–110
Martí y Pérez, José Julián, 62–70
Martínez Campos, Captian General Arsenio, 61–62, 90
Martínez, Governor Bob, 200, 215
Martinez Ybor, Vincente, 80–83
Mas Canosa, Jorge, 221–224, 254
Masó, Bartolomé, 93
Mathews, Herbert, 136
Matos, Huber, 147–148, 195
Maura, Antonio, 84
McIntosh, John Houston, 21, 23
media
    Miami, 216
    see also newspapers
Méndez, Vincente, 179–180
Mendieta, Carlos, 114–115
Menéndez, Bob, 178, 214–215, 224
Menéndez de Avilés, Pedro, 4, 6
Miami
    1950's, 126–142
    1960's, 158–162
    1970's, 183–189
    and Elián González, 256–272
    and Mariel refugees, 208–218
    and refugees, 175–176
    during Machado, 113–117
    ethnic tension, 107–111, 186, 188, 208–209, 218–219
    exiles, 148–151, 158–162
    media, 216
    politics, 221–227
    see also assimilation; Florida
MiGs incident, 244–245
militants, against Castro, 162–164, 178–182, 196–200
Miralles, Juan, 19–20
missile crisis, 162–164, 199, 230
modernismo, 66
Montiel-Davis, Magda, 251
Morales, Colonel Bartolomé, 18
Morales, Pablo, 243–244

Morell de Santa Cruz, Bishop Pedro Agustín, 17
Morón, Pedro, 4
Movimiento de Revolucionario del Pueblo (MRP),
    151, 155
mulatos, 119–120, 182
music, Cuban influence in America, 123–125,
    129–130, 149, 183, 247–249, 255–256

Negrín, José Eulalio, 196–197
New York
    Cubans in, 32–37, 51–52, 70, 74–77, 100–103
        see also Hudson County
newspapers, Cuban-American, 32–33, 45, 58, 63,
    66, 68, 70, 78, 80, 85
Nicaragua, 190, 197, 220, 228
Nuñez, Emilio, 68–69

Ode to Niagara, 31
Ojito, Mirta, 202
O'Laughlin, Sister Jeanne, 259–260, 263
Oliva, Diego de, 4
Oliva, Tony, 171
Olney, Richard B., 91
Omega 7, 196–197
one-and-a-half generation, 185–188
Operation Peter Pan, 162–163

Padilla, Heberto, 177–178
Palmeiro, Rafael, 240
Patria, 66, 68, 70, 85
Pazos, Felipe, 137, 147
Pedroso, Paulina, 187–188
Peña, Mario de la, 243–244
Penelas, Mayor Alex, 261–262, 272
Pérez, Atanasio (Tany), 171–172
Pérez Firmat, Gustavo, 184–185, 226
Pérez Prado, Dámaso, 129–130
Pérez, Roberto Martin, 193–194
Peruvian embassy, 201–204
Pierce, President Franklin, 43–44
Plan Torriente, 179–180
plantados, 193–195
Platt Amendment, 93, 99, 117
political prisoners, 193–195
politics, U.S., and Cubans, 52–57, 214–215,
    221–224, 230, 247, 271
Pope, visit to Cuba, 254–255
Portell Vilá, Herminio, 54
Portes, Alejandro, 217–219
Pozo, Luciano "Chano," 123–125
Prado, Juan, 153
Pride of Havana, The, 120
Prim, Prime Minister Juan, 54–57
Prío Socarrás, President Carlos, 115–117, 125–
    126, 129–130, 134–136, 138–141, 146, 189
Puente, José Eligio de la, 19

Quesada, Gonzalo de, 90
Quitman, General John, 43–44

racial tension, 107–111, 186, 188, 208–209,
    218–219
Radio Martí, 222–223
Radio Pregreso, 250
rafters, 232–240
Rawlins, John, 53–54
Ray, Manuel, 151
Reagan, President Ronald, 219–221
Reed, Dr. Walter, 94–95
reformismo, 28, 29, 31, 46
refugees
    first wave, 158–165
    Freedom Flights, 166–188
    Mariel boatlift, 201–227
    rafters, 233–240
relations
    Cuba-U.S., 189–200
        see also U.S.
Reno, Attorney General Janet, 262–263, 266
resettlement camps, 210–211
Rio Verde expedition, 114–115
Rio Vista, 101–102
Rionda, Manuel, 101–102
riots, Mariel refugees, 206, 210–211
"River View," 101–102
Robaina, Roberto, 253
Robinson, Jackie, 120–121, 138
Rochambeau, Comte de, 23–25
Rodríguez, Arsenio, 129–130
Rodríguez, Douglas, 217
Rodríguez, Manuel and Lyda, 127–128
Rodríguez, María, 166–167
Rodríguez, René, 204–205
Roosevelt, President Franklin Delano, 115–117
Roque, Juan Pablo, 245
Ros Lehtinen, Congresswoman Ileana, 188, 200,
    215, 230, 258
Rosencrans, Major General William, 46
rum, Bacardi, 153–154

Saavedra, Marqués de, 24
Saco, José Antonio, 31–33, 37–38, 47–48
Saladrigas, Carlos, 270–271
San Carlos Club, 103–105
San Carlos Institute, 80, 229
San Román, Bishop Agustín, 206, 210
Sánchez, José, 270–271
Sanchez, Ramón Saul, 265–266
Sandoval, Arturo, 248, 265
Santana, Raisa Teresa, 234
Santos Suárez, Leonardo, 29–30
Sardiñas, Eligio, 100–102
Sargén, Nazario, 164, 180

segregation, 109–111, 188
Serrano, Captain-General Francisco, 46, 48–49
Shafter, General Rufus, 92
Simple Verses, 66
slavery, 26–30, 33, 38, 39, 44, 46, 61, 83
"Small War," 69
social clubs, 103–107, 109–110, 219
"softliners," 250–256
Soles y Rayos de Bolívar, 27
Soto, Hernando de, 4
Soviet Union, support of Castro, 154–158, 162, 189, 220, 229
Spain, independence from, 26–49
Spaniards, and Cubans in Florida, 107–109
Spanish-Ameican War, 90–95
"Special Period," 231–232
sponsors, refugee, 210–211
St. Augustine colony, 4–8
Stepick, Alex, 217–219
sugar, 27, 99–100, 102
Sugar Kings, 138
Suns and Rays of Bolívar, 27

Ten Years War, 48–49, 51–52, 187
tent city, 210
Teurbe Tolón, Miguel, 39–40
13 de Marzo, 232–233
Tiant, Luis, 172
Toral, General Juan José, 92
Torres de Ayala, Laureano, 12
Torriente, Cosme de la, 131
Torriente, José de la, 179–180
tourism, Miami, 126–127
Traconis, Father Francisco, 18
trade
    during British occupation, 16–17, 27
    with Spain, 6–7
    with U.S., 254
    see also embargo
Transfiguration Church/School, 34–35
Treaty of Paris, 17, 92–93
26th of July Movement, 137–142, 147, 199

Unidad Cubana, 230, 251
United Nations Human Rights Commission, 220–221
Urrutia Lleó, Manuel, 137-138, 147, 189
U.S.
    attempts to annex Cuba, 37–44
    attempts to overthrow Castro, 154–158, 162
    attempts to purchase Cuba, 28, 38, 91
    Bay of Pigs, 154–158
    breaking relationship with Cuba, 151–154

el Diálogo, 189–200, 250–256
embargo, 220, 223, 230, 246–249, 250–256, 270
foreign policy regarding exiles, 52–57, 168–174
"Good Neighbor Policy," 115–117
intervention against Spain, 90–95
missiwle crisis, 162–164, 199, 230
policy and Elián González, 258–272
policy under Reagan, 219–221
politics and Cuban-Americans, 52–57, 214–215, 221–224, 230, 247, 271
"rafters"policy, 235–239
"softliners" policy, 250–256
see also assimilation

Valladares, Armando, 193, 195
Varela,Father Félix, 18, 29–37, 239
Varona, Antonio, 151
Velázquez, Loreta Janeta, 46–48
Versalles, Zolio, 171
Versos Sencillos, 66
Villaverde, Cirilo, 30, 40, 42
Virginius, the, 60–61
visits, exiles to Cuba, 191–193, 196, 198, 220
Voluntarios, 50–51, 56, 61, 63

Walsh, Father Bryan O., 162–163
Walters, Ambassador-at-Large Vernon A., 219–220
War
    American Civil, 46–47
    American Revolution, 18–25
    of Independence, 87–90
    Spanish-American, 90–95
    Ten Years, 48–49, 51–52, 187
Washington, George, 19–20, 23–25
Watergate, 175
Welles, Sumner, 115
"wet-dry policy," 239
Weyler, Valeriano, 90
Woman in Battle, The, 47
women, roles, 186–188
Wood, General Leonard, 93, 95
Worth, General William Jenkins, 38–40
writers, 30–31, 62–70, 177–178, 207–208, 224–227

Ybor City, 80–83, 105–111
yellow fever, 94–95

Zayas Bazán, Carmen, 72–74
Zayas, President Alfredo, 99